Medical Law in Ireland

Medical Law in Ireland

Third Edition

Deirdre Madden

This book was originally published as a monograph in the International Encyclopaedia of Laws/Medical Law.

Founding Editor: Roger Blanpain
General Editor: Frank Hendrickx
Volume Editor: Herman Nys

Wolters Kluwer

Published by:
Kluwer Law International B.V.
PO Box 316
2400 AH Alphen aan den Rijn
The Netherlands
Website: lrus.wolterskluwer.com

Sold and distributed in North, Central and South America by:
Wolters Kluwer Legal & Regulatory U.S.
7201 McKinney Circle
Frederick, MD 21704
United States of America
Email: customer.service@wolterskluwer.com

Sold and distributed in all other countries by:
Air Business Subscriptions
Rockwood House
Haywards Heath
West Sussex
RH16 3DH
United Kingdom
Email: international-customerservice@wolterskluwer.com

ISBN 978-90-411-9479-4

e-Book: ISBN 978-90-411-9500-5
web-PDF: ISBN 978-90-411-9521-0

The Author

Professor Deirdre Madden is a graduate of University College Cork, National University of Ireland (BCL, LLM, PhD) and a qualified barrister-at-law. She is a Professor of Law in University College Cork with research interests and publications in the area of medical law and ethics. Professor Madden was author of the Report on Post-Mortem Practice and Procedure (2005) and Chairperson of the Commission on Patient Safety and Quality Assurance which published its Report entitled Building a Culture of Patient Safety in 2008. She was a member of the Irish Medical Council from 2004 to 2013 and is currently a member of the Health and Social Care Professionals Council.Professor Madden has been a member of a number of national expert groups related to medical law, ethics and patient safety, including the National Patient Safety Advisory Group, the Board of the National Office of Clinical Audit, and the National Advisory Committee on Bioethics. Professor Madden also chaired the National Consent Advisory Group for the HSE and is current Chair of the National Assisted Decision-Making Advisory Group. She is an ethics consultant for the Health Information and Quality Authority on Health Information Technology, a member of the Expert Advisory Group for the Citizens Assembly on the 8th Amendment of the Constitution, and a member of an independent review of the role of voluntary organisations in health and social care.
Professor Madden has been an Expert Reviewer on ethics for the European Commission for 15 years; a member of the Research Ethics Committee for the National Longitudinal Study of Children in Ireland; consultant for the National Healthcare Regulatory Authority in Bahrain; former member of the National Council of the Forum on End-of-Life; and an elected Fellow of the Hastings Center in the United States. She has been a Visiting Professor at Colby College, Maine USA; St Louis University, Missouri; and the University of Sydney.

The Author

Table of Contents

List of Abbreviations

ACER	Australian Council for Educational Research
ADM	Assisted Decision-Making
AHD	Advance Healthcare Directive
AHR	Assisted Human Reproduction
BUPA	British United Provident Association
CAHR	Commission on Assisted Human Reproduction
CIS	Clinical Indemnity Scheme
CJ	Chief Justice of the Supreme Court
CPD	Continuing Professional Development
CPR	Cardiopulmonary Resuscitation
CPSQA	Commission on Patient Safety and Quality Assurance
CQA	Continuous Quality Assurance
DNAR	Do Not Attempt Resuscitation
DOH	Department of Health
DPP	Director of Public Prosecutions
ECJ	European Court of Justice
ECtHR	European Court of Human Rights
EEA	European Economic Area
EEC	European Economic Community
EHB	Eastern Health Board
FISH	Fluorescent In Situ Hybridization
FOI	Freedom of Information
FTPC	Fitness to Practice Committee
GCP	Good Clinical Practice
GDP	Gross Domestic Product
GMS	General Medical Scheme
GP	General Practitioner
hESC	Embryonic Stem Cell Research
HIQA	Health Information and Quality Authority

HIT	Health Information Technology
HPAT	Health Professions Admission Test
HPRA	Health Products Regulatory Authority
HRU	Human Rights Unit
HSE	Health Service Executive
ICSI	Intra-Cytoplasmic Sperm Injection
ICT	Information and Community Technology
IEHC	Irish High Court
IESC	Irish Supreme Court
ILRM	Irish Law Reports Monthly
IR	Irish Reports
ISG	Implementation Steering Group
IT	Information Technology
IVF	*In Vitro* Fertilization
J	Judge
LNG-IUS	Levonorgestrel Releasing Intra-uterine Contraceptive Device
LRC	Law Reform Commission
MHC	Mental Health Commission
MLJI	Medico-Legal Journal of Ireland
NGO	Non-governmental Organization
NHO	National Hospitals Office
NTD	Neural Tube Defect
NTMA	National Treasury Management Agency
NTPF	National Treatment Purchase Fund
OECD	Organization for Economic Cooperation and Development
P	President of the Court
PCCC	Primary, Continuing and Community Care
PGD	Pre-implantation Genetic Diagnosis
PPC	Preliminary Proceedings Committee
PRES	Pre-Registration Examination System
PSI	Pharmaceutical Society of Ireland
PVS	Persistent Vegetative State
SCA	State Claims Agency
TD	*Teachta Dàla* (Member of Parliament)

List of Abbreviations

UCC	University College Cork
VHI	Voluntary Health Insurance
WHO	World Health Organization

List of Abbreviations

General Introduction

Chapter 1. General Background of the Country

§1. Geography

1. The island of Ireland contains two jurisdictions: a republic (the Republic of Ireland) and Northern Ireland. This book considers the law in the Republic of Ireland.

2. Ireland is situated in the extreme north-west of Europe between 51.5° and 55.5° north latitude and between 5.5° and 10.5° west longitude. The total area of the island of Ireland is 84,421 square kilometres (32,595 square miles), with the Republic of Ireland covering 70,282 square kilometres (27,136 square miles) and Northern Ireland covering 14,139 square kilometres (5,459 square miles). The greatest length (north-south) is 486 km (302 miles), the greatest width (east-west) is 275 km (171 miles), and the total coastline measures 3,172 km (1,970 miles). The island comprises a large central lowland of limestone with a relief of hills surrounded by a discontinuous border of coastal mountains that vary greatly in geological structure. The longest river is the Shannon, at 230 miles. Although traditionally an agricultural country, Ireland has experienced significant industrial growth in recent decades and maintains strong employment in the chemical, pharmaceutical, and electronic industries.

3. Influenced by the Gulf Stream and with the prevailing winds predominantly from the south-west, the climate is equable and temperatures are fairly uniform over the whole country. The coldest months are January and February, with mean daily air temperatures of between 4°C and 7°C, while July and August are the warmest (14°C–16°C). Extremes of air temperature are rare.

§2. Cultural Composition

4. The island of Ireland is divided between two jurisdictions: a republic of twenty-six counties and Northern Ireland, a territory that shares a border with the Republic of Ireland to the south and west. Northern Ireland consists of six counties and was established as a distinct administrative subdivision of the United Kingdom on 3 May 1921 under the Government of Ireland Act 1920. For over fifty years it was the only part of the United Kingdom to have its own form of devolved government until it was suspended in 1972. Northern Ireland's current devolved government bodies, the Northern Ireland Assembly and Executive, were established by the Northern Ireland Act 1998 but were suspended several times. They were restored on 8 May 2007. Northern Ireland's legal system descends from the pre-1921 Irish legal system. It is based on common law. Northern Ireland is a distinct jurisdiction, separate from England and Wales and Scotland.

5. Northern Ireland was for many years the site of a violent and bitter ethno-political conflict between those claiming to represent Nationalists, who are predominantly Roman Catholic, and those claiming to represent Unionists, who are predominantly Protestant. In general, Nationalists want the unification of Ireland, with Northern Ireland joining the rest of Ireland, and Unionists want it to remain part of the United Kingdom. Protestants are in the majority in Northern Ireland, though Roman Catholics represent a significant minority. In general, Protestants consider themselves British and Catholics see themselves as Irish but there are some who see themselves as both British and Irish. In addition to UK citizenship, people from Northern Ireland are also entitled to Irish citizenship. The campaigns of violence have become known popularly as The Troubles. The majority of both sides of the community have had no direct involvement in the violent campaigns waged. Since the signing of the Belfast Agreement (also known as the Good Friday Agreement) in 1998, many of the major paramilitary campaigns have either been on ceasefire or have declared their war to be over.

6. The Troubles were brought to an uneasy end by a peace process that included the declaration of ceasefires by most paramilitary organizations and the complete decommissioning of their weapons, the reform of the police, and the corresponding withdrawal of army troops from the streets and from sensitive border areas as agreed by the signatories to the Belfast Agreement. This reiterated the long-held British position, which had never before been fully acknowledged by successive Irish governments, that Northern Ireland will remain within the United Kingdom until a majority votes otherwise. *Bunreacht na hEireann*, the Constitution of the Irish State, was amended in 1999 to remove a claim of the Irish nation to sovereignty over the whole of Ireland (in Article 2), a claim qualified by an acknowledgement that Ireland could only exercise legal control over the territory formerly known as the Irish Free State.

7. The new Articles 2 and 3, added to the Constitution to replace the earlier articles, implicitly acknowledge that the status of Northern Ireland, and its relationships within the rest of the United Kingdom and with Ireland, would only be changed with the agreement of a majority of voters in both jurisdictions of Ireland (voting separately). This aspect was also central to the Belfast Agreement, which was signed in 1998 and ratified by referenda held simultaneously in both Northern Ireland and the Republic. At the same time, the British Government recognized for the first time, as part of the prospective, the so-called 'Irish dimension': the principle that the people of the island of Ireland as a whole have the right, without any outside interference, to solve the issues between North and South by mutual consent. The latter statement was key to winning support for the agreement from Nationalists and Republicans. It also established a devolved power-sharing government within Northern Ireland where the government must consist of both Unionist and Nationalist parties.

§3. Political System

8. Ireland is a parliamentary democracy. The national Parliament (in the Irish language, called the *Oireachtas*) consists of the President (*an tUachtaran*) and two houses: the House of Representatives (*Dail Eireann*) and the Senate (*Seanad Eireann*). The executive powers of the State are exercised by, or on the authority of, the government. The Constitution provides that the government shall consist of not fewer than seven and not more than fifteen members. The Prime Minister (*Taoiseach*), Deputy Prime Minister (*Tanaiste*), and Minister for Finance must be members of the *Dail.* The other members of the government may be members of the *Dail* or *Seanad*, but not more than two may be members of the *Seanad.* The government acts collectively and is responsible to the *Dail.* The *Taoiseach* is appointed by the President on the nomination of the *Dail.* He or she must resign on ceasing to retain the support of a majority in the *Dail.* The *Taoiseach* nominates one member of the government to be *Tanaiste.* The *Tanaiste* acts in place of the *Taoiseach* if the *Taoiseach* is temporarily absent or becomes incapacitated.

9. The Attorney General, while not a member of the government, acts as legal adviser to the government and may attend Cabinet meetings. The Attorney General's tenure of office is normally conterminous with that of the government. The *Taoiseach* assigns Departments of State to members of the government. Usually, each member of the government heads one Department of State, but occasionally a minister is responsible for more than one Department. Ministers of State, who are not members of the government, assist government ministers in their parliamentary and departmental work. The maximum number of Ministers of State is fixed by law at seventeen.

10. Bills passed by the *Dail* and the *Seanad* require the signature of the President for their enactment into law. The President may refer certain bills to the Supreme Court (except money bills, or bills expressed to be containing a proposal to amend the Constitution, or bills necessitated by national emergency). The Supreme Court will adjudicate on the constitutionality of the bill. In addition, the President may decline to sign a bill until its contents are put before the people in a referendum.

11. The Irish Constitution (*Bunreacht na hEireann* 1937) provides that the High Court has full original jurisdiction in and power to determine all matters and questions of law or fact, both civil and criminal. The Supreme Court has supreme jurisdiction in cases relating to the constitutionality of legislation and is the Court of Final Appeal. As a consequence of Irish membership of the European Union, the Constitution was amended to provide as follows:

> No provision of this Constitution invalidates laws enacted, acts done or measures adopted by the State which are necessitated by the obligations of membership of the European Union of the Communities, or prevents laws enacted, acts done or measures adopted by the European Union or by the Communities, or by institutions thereof, or by bodies competent under the Treaties establishing the communities, from having force of law in the State.

The President of the Supreme Court is the Chief Justice of Ireland. Courts of limited jurisdiction are the Circuit and District Courts.

12. The primary source of Irish law is the Irish Constitution 1937. It establishes the basic structures of the State and accords specific functions to the President, the *Oireachtas*, and the courts. It also contains provisions that guarantee protection of fundamental human rights that may be enforced through legal action.

13. Legislation is the second source of Irish law and may be divided into acts passed by the British Parliament up to 1800, the Parliament of Great Britain and Ireland (1801–1922), the Parliament of the Irish Free State (1922–1937), and acts of the *Oireachtas* (1937 to date). The courts interpret and apply legislation and are bound by certain rules of statutory interpretation, including the presumption of constitutionality, which provides that all acts passed by the *Oireachtas* are presumed to be constitutional.

14. The third source of law in Ireland is precedent or *stare decisis*, which means that the decisions of higher courts are binding on lower courts. However, the Supreme Court may distinguish or depart from its own previous decisions in certain circumstances.[1] In areas of law where there are no precedents in this jurisdiction, the courts will consider precedents from other jurisdictions but are not obliged to follow them. This has been evident in some areas of medical law where there are similar legislative provisions and/or case law from the United Kingdom drawing on common law precedents. However, in some areas such precedents would not be followed where they conflict with interpretation of Irish constitutional provisions, for example, in relation to abortion, or adolescent autonomy to make healthcare decisions.

§4. Population and Vital Statistics

15. Ireland has a population of 4,757,976 (as of census in 2016).[2] The number of persons aged 65 has risen by 14.4% since 2006 to 535,393 and now represents 11% of the population and the number of persons aged 85 and over has also risen by 22%in that period. The average age is now 36.1 years. Life expectancy for males is 75.1 years, and for women 80.3 years. Persons aged between 25 and 44 years are the fastest growing segment of the population and account for 31.7% of the population. The large increase has been influenced by the high inward migration in recent years. At the time of the 2006 census of the population, 420,000 non-Irish nationals from 188 different countries were resident in Ireland. Since 2006, this figure has risen by 29.7% to 544,357 from 196 different countries. Polish nationals accounted for almost half of the total increase among this group and have overtaken UK nationals as the largest non-Irish group living in Ireland.

16. The number of divorced persons is 87,770 and the number of separated persons is 116,194 with a marital breakdown rate of 9.7%. The average number of children per family has declined in ten years from 2.2 to 1.38.

1. *State (Quinn) v. Ryan* [1965] IR 70; *AG and Minister for Defence v. Ryan's Car Hire* [1965] IR 642.
2. At http://www.cso.ie.

§5. Social and Cultural Values

17. Article 8 of the Irish Constitution (*Bunreacht na hEireann*) designates Irish as the first official language, with English as the second official language. English is, however, the language that is generally used. Almost 1.77 million people (41.1%) in Ireland are able to speak Irish, with the highest proportion of these amongst the school-going population. Just over 1 million of those never or rarely speak the language. In *Gaeltacht* areas where Irish is commonly spoken as the first language, Irish speakers account for over 70% of the population.

18. Article 44 of the Irish Constitution guarantees freedom of conscience and the free profession and practice of religion to all citizens. Eighty-four per cent of the Republic's population is Roman Catholic with the most important non-Christian religion being Muslim with almost 50,000 members. The number of people with no religion has risen by 45% from 2006 to 2011 from 83,500 to 269,800 with the majority in that group being Irish nationals. The Catholic tradition has had a significant influence on the development of health policy in Ireland and the Irish Constitution bears the hallmarks of this in its natural law philosophy.

19. Ireland has the highest rate of third-level degree attainment in the EU, with just over half of all 30–34-year-olds in Ireland completing third-level education. A total of 51.1% of Irish people in this age range have third-level degrees, which is around 16% higher than the EU average of 35.8%.

The proportion of females in full-time education exceeds that of males, with the largest differential evident in the 15–19-year-old age bracket. The most popular branch of study is in the area of social science/business/law followed by health. Engineering/manufacturing and construction are the most prominent branches of study amongst males.

Chapter 2. Description of the Healthcare System

§1. Background to the Irish Healthcare System

20. The provision of healthcare in Ireland is based on a mixture of public and private funding. The State has been involved in the funding and allocation of healthcare resources since the nineteenth century, with many of the principles upon which the healthcare system is presently founded informed by that historical context. The provision of medical relief services and public health in the nineteenth century has been the basis upon which the modern health service has been founded. At the turn of the twentieth century, few people worried about the State's role in ensuring access to high-quality healthcare because the limitations then placed on medicine's ability to conquer disease were such that hospitals remained places of last resort for those with untreatable illness, and for those with insufficient means to access even minimum medical care:[3]

> People did not expect the state to provide for more than a minimum level of medical care for the population. Government in these islands had not yet accepted a general responsibility for the health of the population, nor a duty to make medical facilities available to all at little or no cost to the patient.....Only the medical care of the very poor and the control of infections associated with poverty were considered to warrant public intervention. These responsibilities were known to contemporaries as 'medical relief' and 'public health' respectively.[4]

21. Medical relief was the provision of infirmaries for the care of the sick and diseased poor in each county, financed by public and charitable efforts. A dispensary service operated that divided the country into districts with medical officers and sometimes midwives to attend to the poor. These medical officers, whose recruitment and educational qualifications were assessed under criteria laid down by the Poor Law Commission, had to attend every sick person in the district possessing a ticket entitling them to attendance at home or at the dispensary. These officers were often the medical doctors for the workhouses and soon became responsible for other duties such as vaccination and birth registration, leading to the emergence of the general practitioner (GP) and calls for further development in the health service.[5] At the same time these doctors were free to devote the time not spent on these duties to private practice. These private patients were normally seen at the doctor's house. 'It was taken for granted that private and public patients should be seen in separate premises, since respectable people feared catching infections from the poor.'[6]

3. For a more detailed discussion of medicine and Irish society in the twentieth century, *see* R. Barrington, *Health, Medicine & Politics in Ireland 1900–1970* (Institute of Public Administration 1987).
4. Barrington, *supra* n. 3, at 4.
5. B. Hensey, *The Health Services of Ireland* 8 (2nd ed., Institute of Public Administration 1979).
6. Barrington, *supra* n. 3, at 11.

22. The public health movement developed with the aim of preventing the spread of infectious disease in Ireland and Great Britain. Legislation was enacted to protect water supplies, appoint sanitary inspectors, destroy unsound food, isolate those suffering from infectious disease, and supervise slaughterhouses. However, the apathy with which many local authorities approached their tasks, the poverty of the majority of Irish people, and the opposition to increases in taxation with which to fund these improvements made sure that progress was very slow in this context.

23. Pressure for reform of the system began to grow around the early 1900s as access to medical care began to be viewed as a social right of all citizens, mirrored by an increased role and responsibility for government. Health insurance was introduced in Britain in 1911 to give people some protection against medical costs and loss of income due to ill health and unemployment. Compulsory contributors to the scheme included most wage earners, whose contribution would be boosted by contributions from employers and the State. Others could join on a voluntary basis. This insurance was to entitle the contributor to free attendance by a medical practitioner and free medicine. They would be entitled to maternity and sick benefits as well as disability and sanatorium benefits. The difficulty in the Irish context was its practical applicability here in very different social circumstances. Due to the intervention of many factors – socio-political, religious hierarchical opinion, the resistance of sections of the medical profession, and the financial implications – an insurance-based medical benefit was not introduced to Ireland, and the development of the health systems in Ireland and Britain thereafter continued along different lines.

24. A national health insurance scheme for Ireland was again put forward in the 1930s, although with a different emphasis. Around this time a more modern hospital service was put into place and the National Health Insurance Act 1941 was designed to extend hospital benefits rather than medical benefits. It suffered from problems relating to funding, extensions to the insured person's family, and applicability to those outside the system, such as the self-employed. The consequent lack of attention given to the dispensary service, together with the prevalence of tuberculosis, led to many problems in the early 1940s.

25. Ironically, the emergency during the Second World War advanced the health service in a number of ways due to a widening of access to the service and a focus on strategic plans for the development of a comprehensive system. Deprivation and poverty during these years increased concentration on the control of infectious diseases and pressure for the establishment of a separate department of health, which was set in motion in 1944. The Department of Local Government and Public Health had, by the end of 1945, a strategy for the provision of a free health service and other short-term objectives such as the improved treatment of tuberculosis and other conditions, as well as the protection of the health of mothers and children. 'The challenge was to persuade the government and the medical profession to follow the road charted by the Department.'[7]

26. The Public Health Bill was drafted in 1945 primarily to deal with infectious diseases (which proved controversial in its methodology), but also dealt with the provision of maternity services and the compulsory medical inspection of school children. Although much opposition was voiced to the Bill's provision of powers of

7. Barrington, *supra* n. 3, at 167.

detention and inspection, along the lines of State interference with individual liberty and increasing control over citizens' lives, there was nonetheless a good deal of support for the aim of improvement of the health of mothers and children. However, due to the inevitable interference of personal political ambitions and rumblings within the medical profession about intervention in their practices, the sponsor of the Bill was forced to resign in 1946 when the Bill was at its final stage. Despite this setback, a separate Department of Health was set up in 1946 with the first Minster for Health appointed in 1947.

27. Many of the provisions of the doomed 1945 Bill were restated with some amendments to remove the more controversial provisions. The two most controversial issues remained the impact that a free mother and child health service would have on the medical profession, and the interference with family authority and privacy imposed by compulsory medical inspection in schools. The Catholic hierarchy was also extremely concerned at the direction of State medicine and its interference with the Church's position on contraception, abortion, and sex education. This led to an alliance between the Church and the profession in opposition to the provisions of the Act and the more wide-ranging ambitions for reform of the health services to which the government of the day seemed committed.

28. When pressure was put on the subsequent Minister for Health, Dr Noel Browne, to introduce a mother and child scheme as provided by the Act, much opposition came his way, both political and religious. Although the Minister was heavily committed to other issues such as hospital building programmes and the eradication of tuberculosis, he was obliged to make good on the scheme set out in the Act. His proposals for the introduction of such a scheme emphasized that the services (which provided for children up to 16 years and maternity care for expectant mothers) would be free and voluntary. The Minister also wanted to introduce a medical card, as a substitute for the dispensary tickets that entitled the holder to once-off care. These issues, together with a hostile relationship with the medical profession, led to vociferous opposition to the scheme both from the profession itself and the Catholic hierarchy that eventually caused the Minister to resign, having failed to secure the support of his government colleagues for the introduction of his scheme. The influence of the Catholic Church on politics was clear to all when correspondence between the Catholic hierarchy, the Minister, and the *Taoiseach* was released to the press after his resignation.

29. In the aftermath of this debacle the government fell, and the general election that followed concentrated on health issues as never before. The new Minister for Health tactically decided to introduce a weakened version of the mother and child scheme as part of a wider extension of health services enabled by the hospital building programme and other improvements brought about by his predecessor. Despite the resistance to the idea of a free health service, an uneasy compromise was reached with the profession and the Church, and the Health Act 1953 became law. 'The government conceded nothing on the principle that the state had a responsibility for the medical care of the majority of the population and for the welfare of all mothers and infants … .'[8] However, while the Act introduced many improvements on the system as it existed prior to 1950, the notion of a free health service to all sectors of the population and across all services remained unrealistic in the face of such opposition as existed.

8. Barrington, *supra* n. 3, at 241.

For example, general practice was left unchanged by the Act except for the ability to provide a mother and infant service to lower- and middle-class mothers free of charge. However, in hindsight it did provide a stepping-stone to other changes that followed and showed the profession's members that, in many ways, they had less to fear from a free service than they imagined.

30. Controversy and political disagreement continued to dog the debate surrounding any extensions of the mother and infant scheme to other groups and services. Proposals were put forward and rejected in the 1960s and eventually in 1970 the Health Act was introduced, which, *inter alia*, provided for a scheme to compensate persons of lower income for expenditure on prescribed drugs, and for those suffering from certain diseases, regardless of income. The dispensary system was replaced with a choice-of-doctor scheme that allowed all GPs to treat public patients and that took control from the department over the organization of general practice. Changes were made to health service administration, with the setting up of eight regional health boards. Despite a general election during the time when the Bill was being discussed, government policy remained unchanged and the Bill became law in 1970. The profession became reconciled to working within a system that was publicly funded and centrally planned.

31. In summary, the main factors that give Irish medical services their character are 'the legacy of the nineteenth century, the role of the state as the chief mediating force between the medical profession and the patient … the aspiration for a health service comparable to Britain's and the limits set by the formidable alliance of the Catholic Church and the medical profession'.[9] These characteristics, also shaped by economic factors such as severe cutbacks on health spending in the 1980s[10] followed by increased availability of funding with the birth of the Celtic Tiger in the 1990s, have led to sharp criticism in recent years of the disparity in levels of services available to public and private patients, the growth of private health insurance,[11] and concerns over lengthy waiting lists for treatment.

32. The foundation in 1957 of the Voluntary Health Insurance scheme (VHI) is seen now as having been motivated by a desire to provide private income for the medical profession members who had, with the help of the Catholic Church as outlined above, opposed a comprehensive public health system such as existed in Britain. Private health insurance is generally seen as providing preferential access to healthcare at rates less than the full economic cost, the balance of the costs being provided by the State. The opening of the market to foreign competitors by the Health Insurance

9. Barrington, *supra* n. 3, at 286.

10. 'Between 1980 and 1996 only three EU Member States reduced health spending as a proportion of GDP, and by far the biggest reduction – 23%– was in Ireland. Spending here fell in the 1980s, not only as a proportion of GDP in real terms. In 1989 spending on health was, in volume terms, 6% lower than in 1980. Spending on hospitals was 15% lower.' During this time thirteen other EU states increased their spending on healthcare by 24%. In recent years the disparity across the EU lessened, and Ireland has finally caught up with the EU average in terms of spending on healthcare..

11. Membership of private health insurance schemes currently stands at 47%, leading to fears that the Irish health system will end up more similar in operation to that in the United States, rather than the United Kingdom.

Act of 1994, which saw British United Provident Association (BUPA) enter the market in 1996, was seen as driving an increased motivation for profit-making in the health insurance market. Other companies such as LAYA Healthcare and Irish Life Health have also joined the market providing more choice and competitive prices to consumers. Insurers are required to provide community rating, open access, and lifetime coverage to members. They are also required to provide a minimum level of benefits.

33. In Ireland today, those without private health insurance are either covered by the General Medical Scheme (GMS) or have no cover.[12] Persons whose income falls below a certain threshold can apply for a 'medical card' which enables them to receive free hospital and GP care, free prescriptions (subject to a minimal charge), certain free dental services, midwifery services, and other benefits. For those who do not qualify for the medical card, there is also the possibility of applying for a GP visit only card to cover the cost of attending a general practitioner.[13] These cards are designed primarily for the elderly and social welfare recipients, not for those with low incomes who fall just outside the threshold but cannot pay the insurance premiums. This sector, therefore, remains a sizeable proportion of the population (about 23%) who are not covered by the GMS or by private insurance and who may struggle to meet healthcare charges. Since 1991, the entire population is entitled to free medical care in hospitals, apart from a charge of EUR 100 for attending the Emergency Department and a nightly charge of EUR 75 for persons admitted to hospital. This has not slowed the subscription to private insurance schemes as it is generally felt that private patients are seen faster, more efficiently, and by more highly qualified and specialised doctors.

34. The Department of Health (DOH) and the Health Service Executive (HSE) have paramount responsibility for health service provision in Ireland. The Department's primary role is to support the Minister for Health in formulating and evaluating policies for the health services. The Department also has a role in the strategic planning of health services in consultation with the HSE, the voluntary sector, other government departments, and other interests.

35. Each year, the DOH allocates funding to the HSE. Each HSE Area then makes decisions about how it will distribute available resources to the agencies in its area. The Department takes account of a range of factors in determining what proportion of the funding should be allocated to each HSE Area. These factors include the cost of providing services in the previous year, pay costs, health service developments, and funding for agreed specific items. The budget for the HSE in 2017 is EUR 14.6 billion.

36. At a political level, the Minister for Health has overall constitutional responsibility for the Department. In addition to the Minister for Health, currently, there are four Ministers of State in this Department responsible to the Minister for health promotion, mental health and older people, and the national drug strategy. The administrative (Civil Service) head of the Department is the Secretary General. He or she is the accounting officer. In other words, he or she is responsible to the Parliament (*Dail Eireann*) for ensuring that the money allocated to the Department is spent in the

12. *See* generally E. McAuliffe & L. Joyce, *A Healthier Future? Managing Healthcare in Ireland* (Institute of Public Administration 1998).
13. About 30% of the population. This rate has fallen in recent years as the eligibility criteria have failed to keep pace with changing incomes.

proper manner. The Chief Medical Officer advises the Minister and the Department on medical issues.

37. The HSE has responsibility for delivering public health and personal social services in Ireland. It is a national organization operating throughout Ireland and came into operation on 1 January 2005. So, although the DOH decides health policy in Ireland, the HSE is responsible for delivering services. The HSE is organized into sections called Directorates which have responsibility for and governance over areas such as:

- Primary care.
- Social care.
- Acute hospitals.
- Population Health: involved in health promotion and protection of the health of various groups.
- Mental Health.
- Quality Improvement.

38. As mentioned earlier, all persons resident in Ireland are entitled to receive healthcare through the public healthcare system, which is funded by general taxation. A person may be required to pay a subsidized fee for certain healthcare received; this depends on income, age, and illness or disability. All child health and maternity services are provided free of charge as is emergency care. Everyone living in the country, and visitors to Ireland who hold a European Health Insurance Card, are entitled to treatment in public beds in HSE and voluntary hospitals subject to a charge of EUR 100 for attendance at the emergency department and an overnight charge of EUR 75 for admission.

39. The medical card, which entitles holders to free hospital care, GP visits, dental services, optical services, aural services, prescription drugs, and medical appliances, is available to those receiving social welfare payments, low earners, those with certain long-term or severe illnesses, and in certain other discretionary cases such as where the person's income might be above the income threshold but there are exceptional medical expenses for the family due to illness of a family member. Since 2015 people aged 70 years or over are entitled to a medical card regardless of income. Children under 6 are entitled to free GP visits. Those with slightly higher incomes are eligible for a GP Visit Card, which entitles the holder to free GP visits. People who do not qualify for a medical card must pay for certain healthcare services at a subsidized rate. Those who do not qualify for the exemptions can also be charged for a visit to an out-patient department or an accident and emergency department if the patient has not been referred by a family doctor. Specialist assessments and diagnostic assessments are provided for free.

40. Private health insurance is available to the population for those who want to avail of it. The regulatory body for private health insurance is the Health Insurance Authority. Approximately 47% of the population is covered by private health insurance, and 30% of the population is covered by medical cards. There are fifty-two publicly funded acute hospitals, with an average total of 12,492 in-patient and day beds available.

§2. Regulation of the Healthcare System

41. The challenge of any healthcare system is to provide accessible, effective, and high-quality healthcare, bearing in mind increased demands for services, higher costs of technology, and longer life expectancies. In addition to the prevention and treatment of disease, the promotion of health, support for the disabled, and the protection of children, the health service also has a contribution to make to the wider objectives of society, such as contributing to the economic and social development of the country.[14] The solution to many of the difficulties faced by health systems is not primarily based on funding but rather in the way that services are planned, organized, and delivered.[15] The Irish health system has both public and private elements within it. The majority (approximately 75%) is funded by the government, while the remaining 25% is funded through private health insurance premiums.

42. The State's role in the provision of health services has changed in character from provider of services to the poor, to overall regulation of standards and an increase in management of targets and objectives within the system. It does this through a team made up of government, DOH, advisory and executive agencies, and voluntary organizations. The Minister for Health is responsible for the development and operation of the health services in accordance with legislation and public policy. The Department, which was set up in 1947, supports the Minister in the formulation, development, and evaluation of health policy. Its main objectives include the strategic development of services through interaction with health boards, the voluntary sector, and other government departments; the encouragement of the highest standards of effectiveness, efficiency, equity, quality, and value for money in the health system; to improve accountability at all levels of the health services; to encourage the development of a customer service ethos in the health service; to optimize staff performance; and to represent Irish interests in international forums relating to health issues.[16]

43. Health services in Ireland are provided by a number of different bodies, namely the HSE, the voluntary hospitals and agencies; specialist bodies; bodies established under the Health (Corporate Bodies) Act; and registration bodies. Until the establishment of the HSE in 2005, regional health boards had a statutory responsibility under the Health Act 1970 (as amended by the Health (Amendment) (No. 3) Act 1996) to administer the services provided for in health legislation and by the Minister. There were twelve health boards ranging across geographical areas and based on population size and local planning and development advice. The boards were made up of elected county councillors, professionals, and ministerial nominees who represented user groups. The boards' functions included resource allocation, cooperation with voluntary bodies providing services in the area, and implementing government policy. The Health Act 1970, Part III obliged health boards to be responsible for the provision and maintenance of hospitals, sanatoriums, homes, laboratories, clinics, or healthcare centres. The hospitals, which include regional and county hospitals as well as district,

---

14. R. Barrington, *The Future Political, Legislative and Social Framework of the Health Services*, in *The Irish Health System in the 21st Century* 83–101, at 84 (A. Leahy & M. Wiley eds., Institute of Public Administration 1998).
15. Department of Health (1989) *Report of the Commission on Health Funding*.
16. *Statement of Strategy* (Department of Health & Children 1997).

fever, and orthopaedic hospitals, were managed by the health boards and funding was sought from the budget allocated to each board by the Department of Health.

44. The voluntary health sector also plays an integral role in the provision of health services in Ireland, through identification of community needs and development of appropriate responses. This sector is the major provider of services to those suffering from mental disabilities in the country. Voluntary hospitals, first instigated in the early eighteenth century to cater to the sick poor, are funded by the Department of Health but run by boards comprised of religious and lay members. Private hospitals also exist, managed generally by religious orders and largely financed by the patients themselves or health insurers such as the VHI company. Some funding towards these hospitals is available from the HSE.

45. Specialist bodies also exist where established under specific acts, such as the Food Safety Authority of Ireland and the Health Products Regulatory Authority. These bodies provide an advisory service to the Department of Health on a range of issues such as food safety and regulation of medicines. Other bodies set up under the Health (Corporate Bodies) Act 1961 for the purpose of advising on health policy and the provision of health services on a national basis include the Health Research Board (which promotes, commissions, and conducts medical research), the Blood Transfusion Board (which organizes a blood transfusion service), and the National Rehabilitation Board (which provides guidance, training, information, and public awareness services in the area of people with disabilities.) The registration bodies such as the Medical Council, the Dental Council, The Nursing and Midwifery Board, and the Health and Social Care Professionals Council maintain a register of practitioners, provide for standards of education and training, and provide a disciplinary process to inquire into alleged unprofessional conduct.

46. A national health strategy, *Quality and Fairness: A Health System for You*, was developed in 2001.[17] A National Health Strategy Consultative Forum, representative of key stakeholders in the health services, including health professionals, management, and consumers, was established to advise on the development of the strategy. Following publication of the national health strategy and the associated strategy for primary care, *Primary Care: A New Direction*,[18] the Health Reform Programme was developed to translate the vision into reality and implement the actions set out in the strategy. It was clear that new structures and supporting processes were required to best meet current and future health needs as expressed in the goals and objectives of the strategy.

47. Two independent reports published in 2003[19] arrived at similar conclusions about the system and made comparable recommendations that provide the background for the government decisions on the Health Service Reform Programme. The main findings and recommendations were:

- The multiplicity of health boards and specialist agencies operating in the public health sector had resulted in a complex and fragmented system.

17. *Quality and Fairness: A Health System for You* (Department of Health 2001).
18. *Primary Care: A New Direction* (Department of Health 2001).
19. *Prospectus Report (Audit of Structures and Functions in the Health System)* (Department of Health 2003); *Brennan Report (Commission on Financial Management and Controls in the Health Service)* (Department of Health 2003).

- There was a need for rationalization, standardization, and much improved coordination within the system.
- There was a need for greater clarity of roles, accountability, and responsibility throughout the system, including the roles of the Department and the delivery system.
- There was a need to enhance needs assessment and service planning, with stronger links to funding, activity, and outcome measurement.

48. Another report was commissioned on the staffing requirements of acute hospital services.[20] The outputs from all this work culminated in the announcement of the Health Service Reform Programme in June 2003. The main elements of the Reform Programme were: structural reform, legislation, modernization, and improvement coupled with increased investment and enhanced governance and accountability. The structural aspects of the Reform Programme were:

- Rationalization of health service agencies to reduce fragmentation, including abolition of the health board/health authority structure.
- Establishment of the HSE as a single national entity to manage the health services.
- Restructuring of the DOH.
- Establishment of the Health Information and Quality Authority (HIQA).

49. The HSE was established on 1 January 2005 under the Health Act 2004 and in 2011 the government decided to change the governance of the HSE, replacing the Board of the HSE with a new Health Service Directorate. The HSE (Governance) Act of 2013 was enacted to formally make these changes. The new Directorate is comprised of a director general, chief operating officer, and chief financial officer with national directors of primary care, acute services, social care, health and well-being, and mental health. The Act allows the Minister for Health to issue directions to the HSE on the implementation of Ministerial and Government policies and objectives relating to HSE functions. The Minister may also determine priorities to which the HSE must have regard in preparing its service plan and may specify performance targets for the executive. These changes are seen as part of a much wider process of reform which envisages the eventual dissolution of the HSE although this will require further legislation and careful planning over the coming years.

Further reform took place in 2013 with the re-organization of fifty-two acute hospitals into seven largely autonomous groups located in various geographical regions around the country. The services delivered by these groups include inpatient care, emergency care, maternity services, outpatient, and diagnostic services. There is a Chief Executive of each group who reports to the National Director for Acute Services and is accountable for the group's planning and performance under an accountability framework. In 2016 the HSE also introduced a new funding model for hospital care known as 'Activity Based Funding' which means a specified price is paid to each hospital for each weighted unit of inpatient works and each weighted unit of day-case

20. *Report of the National Task Force on Medical Staffing (the 'Hanly Report')* (Department of Health 2003).

work. Emergency care, outpatient care, and other services will receive block grant allocations.

50. The Health Information and Quality Authority (HIQA) was established on 15 May 2007 under the Health Act 2007. The DOH was restructured to take account of these changes and reflects its current core roles of national policy development and oversight of the operations of the State bodies under its aegis. HIQA[21] was established to underpin patient safety and quality in the newly restructured health service. A core function of HIQA is to set standards on safety and quality of services and to monitor enforcement of these standards in an open and transparent way. Other functions of HIQA include:

- Undertaking investigations into the safety, quality, and standards of services where it is believed that there is a serious risk to the health or welfare of a person receiving services.
- Carrying out reviews to ensure best outcomes/value for money for the resources available to the HSE.
- Inspecting and registering designated residential care services for older people, for example nursing homes, children, and for people with disabilities. Monitoring of foster care services, day facilities, and children's detention centres.
- Undertaking Health Technology Assessments to inform the decision making for safety and quality.
- A central role in health information development and the implementation of the recommendations set out in the National Health Information Strategy.
- Evaluating information available on services provided by the HSE and other service providers and on the health and welfare of the population, identifying information deficiencies, and advising the HSE and Minister accordingly.

51. In addition to establishing the HSE, the Health Act 2004 provided the legal framework for Regional Health Forums established by regulation to allow public representatives to share their views with the HSE on how services are being delivered and managed and a statutory complaints framework to help ensure a high standard of complaints management within the health service. The Health Act 2007 also provided for protected disclosures or *whistle-blowing* safeguards; employees making protected disclosures in good faith and on reasonable grounds about issues of patient safety or patient welfare are protected from penalization in the workplace and from civil liability.

52. Other important pieces of legislation introduced to support the Reform Programme include the Health and Social Care Professionals Act 2005, Pharmacy Act 2007, and Medical Practitioners Act 2007. The Health and Social Care Professionals Act 2005 provides for a system of statutory registration for twelve healthcare and social care professions to ensure that members of the public can be confident that healthcare and social care professionals providing services are properly qualified, competent, and fit to practise. There is an overarching Health and Social Care Professionals Council with separate registration boards for each profession. The first Council was established on 26 March 2007.

21. At http://www.hiqa.ie.

53. The Pharmacy Act 2007 reforms the regulation of pharmacy practice by setting new standards of governance, fitness to practise, and registration for pharmacy. It also lifts restrictions on qualified EU pharmacists setting up in Ireland.

54. The Medical Practitioners Act 2007 provides for an enhanced system of regulation of the medical profession in Ireland. Some of the important changes introduced by the Act include increased non-medical membership on the Medical Council and the statutory obligation on medical practitioners to maintain their professional competence throughout their careers by participation in competence assurance schemes that include peer review and clinical audit.

55. The regulation of other healthcare professionals, including nurses and midwives, who are regulated by the Nursing Board under the Nurses and Midwives Act 2011, follow the same model as for registered medical practitioners. CORU, the Health and Social Care Professionals Council, was established by legislation in 2005 to act as an umbrella body for twelve registration boards covering clinical biochemists, dieticians, medical scientists, occupational therapists, orthoptists, physiotherapists, podiatrists, psychologists, radiographers, social care workers, social workers, and speech and language therapists.

§3. Financing of the Healthcare System

56. Ireland's health system is characterized by a mix of public and private health service funding and provision. Total health spending in 2013 was EUR 18.4 billion, representing 10.5% of Gross Domestic Product (GDP) in Ireland, higher than the average of 9% across Organization for Economic Cooperation and Development (OECD) countries. In terms of health spending per capita, Ireland ranks above the OECD average, with spending of USD PPP of 3,781 in 2011 compared with an OECD average of USD PPP 3,233.

57. The health service remains predominantly tax-funded; approximately 71% of health expenditure came from the government in 2013, 14% came from health insurance payments and 15% came from household out-of-pocket payments.

58. Funding for health services is determined annually in negotiations between the Department of Finance and the DOH. Government revenue, demographic factors, commitments to service provision, national pay policies, and other social, economic, and political considerations all influence budgets. Funding is also provided directly by the Department to voluntary hospitals and other service delivery agencies in the voluntary sector for the funding of some services. Regional health authorities enter into agreement with these agencies directly.

59. The largest single purchaser of primary healthcare services in Ireland is the State. The GMS covers services from GPs and pharmacists. There are approximately 2,500 GPs in Ireland who hold GMS contracts (but who also may see private patients). Each person entitled to a medical card registers with a GP from a list of GPs who have GMS contracts. There is a maximum number of patients that a GP can have on its panel. Under the terms of the GMS contract, GPs undertake to provide free services to those patients registered with them. The GP is paid an annual capitation fee per person in its panel depending on age, gender, and distance of residence from the GP's clinic. There are additional payments for out-of-hours services, special services, and temporary residents. There is also an annual supplement for rural practices, practice secretaries, nurses, locum expenses, and medical indemnity insurance.

60. There are approximately 1,800 pharmacies in Ireland that hold GMS contracts. A person may take a prescription for medication to any pharmacy that has an agreement to dispense GMS prescription forms and will be provided with the prescribed drugs free of charge. Pharmacists are reimbursed on a fee-per-item basis, covering the ingredient cost and a dispensing fee.

61. There is a Drugs Payment Scheme in operation which provides that no individual or family has to pay more than a certain amount (currently EUR 144) per month for the cost of prescribed drugs. The pharmacist recovers the balance of the cost from the GMS Board. There is also a Long-Term Illness Scheme in place whereby any person suffering from a specified illness (e.g., cystic fibrosis, multiple sclerosis) may obtain the prescribed drugs they require free of charge. Eligible persons are issued with a long-term illness book that lists the drugs to which they are entitled, and these will be dispensed free of charge on presentation of the book to their pharmacist. The pharmacist will recover the cost from the GMS.

62. Emergency dental services are also available free of charge to GMS-eligible adults for the relief of pain and free dentures. There are also benefits available for optical and hearing aids.

§4. Sources of Medical Law

63. Medical law in Ireland is a relatively young discipline; it is not codified and therefore a number of sources exist. These include statutory provisions and regulations and case law. The subject area itself crosses a number of different legal areas, including constitutional law, law of torts, and family, contract, and public law, and therefore sources from all of these subject areas may be relevant. The discipline may be regarded as encompassing both private and public law, in the sense that it examines the private relationship between medical practitioner and patient, as well as the public regulatory aspects of how healthcare is delivered. In some countries the subject may be referred to as healthcare law, to indicate that the subject is increasingly concerned with the latter area rather than the former, but in Ireland the expression *medical law* is more commonly used at present.

64. The influence of medical ethics is also relevant as the interaction of medicine, ethics, and the law shows how each discipline engages and influences the other in an attempt to find solutions to dilemmas posed by advances in medical technology and recognition of the rights and interests of those seeking medical treatment. Although *law* is usually reserved for rules that are enforceable by legal sanctions, it can be argued that in this context the concept also encompasses principles and rules that govern medical practice and that emanate from an authoritative source, even if they are not, strictly speaking, legally enforceable. Therefore, another useful source in Ireland includes codes of practice or guidelines issued by the professional regulatory bodies, principally the Medical Council's Guide to Professional Conduct and Ethics.[22]

65. In the international context Ireland also has obligations in the area of medical law. Article 29.4.3 of the Irish Constitution was passed by referendum of the Irish people in 1972 to enable Ireland to join the European Economic Community (EEC). The European Communities Act 1972, as amended by the Single European Act 1992, provides for the integration of Irish law with EU law. The effect of this is to provide that EU law has 'the paramount force and effect of constitutional provisions'.[23] Therefore, Irish medical law is influenced by developments in healthcare policies in Europe.

66. The European Convention on Human Rights and Fundamental Freedoms 1950 was introduced into Ireland by the Human Rights Act 2003. The Human Rights Commission was established in 2001 as a direct result of the Good Friday Agreement of 1998, which provided for the establishment of a Human Rights Commission in this jurisdiction and for a Human Rights Commission in Northern Ireland. Under the Good Friday Agreement, the Commissions are charged with promoting and protecting human rights in their respective jurisdictions and working together to improve the protection of human rights on the island of Ireland.

The Commission aims to ensure that Irish law and practice is in line with the highest international standards, measuring law and practice against the standards set out in the Constitution and in international human rights agreements to which Ireland is a party.

67. The Human Rights Unit (HRU) was established in the Political Division of the Department of Foreign Affairs in 1996. Its main function is to take an overview of Ireland's approach to international human rights issues, so that they are given full attention in all aspects of Ireland's foreign policy. HRU liaises with other Divisions across the Department on international human rights issues and provides domestic policy departments with information on Ireland's international human rights obligations. The HRU also interacts with international and domestic Non-Governmental Organizations (NGOs) on international matters of particular concern to them through policy partnerships. In addition, the HRU coordinates Ireland's participation in international human rights forums such as at the Third Committee of the UN General Assembly, the UN Human Rights Council and the EU Human Rights Working Group (COHOM). The HRU is also responsible for facilitating the ratification of international human rights instruments.

68. Ireland is also a member of the Council of Europe and participates in a programme of cooperation in relation to the development and provision of health services and programmes across Member States. Ireland has introduced regulations to implement the provisions of relevant EU Directives in the area of healthcare, including those concerning clinical trials, data protection, free movement of health

---

22. Known as the Ethical Guide, this document is revised every five years. It is not intended to be a code of practice but rather an articulation of general principles that doctors should take into account along with their own judgment and experience in deciding on how to behave. The most recent edition (8th) was published in 2016 and is available at https://www.medicalcouncil.ie/News-and-Publications/Reports/Guide-to-Professional-Conduct-and-Ethics-8th-Edition-2016-.pdf.
23. *Doyle v. An Taoiseach* [1986] ILRM 693.

professionals, and safety and quality assurance in relation to procurement and storage of human tissue and cells for clinical application.

69. Ireland is a member of the World Health Organization (WHO), which was founded in 1948.[24] WHO is the directing and coordinating authority for health within the United Nations system. It is responsible for providing leadership on global health matters, shaping the health research agenda, setting norms and standards, articulating evidence-based policy options, providing technical support to countries, and monitoring and assessing health trends.

24. At http://www.who.int.

Part I. The Medical Profession

Chapter 1. Access to the Medical Profession

§1. Medical Education

70. There are currently six medical schools in the Republic of Ireland, five of which are university-based medical schools funded by the State (University Colleges at Dublin, Cork, and Galway, Trinity College Dublin, and the University of Limerick) and one of which is an independent institution predominantly funded through fee income (the Royal College of Surgeons of Ireland). Medical schools use the Central Applications Office points score as the criterion for medical school entry. Traditionally, school-leavers obtaining very high points in the Leaving Certificate Examination are the typical entrants to Irish medical schools.

From 2009 on, undergraduate entry to medicine for school-leavers also require completion of a required admissions test within the two-year period immediately preceding admission to the medicine programme. The admissions test selected by the Irish Medical Schools is called Health Professions Admission Test-Ireland (HPAT-Ireland). This test is independently administered by the Australian Council for Educational Research (ACER). The HPAT-Ireland test measures a candidate's logical reasoning and problem-solving skills as well as non-verbal reasoning and the ability to understand the thoughts, behaviour, and/or intentions of people. It does not test academic knowledge and candidates do not require special understanding of any academic discipline.

71. Most medical schools operate a five- or six-year undergraduate degree course. In all medical schools a significant proportion of the programme involves clinical training at approved sites such as hospitals or primary care settings. Traditionally, the first phase of the degree is a pre-clinical phase during which students study basic sciences such as physiology, biochemistry, and anatomy. The second phase is spent largely on clinical placements or rotations in hospitals. In recent years this traditional approach has been changing to a more modern integrated approach with the sciences and clinical experience running at the same time.

72. In recent years graduate entry programmes have been introduced in some medical schools to provide a four-year degree course to those who meet specific graduate entry criteria. Entry to these programmes is based on an honours university degree or equivalent in any discipline such as science, arts, or social sciences. The accreditation of such programmes by the Medical Council (*see* paragraph 73) is based on the standards of the World Federation for Medical Education. This includes participation of external assessors, documentation review, site visit, and inspection of campus and teaching hospitals. As these programmes are relatively new in the Irish context, the development of the programmes will continue to be monitored by the Medical Council.

73. Under the Medical Practitioners Acts 1978–2007, the Medical Council is statutorily responsible for the accreditation of medical schools in Ireland, for the assessment of the quality of educational programmes, and for the registration of graduates as medical practitioners.[25] Section 35 of the 1978 Act states that: It shall be the duty of the Council from time to time to satisfy itself:

(a) as to the suitability of the medical education and training provided by anybody in the state recognized by the Council for such purposes;
(b) as to the standards of theoretical and practical knowledge required for primary qualifications;
(c) as to the clinical training and experience required for the granting of a certificate of experience.

74. The Medical Council is obliged to ensure that the minimum standards required by any Directive of the European Communities relating to education and training are met by the formal qualifications in the State. The Council must satisfy itself as to the suitability of undergraduate medical education and training provided by recognized medical schools and the standard or theoretical and practical knowledge required at the examinations for primary qualification. It must also satisfy itself as to the clinical training and experience required for the granting of a certificate of experience, and the adequacy and suitability of postgraduate education and training. It states that:

> Education and Training are at the heart of the Council's role in developing medicine in the future. Lifelong learning has long been an aspiration of the medical profession. In the medical practice of the twenty-first century this aspiration is fast becoming a reality.
>
> The rigorous process of undergraduate medical education enables the newly graduated doctor to begin an extended period of specialist training in the discipline of his or her choice. On completion of specialist training the newly independent doctor finds him or herself in an environment of rapidly changing scientific knowledge, high patient expectations and increasingly sophisticated healthcare delivery systems.[26]

75. The Council has an Education, Training, and Professional Development Committee that implements the Council's policy for medical education in Ireland. The

25. *Review of Medical Schools in Ireland* (Medical Council 2007).
26. At https://www.medicalcouncil.ie/News-and-Publications/Reports/Guide-to-Professional-Conduct-and-Ethics-8th-Edition-2016-.pdf.

Council strives to ensure the quality of education and training within the medical profession through the following means:

- visiting the medical schools in relation to undergraduate medical education;
- ongoing assessment of the intern year;
- visiting the hospitals approved for the purposes of internship training and temporary registration;
- liaising with the recognized postgraduate training bodies.

76. Each medical school is responsible for devising and delivering its own curriculum, which is then assessed by the Medical Council using national and international best practice, such as the World Federation of Medical Education, as benchmarks as appropriate. Only persons holding qualifications recognized by the Medical Council can be entered on the medical register. Therefore, the Council influences the structure of medical education by withdrawing or according recognition to medical schools.

77. Each medical school has a broadly similar curriculum, five years pre-clinical and clinical education, and a year spent as an intern acquiring further clinical experience. It is regarded as a fundamental part of medical education that students receive a significant part of their education in a clinical environment. Approximately one-half of undergraduate training is delivered in clinical settings, usually in a hospital, but also in some primary and community care facilities. It is usually in the last two to three years of their medical education that students attend clinical settings for lectures, 'bedside' tutorials, and attachment to health service teams in which students follow a variety of team activities, including ward rounds, attendance at out-patient clinics, theatre, and case conferences. This learning method is largely observational as students are not generally expected to interact with patients other than in minor ways. Most of the clinical education is provided by consultant and non-consultant doctors who do not have a specific academic contract and who provide teaching services in a voluntary capacity. The Fottrell Report[27] noted that:

> while there is a weak contractual basis for the training carried out by health professionals, it should be noted that there has traditionally been a strong ethic among doctors to train their successors, and indeed involvement in training is perceived to be integral to professional development.

78. Following graduation, graduates receive internship registration with the Medical Council and must then complete an intern year during which they are employed and paid by the health service and expected to fulfil relevant clinical activities. The intern year is, therefore, the first year of postgraduate training. The vast majority of intern posts are in hospitals, though it is possible to do an internship in general practice. It is the Medical Council's responsibility to approve intern posts, based on approval of the hospital's programme of education and training for the interns. During the twelve-month period, graduates must spend at least three months in an internship in medicine and three months in surgery. The Medical Council will also approve suitable

27. *Medical Education in Ireland: a New Direction* (Department of Health 2006).

posts in obstetrics and gynaecology, emergency medicine, paediatrics, psychiatry, general practice, and perioperative medicine (which includes anaesthesia and pain management).

79. Upon successful completion of this intern year, all graduates are then fully registered by the Medical Council and may choose to progress through a number of postgraduate education streams, for example, surgery, anaesthesia, radiology, pathology, and general practice, which are coordinated by recognized postgraduate training bodies. The Medical Council has functions in relation to the determination of recognized medical specialties and the recognition of bodies granting evidence of satisfactory completion of specialist training.

80. In recent years there has been much discussion on the topic of continuing education and professional development of healthcare professionals. The Medical Council stresses the importance of lifelong learning for doctors and the Council introduced a competence assurance programme to enable doctors to participate in learning activities throughout their careers. The Council states that:

> Good quality patient care requires each doctor to continuously participate in learning activities, to monitor their own performance and to measure their performance against that of colleagues. Each of these elements is contained within the newly introduced Competence Assurance Structures which for the first time formalise the lifelong learning pattern of medical practice from completion of specialist training to retirement.[28]

Similarly, the Report of the Commission on Patient Safety in 2008 stated:

> It is clear that a health professional can no longer be regarded as trained for life upon qualification. Instead what is required are systems of lifelong learning and professional development, with regular competence assurance to ensure that there is a workforce of skilled professionals who are fit for purpose, competent in managing patients' needs, aware of the limits of their own competency and adaptable and capable of responding to changing needs. Continuing Professional Development (CPD) is a key responsibility of individual practitioners, a core function of training bodies and a crucial component of the professional regulatory reforms e.g. the Medical Council's Competence Assurance Scheme.[29]

81. It is also a key issue for employers, who should have systems in place to ensure that all professional staff participate in Continuing Professional Development (CPD) and are provided with adequate time and resources to do so. CPD involves not only the continuous upgrading of clinical skills but also the development of the necessary skills of accessing and appraising evidence, clinical audit and reflective practice, the application of standards, and the monitoring of performance against standards.

82. The Medical Practitioners Act 2007, section 94, introduced for the first time a legal obligation on registered medical practitioners to maintain their professional

28. . At https://www.medicalcouncil.ie/News-and-Publications/Reports/Guide-to-Professional-Conduct-and-Ethics-8th-Edition-2016-.pdf.
29. *Building a Culture of Patient Safety* 99 (Department of Health 2008).

competence throughout their working lives. Part 11 of the Medical Practitioners Act 2007, once commenced, will provide a statutory basis for the development of Professional Competence Schemes in Ireland. Section 91(1) of the Act provides that:

> It shall be the duty of the Council to satisfy itself as to the ongoing maintenance of professional competence of registered medical practitioners.

The Medical Council is charged with the responsibility to satisfy itself as to the ongoing maintenance of the professional competence of registered medical practitioners, and to this end the Council has a duty to develop, establish, and operate one or more Competence Assurance Scheme(s) that will be reviewed periodically. In 2006 the Council published a consensus statement entitled *Performance in Practice, Maintenance of Professional Competence*, which sets out three strands to competence assurance:

- Continuous Quality Assurance (CQA): All doctors will be asked to participate in a CQA programme (fifty hours per year) and align themselves with a postgraduate training body where possible. The Council will monitor those who are unable to align themselves with a postgraduate training body. Doctors will be encouraged to participate in clinical audit and peer review activities (up to 50% of their annual hourly total) as part of their ongoing education.
- Professional Practice Review: A multi-source feedback questionnaire will be used as a quality improvement tool and will be filled out by medical peers, non-medical peers, and patients nominated by the individual doctor. The doctor will receive a confidential summary of the results of the questionnaire and the Council will receive a collective statistical report and a confidential report of the lowest five percentile.
- Performance Assessment: If concerns are expressed about a doctor, he or she might be asked to have his or her performance assessed. A structured assessment will be carried out by two trained peer assessors and one lay assessor according to published standards and benchmarks. Recommendations will be made for the individual doctor accordingly.

83. If a registered medical practitioner refuses or ceases to cooperate with the Scheme, the Council may make a complaint to the disciplinary or Fitness to Practise section of the Council. Healthcare employers are obliged by section 93 of the Act to facilitate the maintenance by the practitioner of his or her professional competence. The section provides as follows:

> 93.– (1) The Health Service Executive shall facilitate the maintenance of professional competence of registered medical practitioners pursuant to a professional competence scheme applicable to the practitioners concerned.
>
> (2) An employer of a registered medical practitioner, not being the Health Service Executive, shall facilitate the maintenance of professional competence of registered

medical practitioners pursuant to a professional competence scheme applicable to the practitioners concerned.

§2. Manpower Planning

I. Freedom of Establishment

84. Under European law, citizens are entitled to freedom of movement, meaning the presence of national borders should not be an impediment to the free market. In relation to medical practitioners this means that in principle, a doctor who is qualified in one EU state should be free to travel to and work in another EU Member State. Issues that have caused some difficulties in recent years centre on the recognition of qualifications from other countries and language proficiency tests.

85. A number of EU Directives were introduced to deal with free movement of persons and freedom of establishment. These were consolidated in 2005 in Directive 2005/36/EC. A person who wishes to carry on a regulated profession in another Member State is obliged to fulfil certain minimum criteria set out in the Directive, and must obtain the equivalent professional and educational qualifications and training in an EU Member State. If these conditions are met, permission may not be refused to an EU citizen to practise in another Member State. If the training is not deemed equivalent, the host state may offer an aptitude test and period of adaptation in the host country.

86. The Medical Council has the statutory function to maintain a register of medical practitioners entitled to practise medicine in the State. To this end, the Council has developed registration rules that apply to applications for registration. The rules outline the four main categories of applicant:

- Category 1: Graduates of Irish medical schools.
- Category 2: EU citizens who graduated in an EU medical school and/or their qualifications are recognized under EU Directive 2005/36/EC (recognition of professional qualifications for EU citizens).
- Category 3: Non-EU citizens who graduated in an EU medical school and/or their qualifications would be recognized under EU Directive 2005/36/EC (recognition of professional qualifications) if they were an EU citizen.
- Category 4: Medical practitioners who have completed recognized internship training, hold full/general registration in another jurisdiction, and do not meet the criteria for any of the above categories.

The Pre-Registration Examination System (PRES) (Levels 2 and 3 of the application process) must be passed by Category 4 applicants for trainee specialist or general registration, unless they are exempt under the Rules Specifying Pre-Registration Exams and Exemptions. Applicants for trainee specialist, general or specialist registration, who are not EU/EEA/Swiss citizens are required to pass or be exempted from the Academic International English Language Testing System.[30]

§3. Licensing of Physicians

87. A person cannot practise medicine in Ireland unless he or she is registered with the Medical Council. Section 41 of the Medical Practitioners Act 2007 provides that certain designated titles may only be used by doctors and that breach of this provision is a criminal offence. The Medical Council is obliged to maintain a general register of medical practitioners.[31] Those entitled to be registered include:

- those registered by the Medical Registration Council pursuant to the Medical Practitioners Acts 1927–1961, and those entitled to be so registered;
- persons awarded any of the primary qualifications specified by the Act;[32]
- citizens of any European Member State who have been awarded a qualification in medicine by a competent body or designated authority pursuant to any Directive adopted by the Council of the European Communities;
- or any person who satisfies the Council that he or she has undergone specified courses of training and passed specified examinations as set out by the Council;[33]
- or any person entitled to be registered pursuant to an order under the Medical Practitioners Act 1927.

88. Applicants who fulfil these conditions are entitled to be registered on submission of a registration fee to the Council.[34] However, the Council is empowered to refuse registration on the grounds of the unfitness to practise medicine of any applicant. Under the 2007 Medical Practitioners Act the register is divided into:

---

30. At https://www.medicalcouncil.ie/News-and-Publications/Reports/Guide-to-Professional-Conduct-and-Ethics-8th-Edition-2016-.pdf.
31. At https://www.medicalcouncil.ie/News-and-Publications/Reports/Guide-to-Professional-Conduct-and-Ethics-8th-Edition-2016-.pdf.
32. Section 27 refers to the Fourth Schedule to the Act, which specifies those primary qualifications as Bachelor of Medicine and Bachelor of Surgery of the National University of Ireland and the University of Dublin, and Licentiates of the Royal College of Physicians of Ireland and of the Royal College of Surgeons in Ireland. This has been amended by s. 6 of the 2002 Act, which allows for graduates of colleges in EU Member States to become interns in Ireland.
33. *See Bakht v. Medical Council* [1990] 1 IR 515, in which the Supreme Court dealt with the case of a doctor who qualified in Bangladesh, was temporarily registered in Ireland for various periods of time, obtained postgraduate qualifications in the State, became an Irish citizen, and was nonetheless unable to receive full registration. The judgment discusses the rule-making functions of the Council under the Act and its powers in relation to registration. Rules made by the Council must be of general application and not merely rules under which a restricted class of doctors can apply.
34. Refusal to register a person who is entitled to registration will be actionable. *See Phillips v. Medical Council* [1991] 1 IR 115.

- The General Division: This is open to those who have completed medical training in Ireland, the EU, or elsewhere and who have completed any required examinations or have satisfactory evidence of experience sufficient to permit registration.
- The Specialist Division: This is open to those who have completed specialist medical training in a specialty recognized by the Council and who can provide evidence from an appropriate body that satisfies the Medical Council.
- The Trainee Specialist Division: This is open to qualified doctors who are practising medicine in an individual identifiable specialist training post, and interns.
- The Visiting European Economic Area (EEA) Practitioners Division: This is for practitioners who are practising medicine in EU Member States and who wish to practise in Ireland only on a temporary or occasional basis. These practitioners must notify the Council of intended periods and scope of practice in Ireland and make declarations as to good standing in their native country.
- Internship registration – This allows a doctor to carry out internship training in a hospital recognized by the Medical Council. Internship registration is open to both graduates of Irish and EU Member State Medical Schools.
- Supervised division – This enables doctors to be registered for a maximum of two years in a supervised individually numbered and identifiable post within a Health Service Executive hospital or service.

89. The Council is obliged by the Act to publish copies of the register (and supplements to it) at specified intervals and keep available for inspection at Council offices the most recently published copy of the register.[35] Only a person registered under the Act may sign a certificate that is required to be signed by a medical practitioner. It is a criminal offence to make any false declaration or misrepresentation to the Council in order to obtain registration.

90. Registration of medical practitioners serves many important functions, not least of which is the maintenance of public confidence in the supervision of educational standards imposed by the Council and adherence to codes of ethical conduct. Indeed, the classic characteristics of a profession would usually include an agreed ethical code, discipline rules, and control of entry and training standards. There is also an expectation among members of the public that doctors will be members of the relevant professional organization.

35. Section 57 of the Act.

Chapter 2. The Practice of Medicine

91. There are a number of professional regulatory bodies in Ireland governing the practice of medicine:

– The Medical Council regulates registered medical practitioners under the Medical Practitioners Acts 1978–2007. Its functions include assuring the quality of undergraduate education of doctors, assuring the quality of postgraduate training of specialists, registration of doctors, disciplinary functions, and providing guidance of professional standards/ethical conduct.
– The Dental Council regulates dental practitioners under the Dental Act 1985. Its roles include the maintenance of a register of dentists and dental specialists, assessment of the adequacy and suitability of dental education and training in the dental schools in the State, disciplinary functions, and advising the dental profession and the public on matters relating to dental ethics and professional behaviour.
– The Nursing and Midwifery Board regulates nurses under the Nurses and Midwives Act 2011. The Board's functions include the registration of nurses, provision of education and training, disciplinary functions, giving guidance to the profession, managing a careers centre to provide a centralized system of processing, and selection of applicants wishing to enter nursing and provision of career advice to nurses and midwives.
– The Pharmaceutical Society of Ireland (PSI) is the regulator of pharmacies under the Pharmacy Act 2007. Its roles include the maintenance of a register of pharmacists and pharmacies, inspection of pharmacy premises, development of codes of conduct for pharmacists, promotion of high standards of education and training, disciplinary functions, and recognition of qualifications of pharmacists from other jurisdictions.
– The Opticians Board regulates optometrists and dispensing opticians under the Opticians Act 2003. It has functions in relation to registration and education and training.
– The Health and Social Care Professionals Council regulates twelve healthcare and social care professions under the Health and Social Care Professionals Act 2005. These cover clinical biochemists, dieticians, medical scientists, occupational therapists, orthoptists, physiotherapists, podiatrists, psychologists, radiographers, social care workers, social workers, and speech and language therapists. The functions of the Council include coordination of the activities of the twelve registration boards established for each of the foregoing professions, enforcement of standards of practice for registrants, disciplinary functions, and promotion of collaboration between the registration boards, including in relation to education and training.

Chapter 3. Illegal Practice of Medicine

92. The Medical Practitioners Act 2007 provides in section 37 that an unregistered medical practitioner shall not practise medicine or advertise his or her services as a medical practitioner. The expression 'practise medicine' is not clearly defined in the Act; it is simply stated to mean 'to engage in the practice of medicine'. This phrase in turn is defined as including 'the practice of surgery and other disciplines of medicine'. Section 38 of the Act provides that a medical practitioner does not contravene section 37 if:

(a) the practitioner is a dentist registered under the Dentists Act 1985 who only practises medicine in the course of, and for the purpose of, the lawful practise of dentistry;
(b) the practitioner is a person registered under the Nurses Act 1985 who only practises medicine in the course of, and for the purposes of, the lawful practice of nursing or midwifery;
(c) the practitioner is a registered pharmaceutical chemist or a registered dispensing chemist and druggist, under the Pharmacy Acts 1875–1977, who only practises medicine in the course of, and for the purposes of, the lawful practise of pharmacy in accordance with those Acts;
(d) the practitioner is a person registered under the Health and Social Care Professionals Act 2005 to practise a profession designated under that Act who only practises medicine in the course of, and for the purposes of, the lawful practise of that profession;
(e) the practitioner only practises medicine in the course of rendering first aid to a person;
(f) the practitioner only practises medicine in the State pursuant to the provisions of section 50 (this section provides that, subject to the conditions set out in the Act, a medical practitioner who is a national of a Member State and lawfully established in medical practice in a Member State may, on visiting the State, practise medicine on a temporary and occasional basis without first being registered, and advertise the practitioner's services as a medical practitioner for this purpose);
(g) the practitioner only practises medicine in any combination of any of the circumstances specified in paragraphs (a)–(f).

93. Section 39 of the Act provides that the Minister for Health may make regulations to designate for the purposes of this Act any title or variants thereof to be used by any registered medical practitioner. This power will only be exercised following consultation with interested parties and organizations, and where the designation of title is deemed to be in the public interest. The Minister will consider the extent to which any class of medical practitioners has a defined scope of practice and applies a distinct and recognized body of knowledge, as well as the degree of risk to the health, safety, or welfare of the public from the incompetent, unethical, or impaired practice of any class of medical practitioners. If the Minister exercises the power under this

Act, section 40 provides that a registered medical practitioner shall not use a designated title other than in accordance with such regulations.

94. Section 41 of the Act provides that persons are guilty of an offence if they practise medicine while unregistered or use a designated title without being so entitled, falsely represent themselves to be a registered medical practitioner, or represent themselves to be registered in a division of the register other than that in which they are so registered. Section 42 provides that an unregistered medical practitioner shall not be entitled to recover fees or expenses incurred in providing services in the course of practising medicine.

Chapter 4. Control over the Practice of Medicine

§1. Professional Liability

95. Although the relationship between a doctor and patient is rarely based on a written contract, nonetheless the principles of contract law may govern the relationship. The courts would undoubtedly be loath to imply a term into the contract that might suggest a guarantee of a specific result of treatment but it would be implicit in the performance of a medical treatment that the doctor would use reasonable care and skill. Therefore, in the event that the patient perceived the doctor to have deviated from acceptable standards of care, he or she could sue for breach of contract in addition to the commission of the tort of negligence.

In extreme cases where harm was suffered by a patient, a doctor could be charged with a criminal offence such as assault, battery, or homicide.

§2. Civil Liability

96. Most legal actions against doctors in Ireland are founded on the principles of negligence as a tort or civil wrong. Negligence is doing or omitting to do something that a reasonable person would do in the circumstances in order to avoid harm to others. This applies whether or not there is a contract between the parties and is based on the 'neighbour principle' set out by Lord Atkin in the English case of *Donoghue v. Stevenson*,[36] in which a woman discovered the decomposed remains of a snail in a bottle of ginger ale she was drinking. She sued the manufacturer of the drink for the illness and distress that was caused to her as a consequence. Although there was no direct contractual relationship between the manufacturer and the plaintiff (she purchased the drink from a retailer who had in turn purchased it from the manufacturer), the Court took the view that the manufacturer should reasonably have foreseen that a person such as the plaintiff might consume the drink and might be affected by any negligence on its part in relation to its manufacture. Lord Atkin described the basis for the imposition of liability as follows:

> You must take reasonable care to avoid acts or omissions which you can reasonably foresee would be liable to injure your neighbour. Who then, in law, is my neighbour? The answer seems to be persons who are so closely and directly affected by my act that I ought reasonably have them in contemplation as being so affected when I am directing my mind to the acts or omissions which are called into question.

36. [1932] AC 562.

97. Therefore, under this principle, one must take care to prevent harm to anyone who might reasonably be affected by one's actions. There are four aspects to establishing a claim of negligence:

- the existence of a duty of care;
- breach of the duty of care by falling below the required standard of care;
- causation, that is, that the harm suffered by the plaintiff was caused by the breach of duty;
- proof of injury or damage.

Medical negligence actions seek to provide compensation to the patient in circumstances where a doctor carried out his or her duty incompetently as result of which the patient was injured. A doctor may also be liable for not doing something, such as failing to diagnose an illness or refer a patient for further tests or specialist treatment.

I. Duty of Care

98. A doctor clearly owes a duty of care to his or her patient. The scope of this duty relates to all aspects of care of the patient – diagnosis, treatment, advice, and counselling. In undertaking the care of a patient, although a doctor does not guarantee a successful treatment outcome, he or she undertakes that he or she has the necessary skill and competence to provide the treatment and will exercise that skill in administering the treatment.

In Irish law a duty of care arises where:

- there is legal proximity between the parties;
- the damage caused by one party to the other is foreseeable;
- there is no strong public policy against allowing the plaintiff's action to succeed.[37]

99. In many cases a patient will be treated in a hospital context in which a clinical team provides multi-disciplinary care and treatment. The hospital, therefore, also owes a duty to the patient to exercise reasonable care to provide a safe system of admission, diagnosis, and treatment by competent healthcare professionals. In *Kelly v. Board of Governors of St Laurence's Hospital*,[38] the plaintiff presented symptoms of epilepsy and was admitted to hospital for tests and observation. He was taken off medication for the purpose of assessment and on the fifth night of his stay in hospital he left the ward unaccompanied and entered a toilet, climbed through the window, and fell 20 feet to the yard, sustaining severe injuries. The hospital was found negligent on the basis that it owed a duty to the patient to take reasonable care to avoid permitting him to be exposed to injury that a reasonable person ought to foresee, and in this case to provide a reasonable nursing service.

---

37. For example, *Ward v. McMaster* [1988] IR 337. The Court found there to be a compelling public interest against allowing plaintiffs to sue the police for negligence during the investigation of criminal offences.
38. [1988] IR 402.

100. Irish law is unclear on the imposition of a legal duty on doctors to treat persons who are not their patients. For example, in circumstances where a doctor happens to come upon the scene of an accident, there is no general obligation on a doctor to provide care. If a doctor chooses to provide assistance, the standard of care expected will be assessed according to the nature of the emergency, the skills of the doctor, and the availability of back-up assistance and facilities. The Medical Council's Ethical Guide advises doctors that they have an ethical responsibility to provide care in emergencies unless they are satisfied that appropriate care will be provided by others. They should also consider their own competence and safety when considering what care they can offer.[39]

101. Although at common law a doctor would not owe a duty unless he or she had undertaken the care of the person, an Australian case called *Lowns v. Woods*[40] may cast doubt on this principle. In that case a doctor who was off duty was asked to come to aid of a nearby child who was having a seizure. He declined to do so. The child suffered brain damage and the doctor was found guilty of negligence on the basis that although he did not have an automatic legal duty to treat someone who was not his patient, in this case he had no satisfactory justification for not attending following a request to do so. Liability was imposed in part due to the provisions of the Australian Medical Practitioners Act 1938, and therefore the principles underpinning liability in this case may not be applicable in Ireland. There are no relevant Irish cases in point.

II. Standard of Care

102. In order to establish negligence on the part of the doctor, the patient must prove that the doctor fell below the standard of care that may be reasonably expected of doctors. Thus, even where the patient has a negative outcome to treatment, this will not necessarily mean that the doctor will be liable as the patient must prove that the negative outcome was caused by a failure on the doctor's part to exercise the necessary level of care and skill as might reasonably be expected in the circumstances. When assessing the standard of care to be expected of doctors, the court will compare the doctor's actions with the practice and standards of his or her peers. The courts acknowledge that there may be differences of opinion between professionals in relation to appropriate treatment and will not hold a doctor liable for following one opinion over another once the course of action is supported by a responsible body of opinion within the profession.

103. In *Daniels v. Heskin*[41] the Supreme Court stated that medical practitioners are liable for injury caused to another person to whom they owed a duty to take care if they fail to possess the amount of skill that is usual in their profession or if they neglect to use the skill that they possess or the necessary degree of care demanded or professed.

---

39. At https://www.medicalcouncil.ie/News-and-Publications/Reports/Guide-to-Professional-Conduct-and-Ethics-8th-Edition-2016-.pdf.
40. (1996) Australian Tort Reports 81.
41. [1954] IR 73.

104. This test was refined in the important case of *Dunne v. National Maternity Hospital*,[42] which concerned the birth of twins, one of whom died at childbirth, and the other of whom suffered severe brain damage. The Supreme Court held as follows:

- The true test for establishing negligence in diagnosis or treatment is whether the doctor has been guilty of such failure as no doctor of equal specialist or general status or skill would be guilty of if acting with ordinary care.
- If the allegation of negligence is based on proof that the doctor deviated from a general and approved practice,[43] that will not establish negligence unless it is also proved that the course he or she did take was one which no doctor of like specialization and skill would have followed had he or she been taking the ordinary care required from a person of his or her qualification.
- If a doctor charged with negligence defends his or her conduct by establishing that he or she followed a practice that was general and that was approved of by his or her colleagues of similar specialization and skill, he or she cannot escape liability if in reply the plaintiff established that such practice has inherent defects that ought to be obvious to any person giving the matter due consideration.
- An honest difference of opinion between doctors as to which is the better of two ways of treating a patient does not provide any ground for leaving a question to the jury[44] as to whether a person who has followed one course rather than the other has been negligent.
- It is not for a judge to decide which of two alternative courses of treatment is preferable. The judge must decide whether the course of treatment followed by the doctor complied with the careful conduct of a medical practitioner of like specialization and skill to that professed by the defendant.

Therefore, doctors are free to follow an accepted standard within the profession and may deviate from accepted practice in certain circumstances without being found guilty of negligence. The doctor must prove that his or her actions were consistent with a body of responsible opinion within the profession. This defence will not apply where the practice is obviously flawed. For example, in *Gottstein v. Maguire and Walsh*[45] the Court held that failing to have someone present in an intensive care unit who was competent to replace a dislodged tracheostomy tube was 'an inherent defect which ought to be obvious to any person giving the matter due consideration'. The general and approved practice followed by the doctor does not have to be universally adopted. It suffices if a substantial number of reputable practitioners holding the relevant specialist or general qualifications adhere to the practice in question. The Supreme Court reserves the right to question the reasonableness of any expert evidence presented before it.

42. [1989] IR 91.
43. The judge went on to clarify that such practice need not be universal but must be approved of and adhered to by a substantial number of reputable practitioners holding the relevant qualifications.
44. At the time of this judgment, it was common to have jury trials of negligence actions. This is no longer the case but the principle remains the same.
45. [2004] IEHC 416.

105. Where there is a difference of opinion between medical experts in relation to diagnosis or treatment of a patient, the court is not entitled to prefer one doctor's opinion over the other. However, where the disagreement is in relation to whether the defendant doctor's actions were negligent, the court may prefer the evidence that seems to be more compelling. In *Griffin v. Patton*[46] a patient was in her seventeenth week of pregnancy when her unborn baby died. When it was discovered that this had happened it was hoped that the dead foetus could be evacuated from the uterus as soon as possible. For this purpose the woman was prescribed dosages of prostaglandins that have a propensity for inducing a termination of pregnancy. Unfortunately, they did not work in this case. The doctor then decided on a surgical procedure involving the evacuation of the uterus through the vagina. All the doctors who gave evidence at the trial agreed that it is incumbent on the doctor carrying out this surgical procedure to satisfy him- or herself that all parts of the foetus are removed. It was common case among the medical experts who gave evidence that without negligence, small pieces of soft tissue can be accidentally left behind. That normally presents no problem because within days they are passed out of the body in the normal way. What was in issue between the medical experts, however, was whether a piece of bone 5.5 centimetres in length and probably a lower limb of the baby could be accidentally left behind in the uterus without there being negligence on the part of the surgeon. Here, it was common case among all the medical experts that a gynaecologist carrying out the procedure that the appellant did carry out had to take all the correct steps to ensure as far as possible that the uterus was properly evacuated and especially of the major bony structures. It was for the judge to decide on the issue of fact as to whether the appellant did that or not. He found that the doctor did not. The fact that one doctor may say in the witness-box that in his opinion, the doctor was not to blame does not in any way oust the normal function of the trial judge on the issues of fact even if the judge takes the view that the doctor giving evidence was giving an honest opinion. The Court took the view that as a matter of fact, the doctor had not carried out an assessment of what was removed from the body. Therefore, the doctor was guilty of negligence.

106. It is acknowledged that medicine is not a risk-free activity and that mistakes, unfortunately, do occur. Doctors will, therefore, only be liable where the decisions they make as to diagnosis and/or treatment are not reasonable. In *Collins v Mid Western Health Board*[47] a GP was found guilty of negligence for failing to take into account in his diagnosis of a patient, a description of the patient's symptoms given by the patient's wife. She had telephoned the doctor in advance of her husband's visit to tell him of her husband's 'very bad headache' and that her husband must be 'very bad' to want to attend a doctor as he usually avoided doctors. The Court found that the doctor was negligent in not taking this into consideration in making his diagnosis of the patient.

107. Doctors have always been expected to keep up-to-date with recent developments in medical diagnosis and treatment by reading medical journals, but the recent introduction of professional competence assurance schemes aims to ensure that doctors also engage in continuing medical education and professional development by attending courses, workshops, and seminars in their field.

---

46. [2004] IESC 46.
47. [2000] IR 154.

III. Causation

108. In order to succeed in an action for negligence against a doctor the patient must establish that the doctor's breach of duty was the cause of the injury or harm complained of. Thus, even where patients have proved that doctors fell below the appropriate standard of care expected of them, patients will not be successful in their actions unless they can show that they would not have suffered the damage they complain of 'but for' the negligence of the doctors. If the injury would have occurred in any event, then causation is not proved and the doctor will not be liable in negligence. In situations where the medical care has been provided by a team or by more than one health professional, it will be a question of fact and degree to what extent each or any of them 'caused' the patient's injury.

109. In *Best v. Wellcome Foundation,*[48] the plaintiff (a child suing through his mother) alleged that the defendant had been negligent in the manufacture of a vaccine that was administered to the plaintiff as a result of which he suffered brain damage. It was established that the particular batch of vaccine was below standard, had an unusually high potency rating, and should not have been released on to the market. The High Court did not accept the evidence of the parents of the plaintiff child that the child had started to have seizures and show signs of distress within a few hours of the vaccination as their GP had not recorded these symptoms and had no recollection of having been told but stated that had he been informed he would have recorded the symptoms on their medical records and referred the child to hospital immediately.

110. The case was appealed to the Supreme Court, which held that Wellcome had been negligent and that the vaccine was capable of causing brain damage. The Court accepted that the baby did suffer seizures within a few hours of receiving the vaccine, that his mother had sought help from the GP who had regarded her as unduly worried and fussy, with the result that the baby was not seen by a specialist for a number of months after the vaccination. In relation to the court's role in hearing expert evidence Finlay CJ said '*I am satisfied that it is not possible either for a judge of trial or for an appellate court to take upon itself the role of a determining scientific authority resolving disputes between distinguished scientists in any particular line of technical expertise. The function which a court can and must perform in the trial of a case in order to achieve a just result is to apply common sense and a careful understanding of the logic and likelihood of events to conflicting opinions and conflicting theories concerning a matter of this kind.*'

111. In order to succeed in his or her action the plaintiff must establish not only that the injury was caused by the doctor's breach of duty but also that it was foreseeable. If the action is brought in negligence, this means that at the time of the breach of duty, the injury was reasonably foreseeable as a consequence. In the majority of medical negligence cases the injury complained of is either the continuance of an illness that the plaintiff alleges ought to have been prevented or cured, or the infliction of a new injury during treatment. In practice the injury is usually reasonably foreseeable given that doctors are expected to be up-to-date with modern medicine and to be au fait with the possible consequences of mistakes.

48. [1992] ILRM 609.

112. In some cases it is alleged that a new intervening act breaks the chain of causation between the original wrongdoer (tortfeasor) and the injury. This is referred to as *novus actus interveniens*. For example, in *Conley v. Strain*[49] the plaintiff was injured in a road traffic accident in June 1984 as a result of which he underwent emergency surgery. Two weeks later while still in the hospital, he suffered a relapse and had a second surgical operation, following which he remained unconscious until November 1984. When he regained consciousness he was found to be suffering from severe disabilities. Although the owner of the car with whom the plaintiff had crashed did not deny negligence, he sought to make the doctor and hospital contributories on the basis that the consequences of the accident were aggravated by the negligence of the doctor, and that such negligence amounted to a *novus actus interveniens*. The plaintiff alleged that the surgeon had been negligent in not seeking advice from a neurosurgeon and having him transferred to a specialist neurosurgical centre. The Court dismissed the action against the surgeon and held that the plaintiff's condition was caused by the road traffic accident in June and the second haemorrhage two weeks later that was a consequence of the accident.

113. In some cases the plaintiff is unable to prove how the medical injury happened as its cause is solely within the knowledge of the medical practitioner. These cases may come within the maxim *res ipsa loquitur* (meaning 'the facts speak for themselves'), which applies where the accident is such that in the ordinary course of things does not happen if those who have the management of such things use proper care. There are three conditions to be fulfilled before the maxim will be applied:

– the defendant must be in control of the thing that caused the plaintiff's injury;
– the accident is of such a nature that it would not have occurred in the ordinary course of events without negligence; and
– there is no explanation for the accident.

114. If these conditions are satisfied then an onus is put on the defendant to provide a reasonable explanation for the injuries sustained by the plaintiff and to establish that they occurred without negligence on his or her part. In *Lindsay v. Mid Western Health Board*[50] the plaintiff underwent an emergency appendectomy, after which he experienced a series of seizures and went into a coma that lasted eighteen years and suffered complete brain damage. The Court took the view that although no act of negligence could be identified, it would be unreasonable and illogical not to require an explanation from the defendant as to why a patient who had undergone a routine medical procedure under general anaesthetic did not return to consciousness. The Court, therefore, regarded this as a correct application of the *res ipsa* principle in evaluating the evidence and inferring facts therefrom.

49. [1988] IR 628.
50. [1993] 2 IR 147.

IV. Damage

115. An award of damages or compensation is the normal remedy sought for breach of duty or negligence by a doctor. The plaintiff normally claims general damages for pain and suffering and special damages for financial loss suffered as a consequence of the injury, such as loss of earnings or the ongoing costs of medical care. Damage can be physical, psychological, psychiatric, or financial. The injury sustained by the plaintiff may result in physical symptoms, including chronic pain, mood disorders, fear, and anxiety,[51] and may lead to loss of employment, all of which may be compensated for.

116. As a matter of policy, courts in some jurisdictions have refused to award damages in certain circumstances even where negligence has been proven, as the courts decline to hold that a 'harm' has been established. The clearest example of such circumstances is 'wrongful birth/life', where a pregnant woman is told, following a prenatal test, that the foetus is normal but she goes on to deliver a child with significant disabilities; or 'wrongful conception' cases where a child is conceived following a negligently performed sterilization procedure. In the case of the former, due to the restrictions on the availability of abortion in Ireland, the woman would have to argue that had she been correctly informed of the disability of her foetus, she would have travelled outside of Ireland for an abortion. It is unclear what the view of the Irish courts would be in such cases. In the latter set of circumstances, in *Byrne v. Ryan*[52] the Court awarded compensation for the negligent performance of a sterilization procedure but did not award compensation for the cost of raising a healthy child born as a consequence of the failed sterilization. The judge followed an earlier English case called *McFarlane v. Tayside Health Board*[53] in which Lord Gill stated:

> I am of the opinion that this case should be decided on the principle that the privilege of being a parent is immeasurable in money terms; that the benefits of parenthood transcend any patrimonial loss, if it may be so regarded, that the parents may incur in consequence of their child's existence; and that therefore the pursuers [plaintiffs] in a case such as this cannot be said to be in an overall position of loss.

The assessment of compensation payable to the plaintiff is subject to the principle that the injury must be sufficiently proximate to the doctor's negligence to be said to have been caused by the breach of duty that should have been foreseeable by the doctor.

§3. Criminal Liability

117. There is no specific criminal legislation governing the doctor-patient relationship in Ireland. However, the general criminal law applies; for example, the

51. The fear must be judged by the court to be a realistic one, such as that as a result of the negligent treatment, the plaintiff will die. *Philp v. Ryan* [2004] IEHC 77.
52. [2007] IEHC 207.
53. [2000] AC 59.

crime of assault may be committed by the act of unlawfully inflicting bodily harm on another person. In the context of medical treatment, a surgical intervention could, therefore, be construed as an assault where the intervention was carried out unlawfully such as in the instance where the patient did not give a valid consent. The law relating to the meaning of informed consent is considered later at paragraphs 176 et seq.

118. Under section 41 of the Medical Practitioners Act 2007, a person who is not a registered medical practitioner commits a criminal offence if he or she practises medicine or advertises his or her services as a medical practitioner; or uses a designated title; or falsely represents as a registered medical practitioner or as a member of a division of the register other than that in which he or she is registered.

119. Under the Misuse of Drugs Acts 1977–2007, certain rules must be followed by doctors, dentists, nurses, and midwives who have legal power to write prescriptions for human use. These rules specify the drugs that may be prescribed and the circumstances in which they may be prescribed. These rules are designed to ensure that there are sufficient controls in place in relation to drugs that have potential for abuse and misuse. Healthcare professionals who commit an offence under these acts and regulations may also face disciplinary sanctions imposed by a relevant professional body such as the Medical Council.

§4. Vicarious Liability

120. A person who employs others is generally liable for the negligence of his or her employees when acting in the course of their employment but not for the negligence of independent contractors. Traditionally hospital consultants in Ireland were considered to be independent contractors rather than employees, and therefore hospitals were not considered vicariously responsible for negligence on the part of consultants. The basis for this was the 'control' test, which examines the extent to which one could be said to control the acts of the other. Given that hospitals did not exercise control over doctors other than in relation to administrative matters, it was generally considered that hospitals were not in sufficient control to be vicariously liable. Over time, this principle has been eroded and it is now the case that the hospital is responsible for all medical staff who treat patients. To establish liability of the part of the hospital it must be established that the negligent person is (or was at the relevant time) an employee, and that the negligence took place in the course of the person's employment.

121. In private healthcare institutions it is more difficult to establish an employment relationship between the doctor and the hospital, as the relationship is usually one in which the doctor rents rooms and facilities from the hospital but is not answerable to or controlled by the hospital. In *Bolton v. Blackrock Clinic* [1994] IEHC 12, Geoghegan J held that as the plaintiff was a private patient of the doctors in a private hospital, 'the question of vicarious liability may not arise'. It is unclear whether vicarious liability would arise in the context of a doctor treating private patients in an institution in which the doctor is also employed to treat public patients.

122. In Ireland, up to July 2002, diverse insurance and indemnity arrangements meant that each defendant to a claim – hospital, health board, consultant, hospital doctor or nurse – was represented by a separate legal team. This led to an unnecessarily adversarial approach to the resolution of claims, duplication of effort, considerably lengthened time taken to process a claim, and added significantly to claims' costs. The commercial insurance market at that time had reached a point whereby it was no longer willing to provide insurance cover to obstetricians/gynaecologists or to hospitals with obstetric units due to the escalation in the size of court awards and costs in cases of birth-related cerebral dysfunction.

123. The Clinical Indemnity Scheme (CIS)[54] was established in 2002, in order to rationalize pre-existing medical indemnity arrangements by transferring to the State, via the HSE, hospitals, and other health agencies, responsibility for managing clinical negligence claims and associated risks. Under the CIS, which is managed by the State Claims Agency (SCA), the name used by the National Treasury Management Agency (NTMA) when carrying out its claims' and risk management functions, the State assumes full responsibility for the indemnification and management of all clinical negligence claims, including those that are birth-related.

124. The CIS is funded on a 'pay-as-you-go' basis: payments in respect of compensation and costs made by the SCA are reimbursed to it by the Department of Health and Children. The scheme covers the following:

- All HSE facilities, public hospitals, and other agencies providing clinical services.
- Non-consultant hospital doctors, nurses, and other clinical staff employed by health agencies whether permanent, locum, or temporary.
- Consultant hospital doctors are covered with effect from 1 February 2004 in respect to alleged clinical negligence incidents on or after that date.
- Clinical support staff in pathology and radiology services.
- The clinical activities of public health doctors, nurses, and other community-based clinical staff.
- Dentists providing public practice.
- Certain other ancillary healthcare providers. Participating enterprises are specified in Schedule 1, Part 1 of the NTMA (Delegation of Functions) Order 2003 [SI No. 63 of 2003].

125. The CIS does not cover employer's liability or public liability claims against health agencies. These are already covered under policies of insurance with commercial insurers. The CIS covers only claims alleging medical malpractice or clinical negligence and the associated risk management issues. All clinical claims arising from the diagnosis, treatment, and care of patients are covered, including all services of a diagnostic or palliative nature. The scheme provides representation at coroner's inquests for agencies and individual practitioners where this is requested. The CIS covers personal injury claims against staff employed by agencies covered by the CIS that provide emergency treatment on the island of Ireland.

126. The CIS will cover claims from patients whose treatment was part of a clinical trial or other approved research project subject to certain criteria. The trial must have received approval from the relevant Ethics Committee and be designed by an enterprise, or any of its employees, covered by the CIS. Where a trial is sponsored

54. At http://www.stateclaims.ie/ClinicalIndemnityScheme/introduction.html.

by external organizations such as pharmaceutical companies, the CIS cover extends to treatment only and does not cover product liability or claims arising from trial design or protocol.

127. The CIS does not provide representation at disciplinary proceedings or before professional regulatory bodies. Nor does it provide representation for agencies or individual practitioners at inquiries. It does not provide cover for Good Samaritan Acts outside the jurisdiction of the island of Ireland. The CIS does not generally cover private hospitals. Doctors who are not covered by the CIS may take out private indemnity cover with a medical indemnifier. The Medical Council provides in its Guide to Professional Conduct and Ethics (8th edn) that all medical practitioners must ensure that they have adequate professional indemnity for the services they provide. There is also a proposal to introduce legislation shortly (entitled the Medical Practitioners (Professional Indemnity) (Amendment) Bill) which will make medical indemnity cover compulsory for all practicing doctors by requiring that before the Medical Council can issue a certificate of practice to the practitioner, written evidence of the appropriate insurance being in place must be produced to the Council.

§5. Quality Assurance

128. A number of stakeholders have important roles in relation to quality assurance in the Irish health system. The Medical Council has a role in relation to assuring the quality of medical education and training, registration of medical practitioners according to agreed admissibility criteria, and in the exercise of its disciplinary functions under statute. Section 7 of the Medical Practitioners Act 2007 also obliges the Council to specify and keep under review standards for the maintenance of professional competence of registered medical practitioners, and specify standards of practice for registered medical practitioners, including the establishment, publication, maintenance, and review of appropriate guidance on all matters related to professional conduct and ethics for registered medical practitioners. This function of the Council constitutes an important aspect of quality assurance of medical and professional-standards.

129. The HSE, which was established in 2005, includes within its structure the Directorate of Quality Improvement to support the assurance of good governance in relation to all the services provided by the HSE. It has responsibility for implementing a national quality and risk management standard.

130. HIQA, which was established in 2007, also has a core function in setting standards on safety and quality of services and in monitoring enforcement of those standards in an open and transparent way. HIQA also undertakes national quality assurance reviews of priority service areas such as symptomatic breast disease and hygiene.

131. In 2007 the Commission on Patient Safety and Quality Assurance was established by the Minister for Health to develop proposals for a health-service-wide (encompassing both the public and private sectors) system of governance based on corporate accountability for the safety and quality of health services. The Commission was asked to provide a framework including mechanisms and arrangements to enable the verifiable implementation of nationally agreed-upon managerial and clinical standards. As a component of this framework the Commission was asked to make recommendations in relation to the following areas in particular:

- a system of leadership for clinicians and managers that would underpin robust corporate accountability for institutional and clinical performance;
- a statutory system of licensing for public and private healthcare providers and services;
- the process of quality assurance of clinical services (with an emphasis on clinical outcomes) for public and private healthcare providers and services;
- procedures for healthcare professionals and managers to anticipate risks and promote good performance through effective risk identification, and near-miss and critical incident reporting;
- the participation of patients and carers and support staff in engaging with healthcare providers on health services planning and the quality of care received;
- the participation by all healthcare staff in audit programmes that will aim to ensure quality improvement and that trends in adverse clinical events, complaints, adverse drug reactions, and adverse events with medical devices are effectively analysed and disseminated;
- the means to ensure that evidence-based practice is supported and applied routinely in everyday practice;
- the governance of regulatory bodies in the health system and ways in which effective integration can be enabled between the various bodies.

132. The Commission's report, entitled *Building a Culture of Patient Safety*,[55] was published in August 2008 and accepted by the government as the roadmap for the future development of safety and quality assurance measures in the health system. The background to the establishment of the Commission was a series of investigations and reports in recent years in Ireland that demonstrated, amongst other things, weak governance structures, lack of clinical audit, lack of senior clinical leadership, lack of structured incident reporting, inconsistent analysis of adverse events, lack of clarity of reporting relationships, and poor working relations between clinicians and management. The Commission described its vision of a safe and quality framework for the Irish health system as follows:

> Knowledgeable patients receiving safe and effective care from skilled professionals in appropriate environments with assessed outcomes.

Its 134 recommendations focus on the following themes:

- Patient and service-user involvement in health service design and policy: These recommendations include developing a national network of patient advocates to work with organizations on patient safety; service providers and policy makers must demonstrate robust patient involvement in all healthcare policy development; patients must be supported in raising concerns at the point of care; and there must be a public information system to signpost paths through the system. There should

55. At http://health.gov.ie/wp-content/uploads/2014/03/en_patientsafety.pdf.

also be national standards for open disclosure following an adverse event, legal protection for open disclosure and training, and support and research on the consequences of adverse events for patients and their families.

- Governance, leadership, and accountability: These recommendations include the need to develop key national clinical leadership roles, education programmes in healthcare leadership, and nationally agreed-upon standards of governance as part of a new licensing framework. The chief executive in each organization must be responsible and accountable for patient safety and a system of clinical directorates must be supported. The 'responsible clinician' must be clearly identified for each episode of care. Governance structures may vary but as a minimum should include a board of management comprised of representatives of health professionals and laypeople. The board must review governance systems on a regular basis and should be under a legal duty to put in place and monitor safety arrangements.
- Education, training, and research: There should be pre-employment mandatory induction training for all healthcare workers that includes a module on patient safety. There should be a strong emphasis on patient safety in education of all healthcare professionals and an active research programme on patient safety. Competence Assurance Schemes developed by regulatory bodies should include patient safety modules. There should be management training programmes and training for clinicians with management responsibilities. The competencies of health service managers should be clearly identified.
- Licensing of service providers: A mandatory licensing regime should be introduced for all healthcare providers, public and private. This system, which will be new to Irish healthcare, should commence with application to acute hospitals and other facilities based on analysis of potential risk. There should be a general licence for hospitals and also specific licences for services provided within the hospitals that are linked to compliance with stated core standards. Standards should be enforcement through inspection and imposition of sanctions if necessary by HIQA. Licences should be subject to renewal every three years.
- Professional regulatory bodies: There should be greater collaboration on professional standards and education and training of healthcare professionals. In relation to fitness to practise processes, there should be greater separation of function and independently appointed and trained panels of adjudicators. Healthcare providers not currently covered should also be identified and considered for regulation.
- Credentialing and privileging professionals: There should be a single database to which healthcare employers can inquire regarding a potential employee's qualifications, registration status, and civil claims. This could be used for assessing competence and privileging practitioners. An alert notice system should be developed to enable concerns relating to a practitioner's competence to be circulated between employers in order to protect patients. Employers should only employ in consultant posts those who are on the specialist register.
- Evidence-based practice and clinical audit: A leadership role should be assigned in analysis of international evidence and research for use in policy guidance. There should be evidence-based service frameworks covering major health conditions. In relation to clinical audit, this should be mandatory for individuals

and licensed facilities with an exemption from disclosure under the Freedom of Information Acts or in litigation.

- Adverse event reporting: There should be a national mandatory reporting system for serious adverse events with a complementary voluntary system for non-serious events and near-misses. There should be a national agency to provide leadership, analysis, feedback, and dissemination throughout the system, with clinical leaders who would have responsibility to ensure that there are effective reporting arrangements in place. The reporting system should facilitate patient and family reporting and be exempt from disclosure under Freedom of Information legislation and legal discovery.
- Medication safety: There should be a national analysis of possible solutions to the problems of unlicensed medicines and medicine shortages. Formal medication reconciliation systems and tracking audits should be developed.
- Health information and HIT: Health Information Technology (HIT) should have a patient-centred approach and the necessary Information and Community Technology (ICT) infrastructure requirements should be provided to enhance safe patient care. There should be a unique health identifier and an electronic health record system in place.

A National Patient Safety Advisory Group was established in 2011 to facilitate the process of continuing to drive the patient safety agenda forward at national level and to provide for continuity of high level engagement of the relevant stakeholders. A Patient Safety First initiative was launched in 2011 to outline the many ongoing patient safety activities in Ireland.[56]

§6. Review Boards

133. See §7.

§7. Disciplinary Organizations

I. Order of Physicians

134. The Medical Council of Ireland was established by the Medical Practitioners Act 1978 and commenced operation in April 1979. It has twenty-five members comprised of elected and appointed members. Historically the Medical Council had a majority of medical members (twenty-one) but the 2007 Medical Practitioners Act substantially changed the composition of the Council by requiring that ten of the twenty-five members must be doctors, eleven must not be doctors, and the remaining four may/may not be doctors depending on the nominations made by the HSE and approved bodies delivering undergraduate medical education. Therefore, the Act facilitates the appointment of a lay majority though it does not guarantee it. Membership of the Council since the

56. At http://www.patientsafetyfirst.ie/index.php/home.html.

introduction of the 2007 Act has been a majority of lay people. Members of the Council hold office for five years.

135. The Council is a statutory body entrusted with important functions to be performed in the public interest. Section 6 of the Act states that the object of the Council is to 'protect the public by promoting and better ensuring high standards of professional conduct and professional education, training and competence among registered medical practitioners'. Contrary, perhaps, to public opinion, the Council is 'not a body established to manage the affairs of the medical profession or to protect its interests'.[57]

136. The Medical Practitioners Acts 1978–2007 repealed the Medical Practitioners Acts 1927–1961. The principal functions of the Council are set out by the 1978 Act as amended by the 2007 Act, as: the maintenance of a register of medical practitioners, the supervision of the standards of medical education and training of doctors, the control of postgraduate training of specialists, the imposition of disciplinary procedures, and the development of professional-standards of ethical conduct. The Council has committees dealing with, *inter alia*, education and training, registration, fitness to practise, and ethics. These committees generally meet on a monthly to quarterly basis.

137. As part of its statutory functions, the Medical Council is obliged to convene a Fitness to Practise Committee (FTPC) of the Council to hear inquiries into the conduct of registered medical practitioners. An application for an inquiry may be made either by the Council itself or by any other person. An inquiry may be sought on the following grounds (section 57):

(a) professional misconduct;
(b) poor professional performance;
(c) a relevant medical disability;
(d) a failure to comply with a relevant condition;
(e) a failure to comply with an undertaking or to take any action specified in a consent given in response to a request made under section 67(1);[58]
(f) a contravention of a provision of the Medical Practitioners Act 2007;
(g) a conviction in the State for an offence triable on indictment or a conviction outside the State for an offence consisting of acts or omissions that, if done or made in the State, would constitute an offence triable on indictment.

Section 57(2) provides that a complaint may be made on the grounds of professional misconduct or poor professional performance notwithstanding that the matter to which the complaint related occurred outside the State.

57. *Philips v. The Medical Council, the Minister for Health, Ireland and the Attorney General* [1991] 2 IR 115, per Costello J.
58. Section 67(1) provides that the FTPC may, at any time after a complaint is referred to it, request the doctor to give an undertaking to not repeat the conduct complained of, or to undertake to be referred to a professional competence scheme and comply with any requirements imposed in that regard, consent to undergo medical treatment, or consent to being censured by the Council.

II. Procedure

138. The Medical Practitioners Act 2007 introduced a number of changes to the disciplinary process within the Medical Council. The Council has two committees pertaining to disciplinary matters: the Preliminary Proceedings Committee (PPC) and the FTPC. Under the Act, the FTPC must have a non-medical majority. The PPC, which includes both medical and non-medical members of the Council as well as other members who may be appointed by the Council to assist the Committee, considers all applications for inquiries. The Committee must decide whether or not there is sufficient cause to warrant the holding of an inquiry or that the complaint does not come within the remit of the Council.[59] This decision is passed on to the Council, which may then consider that no further action is required, or that the Committee should hold an inquiry into the matter. It must duly inform the Committee and the applicant. If the Committee is of the opinion that there is a prima facie case for holding the inquiry or has been so directed by the Council, the Committee will refer the complaint to the FTPC to hear the inquiry.

139. The medical practitioner who is the subject of the complaint must be notified of the referral to the FTPC, the nature of the complaint, the evidence supporting the complaint, the right to be legally represented, and the right to apply for the inquiry to be held in private.

140. The Chief Executive of the Council collects evidence in the case for presentation to the inquiry team.[60] The person against whom the complaint has been made is given notice of the evidence in the case and has the opportunity to be present at the hearing of the case, or be legally represented at the inquiry. In practice, both the doctor and the chief executive are usually legally represented. The Committee has the powers, rights, and privileges of the High Court in relation to the calling and examination of witnesses, and the production of documents. Refusal to attend a hearing following a summons by the Committee to do so, or failure to produce documents called for by the Committee, or any other conduct that would constitute a contempt of court, is an offence.[61] Witnesses have the same immunities and privileges as in the High Court. The inquiry team also has the assistance of a legal assessor who is present to give legal advice to the team and to ensure that fair procedures are observed.

141. The evidential burden of proof in cases brought before the Committee is on the person making the allegations. In *O'Laoire v. Medical Council*,[62] the Supreme Court discussed whether the standard of proof was the civil or criminal standard. The FTPC had decided the case in question on the basis of proof beyond a reasonable doubt. O'Flaherty J took the view that, although the criminal standard of proof ought to be confined to criminal trials to which that standard is particularly suited, in civil

---

59. According to the Medical Council, 300–400 complaints are made by patients against their doctors each year. Only about 10% of these give rise to full inquiries.

60. The relationship between the Committee and the Registrar was described by Costello P in *Barry v. The Medical Council* [1998] 3 IR as analogous to that between the chairman of a tribunal and solicitor and counsel employed by him to present the evidence, rather than that which exists between prosecutor and the judge in a criminal trial.

61. Section 45(7).

62. Supreme Court, 185/95, 25 Jul. 1997.

hearings such as this one the evidential burden must be commensurate with the gravity of the matter at hand. He said:

> The essence of a disciplinary enquiry into alleged professional misconduct, such as concerned the Committee and the trial judge here, is to find out by clear evidence the pith and substance of the misdeed being investigated and decide whether the case has been established against the person, always bearing in mind the grave consequences that such a finding will, in general, have for the person whose conduct is called in question but also remembering that the public has an interest in making sure that proper standards of professional conduct are upheld. The graver the allegation the greater will be the care which the tribunal or court will take to make sure that the case has been brought home against the person whose conduct is impugned.

He went on to discuss cases from the United Kingdom,[63] Canada,[64] Australia,[65] and New Zealand[66] with which he was satisfied that the Irish decisions on the point concurred.

142. An important issue, which has in the past exercised both the Medical Council and the courts, is whether the FTPC should hold its inquiry in public or in private. This was at the heart of *Barry v. The Medical Council*,[67] in which the practitioner, who was the subject of an inquiry by the FTPC, wished to have the hearing in public in order to vindicate his character, in circumstances in which the complaints against him had received much damaging advance publicity. The Committee refused on the basis that it had discretion under the scheme of the Act in any case and in this case had exercised its discretion in favour of a private hearing. This was grounded on the nature of the allegations against the practitioner in this case being of an intimate personal nature, a fact that may deter those making the complaints from giving evidence in public.

In the High Court the applicant claimed that he had a constitutional right to fair procedure and that this required a public hearing of the allegations made against him. He relied on the provisions of Article 6(1) of the European Convention on Human Rights, which provides as follows:

> In the determination of his civil rights and obligations or of any criminal charge against him, everyone is entitled to a fair and public hearing within a reasonable time by an independent and impartial tribunal established by law. Judgement shall be pronounced publicly but the press and public may be excluded from all or part of the trial in the interests of morals, public order or national security in a democratic society, where the interests of juveniles or the protection of the private life of the parties so require, or to the extent strictly necessary in the

63. *Reg v. Home Secretary, Ex-p Khawaja* [1984] AC 74; *R v. Wolverhampton Coroner* [1990] 2 All ER 759.
64. *Rizzo et al. v. Hanover Insurance Co.* [1990] 68 DLR (4th) 420.
65. *Neat Holdings PTY Ltd v. Karajan Holdings PTY Ltd* [1992] 67 ALJR 170.
66. *Back v. National Insurance Company of New Zealand Ltd* [1996] 3NZLR 363.
67. [1998] 3 IR.

opinion of the court in special circumstances where publicity would prejudice the interests of justice.

143. The applicant accepted that the Convention was not part of Irish law but argued that in giving effect to the notion of fair procedures under Article 40.3 of the Constitution, the Court should be guided by internationally accepted norms enshrined in the Convention.[68] He also pointed out that Article 34 of the Constitution provides that justice is to be administered in public, save in limited cases prescribed by law. However, the applicant did not argue that the Committee infringed this article as it was accepted that the Committee does not administer justice. In order to have any legal effect the Council must accept the Committee's decision and apply for confirmation to the High Court, which, sitting in public, *determines* the dispute. Costello P accepted the Committee's argument that it had a statutory discretion as to whether to hold its hearings in public or in private. In light of the intimate private details of the case and the reluctance of some witnesses to proceed with giving evidence in public, he held that the Committee had correctly applied the principles contained in Article 6(1) of the Convention in this case. This was on the basis of the right to privacy of others and the interests of justice.[69]

144. The Supreme Court unanimously agreed that the Committee has discretion under the Act to conduct its proceedings in public. Barrington J said:

> While the Act contemplates that proceedings before the Fitness to Practise Committee shall be in private it does not require it. I can see no reason why the Committee should not hold its proceedings in public if all parties were agreed and if the Committee itself thought it was the proper thing to do.

The Supreme Court also agreed that the Committee had properly exercised its discretion on the facts of this case.

145. An important change was introduced in the Medical Practitioners Act 2007, section 65 which now provides that a hearing before the FTPC shall be held in public unless the medical practitioner or a witness who will be required to give evidence at the hearing requests that it be held in private and the Committee is satisfied that it would be appropriate in the circumstances to hold the hearing (or part of it) in private. This has resulted in greater openness and transparency for the public in relation to the

68. The applicant relied on the decision of the European Court of Human Rights (ECHR) in *Diennet v. France* [1995] 21 EHRR 554 where, in similar circumstances, a French doctor successfully argued that Art. 6(1) of the Convention was breached by the fact that he did not receive a public hearing before the disciplinary section of the National Council of the French Medical Association. However, Barrington J in the Supreme Court pointed out that in this case the applicant had appealed the decision of the Disciplinary Committee to the French Conseil d'Etat on a point of law only. There was no rehearing of the case, and therefore it was possible for the Court to agree that there had been no public hearing of an issue that touched on his civil rights, contrary to the Convention. In the instant case the applicant had the right to appeal the decision of the Medical Council to the High Court where he would be entitled to a full rehearing and possibly rehearing in public.

69. Arguments made on the basis that there was no objective separation of the functions of prosecutor and adjudicating tribunal in this case were also rejected by the Court.

way in which the Medical Council conducts inquiries. However, this provision has been criticized because it can lead to increased media and public attention on the medical practitioner which can sometimes be seen as unfair particularly if he or she is not found guilty of professional misconduct at the conclusion of the inquiry.

III. Professional Misconduct

146. Section 46 of the 1978 Act provided that where a registered medical practitioner has been found to be guilty of professional misconduct or to be unfit to engage in the practice of medicine because of physical or mental disability, or has failed to pay the appropriate retention fee, the Council may decide that the name of that person should be erased from the register, or that during a specified period registration of his or her name in the register should not have effect. A person to whom such a decision applies may apply to the High Court within twenty-one days for cancellation of the decision. If such an application is not made, the Council may apply ex parte to the High Court for confirmation of the decision. The High Court shall, unless it sees good reason to the contrary, confirm the Council's decision.

147. The meaning of professional misconduct is defined in the *Medical Council's Ethical Guide* as:

> conduct which doctors of experience, competence and good repute consider disgraceful or dishonourable; and/or conduct connected with his or her profession in which the doctor concerned has seriously fallen short by omission or commission of the standards of conduct expected among doctors.[70]

148. There have been a number of judicial decisions in relation to the meaning of professional misconduct in this context. One of the most important cases is *O'Laoire v. The Medical Council*[71] in which the Court defined professional misconduct as follows:

(1) Conduct which is 'infamous' or 'disgraceful' in a professional respect is 'professional misconduct'.
(2) Conduct which would not be 'infamous' or 'disgraceful' in any other person, if done by a medical practitioner in relation to his profession, that is, with regard either to his patients or to his colleagues, may be considered as 'infamous' or 'disgraceful' conduct in a professional respect.
(3) 'Infamous' or 'disgraceful' conduct in turn is conduct involving some degree of moral turpitude, fraud, or dishonesty.
(4) Conduct which could not properly be characterized as 'infamous' or 'disgraceful' and which does not involve any degree of moral turpitude, fraud or dishonesty may still constitute 'professional misconduct' if it is conduct connected with his profession in which the medical practitioner concerned has seriously fallen short,

70. At http://www.medicalcouncil.ie/News-and-Publications/Reports/Guide-to-Professional-Conduct-Ethics-8th-Edition.html.
71. 27 Jan. 1995, unreported.

by omission or commission, of the standards of conduct expected among medical practitioners.

149. In the later case of[72] *Prendiville and Murphy v. The Medical Council* it was successfully argued that although the Guide published by the Medical Council is no more than a guide and need not be absolutely precise, it is reasonable for medical practitioners to expect that the Guide would give an indication in general terms of what the Council understands professional misconduct to mean. The judge recognized that the notion of professional misconduct can change from time to time because of changing circumstances and new eventualities. He was of the view that it is impossible to catalogue what may amount to professional misconduct but that the Council should identify the essential elements of the concept. Kelly J also took the view that the medical practitioner against whom a finding of misconduct has been made is entitled to at least a general explanation of the basis for the decision.

150. The Medical Practitioners Act 2007 provides in section 57 that a person may make a complaint concerning a registered medical practitioner on one or more of the following grounds:

(a) professional misconduct;
(b) poor professional performance;
(c) a relevant medical disability;
(d) failure to comply with a relevant condition;
(e) failure to comply with an undertaking or to take any action specified in a consent given under this Act;
(f) contravention of a provision of this Act;
(g) conviction in the State for an offence triable on indictment or a conviction outside the State for an offence consisting of acts or omissions that, if done or made in the State, would constitute an offence triable on indictment.

151. The meaning of professional misconduct in section 57 is not described in the Act but is interpreted in the same way as explained earlier in paragraphs 146–147. Complaints in this category are mainly in relation to clinical care such as incompetence, misdiagnosis, poor prescribing practice, adverse outcomes or lack of hygiene. The other important new ground of complaint contained in section 57 is poor professional performance. This is described in the Act as 'a failure by the practitioner to meet the standards of competence (whether in knowledge and skill or the application of knowledge and skill or both) that can reasonably be expected of medical practitioners practising medicine of the kind practised by the practitioner.' In *Corbally v. the Medical Council*[73] the Supreme Court delivered the first judgment on the meaning of poor professional performance. The court held that before a practitioner could be subjected to the ordeal of a public hearing, there must be reason to believe that what can be proved against him is something of a serious nature. The court was very conscious of the devastating consequences of a public hearing for medical practitioners and although there may be many matters which may aggrieve patients, the Medical Council must be capable of

72. *Prendiville and Murphy v. Medical Council* [2007] IEHC 427.
73. [2015] IESC 9.

making the decision that such matters will not proceed to any inquiry unless they are serious in nature. Therefore, as a result of this case, the test to be applied to complaints of poor professional performance (whether in relation to a once-off incident or a series of incidents) is that of 'seriousness'. Following this judgment, the difference between professional misconduct (a serious falling short of standards) and poor professional performance remains unclear.

IV. Sanctions

152. Section 46 of the 1978 Act empowers the Council to impose sanctions, including erasure or suspension from the medical register, provision of advice, admonishment or censure, or the attachment of conditions to the retention of the name of a medical practitioner on the medical register. This section was considered in a number of cases such as *M. v. The Medical Council and the Attorney General.*[74] The plaintiff applied to the High Court under section 46 for an order cancelling the decision of the Council to remove his name from the register. The plaintiff claimed, *inter alia*, that sections 45 and 46 of the Act were unconstitutional,[75] and that the Council's decision was, therefore, null and void. He alleged that the powers vested in the FTPC or in the Medical Council by the 1978 Act were powers to administer justice that, due to the fact that their effect would be to deprive him of his livelihood by striking him from the register of medical practitioners, could not be considered to be limited powers under Article 37 of the Constitution.[76] He also alleged that the procedures set out by the Act were unfair and inconsistent with Article 40 of the Constitution[77] in that his case came before the Court with a predetermination of guilt from the Council. He claimed that there was no prohibition on the Council from publishing its findings that the practitioner was guilty of misconduct, which was a failure to vindicate and defend the practitioner's good name under Article 40.

153. The Council argued that its functions did not constitute the administration of justice as they lacked the finality or enforceability necessary to that function by virtue of the fact that the decision of the Council was not effective unless confirmed by the Court. It was also argued that it was in the public interest that publication be made of the fact that his colleagues had found the doctor guilty of misconduct.

74. [1984] IR 485.
75. Article 34, s. 1 of the Constitution provides 'Justice shall be administered in courts established by law by judges appointed in the manner provided by this Constitution, and, save, in such special and limited cases as may be prescribed by law, shall be administered in public.'
76. Article 37 of the Constitution provides 'Nothing in this Constitution shall operate to invalidate the exercise of limited functions and powers of a judicial nature, in matters other than criminal matters, by any person or body of persons duly authorised by law to exercise such functions and powers, notwithstanding that such person or such body of persons is not a judge or a court appointed or established as such under this Constitution'.
77. Article 40.3.2 provides 'The State shall, in particular, by its laws protect as best it may from unjust attack and, in the case of injustice done, vindicate the life, person, good name, and property rights of every citizen.'

Finlay P distinguished the facts of *In Re the Solicitors Act 1954*,[78] in which the disciplinary committee of the Law Society had the power to determine complaints of professional misconduct against solicitors, strike their names off the register, and award restitution and costs. He said that there was 'a very striking difference between the extent and nature of the powers there conferred on the disciplinary committee and the powers conferred by the Act of 1978 on the Committee and the Council'. He went on to explain that the only power the Committee or the Council had was to initiate proceedings in the High Court that may lead to an order suspending the practitioner from his or her practice, erasing his or her name from the register, or the other sanctions provided by the Act. He adopted the test laid down in the *Solicitors Act Case* that the essential question here was whether the tribunal in question had power by its determination to impose liability or affect rights. In this case the only powers of the Council that could be said to be final were the publication of a finding of misconduct or unfitness to practise, and the Council's power to advise, admonish, or censure a practitioner. Even if these powers could be said to affect the rights of the practitioner in the present context, these functions would be so clearly limited in their effect and consequence as to come within the exception provided by Article 37 of the Constitution.[79]

154. The plaintiff also argued that there was a lack of fair procedure in the manner by which his application came before the High Court with a badge of guilt arising from a finding of the Committee. In rejecting this contention Costello P equated any such implication or imputation that might arise from such a finding by a professional body with the implication or imputation that arises from a decision on the part of the Director of Public Prosecutions (DPP) to prosecute an accused person. Accordingly, this ground also failed. However, it may be questioned whether this is in fact a correct interpretation of the position in relation to the DPP where it would be inconsistent with the constitutional right to fair procedures to have any implication of guilt arising in a criminal prosecution prior to a court hearing. Despite the seriousness of the decision to strike a practitioner from the Register, it is not a criminal prosecution and the two situations are not comparable.

155. The plaintiff also challenged the constitutionality of the Council's power to publish the fact that the Committee had reached a decision as to the practitioner's conduct. Costello P held that Article 40.3.2 does not guarantee to protect a person from every statement that may damage his good name. The common good may require, as in these circumstances, that a decision reached as to the conduct of a person carrying out a profession affecting the public be made known to the public:

> In the case of a person practising medicine, the public have a clear and identifiable interest to be informed of a responsible view reached by his colleagues with regard to his standard of conduct or fitness. I cannot see that the absence from the statute of a prohibition on the publication of an adverse finding of the Committee [where they have made a finding of misconduct or of unfitness] can be a failure to protect the good name of the practitioner from an unjust attack.[80]

78. [1960] IR 239.
79. [1984] IR 485 at 497.
80. [1984] IR 485 at 500.

156. According to the Court, the practitioner's right to have a full public hearing before the High Court during which he may completely vindicate his good name and reputation constituted a sufficient protection of his good name so as to make the scheme of the Act consistent with Article 40. This would seem to be a sensible approach bearing in mind the clear necessity of protecting the public from unfit practitioners. Once appropriate safeguards have been observed from a procedural point of view and the Committee has reached a decision on the practitioner's conduct, it would not be inappropriate for the Committee to publish its findings in that regard.

157. In *Casey v. The Medical Council*,[81] the plaintiff argued that the Council's power to attach conditions to the retention of his name in the register was *ultra vires* of the Council. The plaintiff complained that although the Committee considered that there was insufficient evidence to find him guilty of misconduct, the Council advised him to avail of continuing medical education and professional development courses in his field, keep more comprehensive clinical notes, attend a course in communication skills, and, where appropriate, consider the presence of a chaperone when dealing with patients. These conditions were attached to the retention of his name in the register and were to be reviewed after one year. The plaintiff argued that the Council had no power to make such a decision and had, therefore, acted *ultra vires*.

158. The plaintiff's argument was grounded on the contention that in the absence of a finding of misconduct by the Committee, the Council had no power under the Act to do any of the things it purported to do. By imposing conditions on the retention of his name on the register the Council was in effect reversing the findings of the Committee, which had heard all the evidence and the witnesses in the case. The plaintiff relied on the judgment of Finlay P in *In Re M., a Doctor*,[82] in which the judge was said to have demonstrated the correctness of the plaintiff's case that before a power could be exercised under section 47 of the Act, there must have been a finding of guilt by the Committee. The Council argued that not only was it entitled to invoke the powers in question, but ought to do so having regard to the public interest and the care of patients. The Council sought to rely on *M. v. The Medical Council and the Attorney General*[83] in which Finlay P had considered the provisions of section 47. However, in that case he had taken the opposite view, namely that the Council could exercise its powers under the section irrespective of the precise findings of that enquiry by the Committee.

159. Kelly J held that there was nothing in the words of section 47 or 48 that would require as a condition precedent to their being acted upon by the Council a finding of guilt on the part of the practitioner who has been the subject of an inquiry by the Committee. 'Under the express terms of each section all that is required in order to trigger the entitlement of the Council to utilize them is that there should have been an inquiry held and a report made by the Committee pursuant to section 45 of the Act.' He disagreed with Finlay P in *In Re M., a Doctor*, taking the view that the learned judge had not accurately described the statutory provisions in that case. There was, he held, no basis for indicating that the Council's powers could only be exercised where the practitioner had been found guilty of misconduct. Such a view was inconsistent

81. [1999] Unrep. High Court (4 Jun. 1999).
82. [1984] IR 479.
83. [1984] IR 485. Both this and *In Re a Doctor* [1984] IR 479, discussed below, relate to the same doctor and were decided by Finlay P.

with the express provisions of the Act and also with his own views in the later decision, *M. v. The Medical Council and the Attorney General*, with which Kelly J agreed.

160. As regards the issue of where the public interest lies in such cases, it had been contended by the plaintiff that section 51 of the Act, which enables the Council to apply to the High Court to suspend a practitioner's registration for a specified period, was sufficient protection for the public. Kelly J took the view that although it was quite clear from the wording of that section that the Council had a role to play in the protection of the public interest, section 51 was not the only way in which this might be achieved. On the contrary, that section was reserved for exceptional cases in which a doctor ought to be suspended in the public interest:

> There must be cases where the Council would, from the point of view of protecting the public, wish to bring about an improvement in the standards of an individual practitioner. It would be absurd that in every such case where the Council desired so to do it would have to invoke the provisions of Section 51. To contend that this is the only mechanism that the Council is given by the Legislature in order to address the public interest is, in effect, to advocate the use of the proverbial sledge hammer to crack a nut with consequent hardship being suffered by the unfortunate medical practitioner who would be the recipient of such force.

161. Accordingly, the Medical Council was held not to have acted *ultra vires* in its decision to attach conditions to the plaintiff's registration. In reaching this decision the Court recognized the complexity of the medical relationship and the seriousness of any finding of misconduct. On examination of the doctor's conduct in this case the Committee was of the opinion that although certain aspects of his practice needed improvement, such as communication and note-taking, there was not the level of misconduct involved as to justify a recommendation that he be struck off the register. The plaintiff's argument that it was essentially *all or nothing* so far as the imposition of any sanctions was concerned does not take account of the pragmatic approach taken by the Council in fulfilment of its function in protecting the public.

162. Another power of the Council following a hearing by the FTPC is to 'advise, admonish or censure' a practitioner in relation to his or her professional conduct. It was argued in *Okechuku Anachebe v. The Medical Council*[84] that the sanctions that the Council could impose by way of recommended erasure from the register had such grave consequences for a practitioner that they constituted an administration of justice, a function reserved for the courts by the Constitution. It was for this reason that the confirmation of the High Court was required for such an action and that the practitioner had the right to appeal to the High Court to set such a decision aside. The power of the Council to refuse to renew temporary registration and to censure the practitioner in relation to his conduct were no less serious sanctions for the practitioner, and yet no right of appeal to the High Court was given by the Act to the practitioner in such instances. Morris P held that the power that was exercised in this case was to censure the plaintiff in relation to his professional conduct and that no right is given to the practitioner to apply to the court to set that decision aside. 'This is because the sanction of advice, admonishing and censuring is not of sufficient gravity.' This further recognizes

84. Unrep. High Court 12 Jul. 2000.

the point that a gradation of misconduct exists in relation to medical professionals and that while serious sanctions may be imposed at one end of the scale, it is also necessary to acknowledge that, in keeping with the Council's role in protection of the public interest, less serious penalties may also be appropriate in certain circumstances. It is seen as being impractical to give a right of appeal in such cases where the livelihood of the practitioner is not threatened.

163. The Medical Practitioners Act 2007 provides in section 71 for the power of the Council to impose the following sanctions:

(a) an advice or admonishment, or a censure, in writing;
(b) a censure in writing and a fine not exceeding EUR 5,000;
(c) the attachment of conditions to the practitioner's registration, including restrictions on the practice of medicine that may be engaged in by the practitioner;
(d) the transfer of the practitioner's registration to another division of the register;
(e) the suspension of the practitioner's registration for a specified period;
(f) the cancellation of the practitioner's registration;
(g) a prohibition from applying for a specified period for the restoration of the practitioner's registration.

164. A decision to impose a sanction (other than that referred to in section 71(a)) must be confirmed by the Court before it will become effective. A doctor may appeal the Council's decision (other than a decision to impose a sanction under section 71(a)) to the Court within twenty-one days of receipt of notification of the imposition of a sanction by the Council. The Court may, on appeal, consider any evidence adduced or argument made, whether or not adduced or made to the FTPC (section 75(2)). The Court may either confirm or cancel the decision, substitute a different/no sanction, and give directions to the Council. Where a doctor does not appeal the Council's decision within the stated time period, the Council must make an application to the Court for confirmation of the decision. This is done on an ex parte basis and the Court will confirm the decision unless the Court considers there is good reason not to do so.

165. The Council also has an important power under section 60 to make an ex parte application (without notice to the doctor) to the Court for an order to suspend a doctor's registration immediately, whether or not the doctor is the subject of a complaint, if the Council considers that the suspension is necessary to protect the public until further steps are taken. This may arise in circumstances where the Council becomes aware (through a complaint or other notification) that a doctor's competence or behaviour may be putting the safety of patients at risk. In such cases, the Council may feel it necessary to immediately remove the doctor from practise in order to protect patients. If the Court accepts the Council's application, the doctor must immediately stop practising medicine and the Council must hold a full inquiry as quickly as possible so that the doctor has the opportunity to defend the allegations. The court is conscious that the doctor has a right to his/her good name and the right to earn a livelihood through his or her practise so it must be satisfied that removing the doctor from practise is necessary in the public interest.

§8. Professional Codes

166. Section 69(2) of the Medical Practitioners Act 1978 provides that 'it shall be a function of the Council to give guidance to the medical profession generally on all matters relating to ethical conduct and behaviour'. In this context the Medical Council publishes a set of ethical guidelines on a five-year basis that is designed to be applied by doctors in various situations.

167. Although the Guide to Professional Conduct and Ethics published by the Council does not have binding force in law, it is important for the internal regulation of the profession and it lays down what is ethical medical practice in Ireland. The Council states that these guidelines are not rules that will provide the doctor with an answer to every difficult issue. Rather they are principles that ought to be used by doctors together with their judgment, experience, knowledge, and skills in each situation. It, therefore, does not generally catalogue behaviour that may be deemed to be unprofessional but sets out broad principles against which doctors may judge the situation in which they find themselves.

168. It is possible that the Guide may be indirectly incorporated into law through case law in the same way as the guidelines of other professional bodies such as accountancy bodies in tax and accountancy cases. In the case of the latter, the guidelines are seen as a body of professionally desirable standards for the accountancy profession, departure from which would be strictly scrutinized. Although the Medical Council's current Guide is not as detailed and specific, it could be argued that the principles set out therein should be regarded in a similar fashion. In the absence of legislation, a court may, therefore, decide that although not of binding legal force, departures from the Guide may constitute a breach of professional duty for the purposes of establishing negligence unless justified by the specific circumstances of the case. A patient may also argue that he or she had a legitimate expectation that the Guide would be adhered to by the doctor and that this formed an implied term of the contract with the doctor.

169. The current Guide (8th edn (2016))[85] deals with issues such as professional conduct; responsibilities to patients; medical records and confidentiality; consent to medical treatment; professional practice,. advertising, social media, dealing with adverse events, open communication to patients, reporting of alleged abuse, and how to deal with concerns in relation to a colleague's competence. Its provisions are mentioned throughout this text where relevant.

170. The Medical Practitioners Act 2007, section 7(2)(i) provides that the Council shall:

> Specify standards of practice for registered medical practitioners, including the establishment, publication and maintenance and review of appropriate guidance on all matters related to professional conduct and ethics for registered medical practitioners.

Section 7(3) provides that this function referred to at subsection (2)(i) shall include:

---

85. At http://www.medicalcouncil.ie/News-and-Publications/Reports/Guide-to-Professional-Conduct-Ethics-8th-Edition.html.

Standards of practice relating to advertising by registered medical practitioners, or classes of registered medical practitioners, and in connection therewith, the disclosure of appropriate information relating to the fees to be charged for the medical services the subject of such advertising.

These parts were commenced by Statutory Instrument No. 231 of 2008, on 3 July 2008. It appears that the wording of the 2007 Act is wider than the equivalent provisions of the 1978 Act and therefore, there is a different and more extensive obligation imposed on the Council since 2008 in respect of the publication of standards of practice for the profession. It is not clear from the Act itself what exactly 'standards of practice' means, but it may be linked with the inclusion in the 2007 Act of new grounds for complaint against registered medical practitioners, specifically that ground that relates to 'poor professional performance'. This may impose an obligation on the Council to publish the standards of practice against which a registered medical practitioner's professional performance would be measured in the context of a complaint against him or her.

§9. Biomedical Ethics Committee

171. There are a number of clinical ethics committees and research ethics committees in hospitals, universities, and other institutions in Ireland. The Regulations on Clinical Trials introduced in 2006 require the establishment of a national research ethics committee supervisory body to recognize and monitor local ethics committees. The DOH has undertaken this role and has recognized a number of local ethics committees for the purposes of compliance with the regulations. It is understood that this responsibility will be transferred to the Health Information and Quality Authority in 2017 when new legislation is enacted.

172. The National Advisory Committee on Bioethics was established by the Minister for Health in 2012 to advise the Minister on the ethical and social implications of scientific developments in human medicine and healthcare.[86] Its role is to provide advice in the form of expert reports on priority issues of national significance as requested by the Minister, to provide recommendations and assistance towards the development of healthcare policy and legislation, and to represent Ireland at international fora on bioethics.

86. At http://health.gov.ie/national-advisory-committee-on-bioethics/.

Part II. The Physician-Patient Relationship

Chapter 1. General Description

§1. Rights and Duties of Physicians and Patients

173. In Ireland there is no specific legislation governing the relationship between doctor and patient. Certain aspects of the relationship are governed by common law principles, and others are dealt with by professional guidelines issued by regulatory bodies such as the Medical Council, discussed in paragraphs 134 et seq.

174. Given the way in which Irish healthcare is currently funded, with the State paying for all or some of the healthcare of many people, this may be seen to have an impact on the relationship between the doctor and patient though it does not alter the legal features of this relationship. Where a person receives medical care provided through public funding there is no direct contractual relationship between doctor and patient; the contract exists between the doctor and his or her employer, that is, the State. Part of that employment contract will inevitably entail the discharge of certain functions in the care of patients. On the other hand, where a patient pays a doctor from private funds, a contractual relationship comes into existence between doctor and patient. Despite this difference in the legal basis for the relationship between doctor and patient, the duties and responsibilities of the doctor toward the patient remain the same; that is, irrespective of who pays him or her, the doctor must discharge his or her duty to provide competent treatment to the patient and protect the patient's best interests.

175. In the event that the patient suffers injury as a result of treatment, in the case of a private patient the doctor and/or healthcare institution may be sued directly by the patient. If the patient is a public patient, the legal action will be against the institution that employed the doctor. The institution is indemnified by the CIS. *See* paragraph 123.

§2. Informed Consent

176. In order to avoid actions in civil or criminal law, consent must have been given by the patient or on his or her behalf. This is to give legal effect to the ethical principle that each person has a right to self-determination. The law relating to consent is of the utmost importance in medical law as it serves as means of protecting and preserving the right of a patient to decide what is to happen to him or her. The fundamental significance of consent in legal terms is reflected in judicial statements worldwide. For example, in the United States, Justice Cordozo stated:

> Every human being of adult years and sound mind has a right to determine what shall be done with his own body; and a surgeon who performs an operation without his patient's consent commits an assault, for which he is liable in damages.[87]

177. The Guide to Professional Conduct and Ethics of the Medical Council (8th edn 2016) [88] advises doctors to ensure that informed consent has been given by a patient before any medical treatment can be carried out. Paragraph 9.2 states:

> You must make sure that patients have given their consent before you provide any medical investigation, examination or treatment. Consent is required by law and is an essential part of respect for patients' autonomy. Patients have the right to decide what happens to their own body. They also have a right to refuse medical treatment or withdraw consent.

There are a number of constituent elements to the giving of a valid consent – capacity of the patient, disclosure of relevant information, and the voluntary giving of permission by the patient.

178. In 2013 the Health Service Executive (HSE) launched a new National Consent Policy to provide one overarching HSE policy to guide staff. The policy extends to all interventions conducted by or on behalf of the HSE on service users in all locations. It includes social as well as healthcare interventions and applies to those receiving care and treatment in hospitals, in the community and in residential settings.[89] It provides useful guidance for health and social care professionals in relation to the application of principles of informed consent in practice, assessment of decision-making capacity, consent in the treatment of children and minors, do not resuscitate orders, and clinical research.

---

87. *Schloendoff v. Society of New York Hospital* [1914] 211 NY 125.
88. At https://www.medicalcouncil.ie/News-and-Publications/Reports/Guide-to-Professional-Conduct-and-Ethics-8th-Edition-2016-.pdf.
89. At http://www.hse.ie/portal/eng/about/Who/qualityandpatientsafety/Advocacy/National_Consent_Advisory_Group/National_Consent_Policy.html.

I. Capacity to Give Consent

179. It is presumed that all adults have capacity to give consent to medical treatment on their own behalf.[90] In relation to minors, the Non-Fatal Offences against the Person Act 1997 provides in section 23 that 'the consent of a minor who has attained the age of 16 years to any surgical, medical, or dental treatment which, in the absence of consent, would constitute a trespass to his or her person, shall be as effective as it would be if he or she were of full age; and where a minor has by virtue of this section given an effective consent to any treatment it shall not be necessary to obtain any consent for it from his or her parent or guardian.' This is taken to mean that a person over the age of 16 years can give consent to surgical, medical, or dental treatment without the necessity to get consent from the parents. It is not clear whether persons under the age of 16 can give consent, nor is it clear whether the Act also applies to a refusal of treatment.

II. Assisted Decision-Making (Capacity) Act 2015

180. The issue of how capacity is to be determined in the Irish context is now dealt with by the Assisted Decision-Making (Capacity) Act 2015 (hereafter referred to as the ADM Act).[91] This long-awaited Act has not been fully commenced at this time but is expected to be commenced during 2017. The Act enshrines the presumption of capacity in section 8(2) and it states in section 8(3) that a person shall not be considered to be unable to make a decision unless all practicable steps have been taken without success, to help him or her to do so. These provisions are important in setting out the requirement to provide assistance and information to the person in a manner that is specific to their needs. This recognizes the need for a range of communication styles to enable persons with different abilities to make their own decisions. The ADM Act also states that the fact that a person is only able to retain information for a short time does not render him or her incapable of making a decision. It states that a person who is regarded as incapable of making a decision in relation to one particular matter is not, therefore, incapable of making a decision on any other matter. Thus the test for capacity is both time-specific and issue-specific. A person is not rendered incapable of making a decision merely because they made an unwise or irrational decision.

181. The Act provides a number of Guiding Principles which are applicable where an intervention is to be made in relation to a relevant person. These include the requirement that there shall be no intervention unless it is necessary to do so; an intervention must be made in a manner that minimizes the restriction of the person's rights and freedom of action, have due regard to the need to respect the person's right to dignity, bodily integrity, privacy, autonomy and control over his or her financial

90. Assisted Decision-Making Capacity Act 2015 http://www.irishstatutebook.ie/eli/2015/act/64/enacted/en/html section 8; http://www.hse.ie/portal/eng/about/Who/qualityandpatientsafety/Advocacy/National_Consent_Advisory_Group/National_Consent_Policy.html; para. 10.1 https://www.medicalcouncil.ie/News-and-Publications/Reports/Guide-to-Professional-Conduct-and-Ethics-8th-Edition-2016-.pdf.

91. At http://www.irishstatutebook.ie/eli/2015/act/64/enacted/en/html.

affairs and property; be proportionate to the significance and urgency of the matter the subject of the intervention; and be as limited in duration as possible. These provisions mean that when deciding on how to proceed, the option chosen should be the least restrictive one. The relevant person must be encouraged and facilitated to participate as fully as possible in the intervention. The relevant person's past and present will and preference must be given effect to as far as they are reasonably ascertainable. The beliefs and values of the relevant person must also be taken into account. The views of any person named by the relevant person as someone to be consulted must also be considered. The intervener must at all times act in good faith and for the benefit of the relevant person. This last provision demonstrates a move away from the expression 'best interests' to avoid the often-criticized paternalism inherent in that approach to persons who lack capacity and which is thought to be contrary to the rights of persons with disabilities. The intervener may also consider the views of any person engaged in caring for the relevant person, any person who has a bona fide interest in the welfare of the relevant person, and healthcare professionals. It is worth noting in this context that the intervener is not obliged to consult with such persons as the intervener may be aware of disagreements between family members or may not actually be aware of the wishes of the relevant person.

182. The 2015 Act also provides for a range of new decision-making support options designed to enable and support the relevant person to make their own decisions. This puts in place a flexible functional approach which supports people at all stages and of all abilities to make their own decisions. This is in keeping with the UN Convention on the Rights of Persons with Disabilities.[92] The options include: – a decision-making assistant appointed by the relevant person who may assist the relevant person in making decisions in relation to personal welfare and/or property and affairs. The assistant is not entitled to make a decision with or on behalf of the relevant person – the assistant's role is to assist, advise, and support the relevant person only:

- A co-decisionmaker appointed by the relevant person to jointly make decisions with the relevant person in relation to personal welfare and/or property and affairs. This will be a relative or friend of the relevant person who has had personal contact with the relevant person over a period of time such that a relationship of trust exists between them. The co-decisionmaker's role is to assist the relevant person by assisting him/her in obtaining and understanding relevant information, discussing the relevant options and likely outcomes of a decision, assisting the relevant person in expressing their will and preferences, and making a decision jointly with the relevant person.
- In circumstances where the relevant person lacks capacity to appoint a decision-making assistant or a co-decisionmaker, a court application may be made to appoint a decision-making representative who will act as the agent of the relevant person for the purpose of making specified decisions in relation to personal welfare, property, and affairs. The court may alternatively make the decision concerned if the matter is urgent. In either case the court must consider any advance healthcare directive make by the relevant person and ensure that the

92. Convention on the Rights of Persons with Disabilities (adopted 13 Dec. 2006, entered into force 3 May 2008) 2515 UNTS 3 (CRPD).

court's order or the decision of the decision-making representative is consistent with such directive. Similar provisions apply in the case of any enduring power of attorney made by the relevant person. The decision-making representative is not empowered to prohibit contact between the relevant person and any other person, may not refuse life-sustaining treatment or consent to its withdrawal. They may not restrain, either physically or by chemical means, the relevant person unless there are exceptional emergency circumstances which justify restraint to prevent imminent serious harm to the relevant person or any other person, and the restraint is a proportionate response to the likelihood and seriousness of such harm.

183. Part 7 of the 2015 Act provides that a person (called the donor) may appoint another person as decision-maker (called an attorney) to make decisions on his/her behalf in the event of the donor's subsequent lack of capacity. This is referred to as an Enduring Power of Attorney. The attorney is empowered to make personal care decisions on behalf of the donor, including decisions as to where and with whom the donor should live, who the donor should see, what rehabilitation the donor should receive, the donor's diet and dress, inspection of the donor's personal papers, housing and social welfare benefits for the donor, and healthcare decisions other than refusal of life-sustaining treatment.

184. Part 9 of the Act establishes a new office called the Director of the Decision Support Service. The functions of the Director will include (not an exhaustive list): raising public awareness of the Act; promoting public confidence in the new processes provided for in the Act; providing information to the decision-making supporters described in paragraph 180; supervising compliance of decision-making supporters with the Act; providing information and guidance to organizations in the State in relation to their interaction with relevant persons; and to establish a website to enable the public to understand the operation of the Act. The Director may publish Codes of Practice to provide such guidance as is required under the Act. The Director may also investigate any complaint made in relation to any action of a decision-making supporter.

185. The Mental Health Act 2001, which applies to persons suffering from a mental disorder, provides that a patient's voluntary consent to treatment must be obtained provided he or she is capable of 'understanding the nature, purpose, and likely effects of the proposed treatment'.[93] Information must be given in a manner that the patient can understand. Treatment may only be given where necessary to safeguard the life of the patient, restore his or her health, alleviate his or her condition, or relieve his or her suffering.[94] Certain specific treatments, such as psycho-surgery, electro-convulsive therapy, and continued prescribed medication, require additional safeguards such as second specialist opinions and the approval of a Mental Health Tribunal. Despite the welcome attempt to clarify the legal position relating to those individuals who suffer from a mental disorder, the Act is irrelevant to the majority of people with

93. Section 56(a).
94. Section 57.

mental illness, dementia, or mental disability, whose conditions do not come within the definitions in the Act.[95]

186. If an individual is assessed and found to be competent, then he or she is entitled, as a competent adult, to make a decision regarding medical treatment without recourse being had to parents or guardians. The issues may be considered by his or her family or carers to be different in the context, for example, of capacity to marry or enter a sexual relationship. However, if the individual is deemed competent to make such a decision, then respect for his or her autonomy demands that the decision be adhered to.

III. Refusal of Consent

187. It is important also to examine the circumstances in which a person's capacity to make medical decisions may be challenged. As outlined above, there is a presumption in Irish law that an adult has capacity to make their own decisions, including the right to refuse medical treatment. Even before the passage of the Assisted Decision-Making (Capacity) Act 2015, the courts have expressed this principle in relevant cases such as *In Re a Ward of Court* [96] in which O'Flaherty J. said 'there is an absolute right in a competent person to refuse medical treatment even if it leads to death'.

188. A person may make a decision in favour or against treatment for a wide variety of reasons, some of which may appear to others to be unreasonable or irresponsible. All such decisions must be respected as an exercise of autonomy. However, there does inevitably come a point where the rationale behind the decision is so bizarre as to lead to suspicions as to the person's capacity. Whether this is a clash of individual value systems or an imposition on individual freedom by claims of societal interests is a matter for debate elsewhere. What is crucial is that the decision is not overridden on the basis of instinctive beliefs that 'no one in their right mind' would have made such a decision, and that, therefore, the patient must be viewed as lacking capacity. If the patient is able to understand and process the information given regarding the diagnosis and treatment options and communicate their decision, then the patient must be respected in the decision he or she makes as a result of that understanding. There may be concern that a person might be sufficiently capable to comprehend the information but may be so influenced by factors such as fear, pain, distress, and so on, that his or her capacity to actually make the decision is impaired. It is important here to start from the presumption of capacity and to look at the decision-making process itself and not the result or outcome of the decision.

189. A case which considered the issue of capacity to give consent or refuse treatment is *Fitzpatrick and Ryan v. FK and the Attorney General.*[97] The facts of this case were that K, a 23-year-old African woman from the Congo, gave birth to a baby in an Irish hospital in 2006. Shortly thereafter she suffered a massive post-partum

95. *See* further M. Donnelly, *Legislating for Incapacity: Developing a Rights-Based Framework*, 30 DULJ 394 (2008).
96. [1996] 2 IR 79.
97. [2008] IEHC 104.

haemorrhage resulting in cardiovascular collapse. As blood was being prepared for immediate transfusion, the medical team was informed that K would not accept blood for religious reasons. The medical team was concerned that K would die without a blood transfusion and called the Master of the hospital (the most senior obstetrician in the maternity hospital with responsibility for clinical governance). Following discussions with K, during which she repeated her refusal of blood, the Master had doubts regarding her capacity to make such a decision and decided to apply to the High Court for an emergency order giving the hospital authority to transfuse K.

190. The judge made the order authorizing the hospital to administer blood to K, including all appropriate steps by way of restraint. The Master informed K of the court order and she was transfused following the administration of a sedative. She subsequently made a full recovery. She later claimed that the court order should not have been given, that the transfusion was unlawful, and therefore constituted an assault and trespass to her person, and that she was entitled to refuse all or any medical treatment by virtue of her Constitutional rights and under Articles 8 and 9 of the European Convention on Human Rights.

191. Judge Laffoy was of the view that it could not be argued that a competent adult is not free to decline medical treatment. She referred to the *Ward of Court* case cited above in support of this conclusion. Thus the question that arose on the facts of this case was whether K had capacity to refuse the blood transfusion. This question had not been determined by an Irish court up to this point, and therefore Laffoy J also examined relevant case law from other jurisdictions in her judgment. She also referred to the LRC's report on *Vulnerable Adults and the Law*, in which the Commission recommends that 'capacity will be understood in terms of an adult's cognitive ability to understand the nature and consequences of a decision in the context of available choices at the time the decision is made'.

192. Laffoy J held that the principles applicable to the determination of capacity are as follows:

(a) There is a presumption that an adult patient has the capacity, that is to say, the cognitive ability, to make a decision to refuse medical treatment, but that presumption can be rebutted.

(b) In determining whether a patient is deprived of capacity to make a decision to refuse medical treatment whether: (a) by reason of permanent cognitive impairment, or (b) temporary factors … , the test is whether the patient's cognitive ability has been impaired to the extent that he or she does not sufficiently understand the nature, purpose, and effect of the proffered treatment and the consequences of accepting or rejecting it in the context of the choices available (including any alternative treatment) at the time the decision is made.

(c) … The patient's cognitive ability will have been impaired to the extent that he or she is incapable of making the decision to refuse the proffered treatment if the patient:

- has not comprehended and retained the treatment information and, in particular, has not assimilated the information as to the consequences likely to ensue from not accepting the treatment;

- has not believed the treatment information and, in particular, if it is the case that not accepting the treatment is likely to result in the patient's death, has not believed that outcome is likely; and
- has not weighed the treatment information, in particular, the alternative choices and the likely outcomes, in the balance in arriving at the decision.

(d) The treatment information by reference to which the patient's capacity is to be assessed is the information which the clinician is under a duty to impart – information as to what is the appropriate treatment, that is to say, what treatment is medically indicated, at the time of the decision and the risks and consequences likely to flow from the choices available to the patient in making the decision.
(e) In assessing capacity it is necessary to distinguish between misunderstanding or misperception of the treatment information in the decision-making process ... on the one hand, and an irrational decision or a decision made for irrational reasons, on the other hand. The former may be evidence of lack of capacity. The latter is irrelevant to the assessment.
(f) In assessing capacity, whether at the bedside in a high dependency unit or in court, the assessment must have regard to the gravity of the decision, in terms of the consequences which are likely to ensue from the acceptance or rejection of the proffered treatment.

193. Having regard to the nature of the evidence presented in relation to K's capacity, the Court was satisfied that K had been given the information necessary, in layman's terms, to enable her to make an informed decision in relation to the blood transfusion. The relevant factors to be taken into account in this case were that K's medical status was seriously compromised following a long labour, a difficult delivery, and a massive haemorrhage. There were communication difficulties due to the fact the K's first language was not English, and the hospital believed that K had no family members in the country to support her at that time. Laffoy J concluded that K's capacity at the relevant time was impaired to the extent that she did not have the ability to make a valid refusal to accept the appropriate medical treatment that was proffered to her, a blood transfusion. Therefore, the administration of the transfusion was not unlawful or in breach of her Constitutional rights.

194. The Assisted Decision-Making (Capacity) Act 2015 provides in section 83(2) that an adult with capacity is entitled to refuse treatment for any reason (including a reason based on his or her religious beliefs) notwithstanding that the refusal appears to be unwise, not based on sound medical principles, or may result in his or her death. This provision, therefore, puts on a statutory footing the principles outlined above arising from case law on this matter.

IV. Disclosure of Information Prior to Giving Consent

195. Irish criminal law provides that it is an offence of battery to touch another person without consent or other lawful reasons. It might, therefore, be thought that the criminal law would provide a potential breeding ground for cases involving medical procedures where valid consent had not been given. However, the criminal law has not traditionally been used to ground a case based on the absence of consent in Ireland. Rather, allegations that information was not disclosed generally form part of civil actions for medical negligence, in other words the patient alleges that had s/he been properly informed of the risks of treatment s/he would not have consented. Therefore, the consent given was not 'informed'.

196. The right to be informed is also seen as incorporated in the constitutional right of respect for bodily integrity, which includes the right to make autonomous decisions in relation to one's own body. This implies that there is an obligation on the medical practitioner to inform the patient about matters relating to the illness, the proposal procedure to be carried out, and any possible harmful consequence arising from the procedure. The standard expected of the doctor in these circumstances is the same as that expected in relation to the care to be exercised in the giving of treatment.

197. In *Dunne v. National Maternity Hospital*[98] the Supreme Court held that in order to prove negligence against a medical practitioner, the court must be satisfied that the medical practitioner was 'guilty of such failure as no medical practitioner of equal specialize or general status and skill would be guilty of if acting with ordinary care'.[99] This is referred to as the 'professional standard' or 'reasonable doctor' test. It is essentially the means by which the court equips itself to make a judgment on whether or not the doctor acted with reasonable skill and care.

198. One of the difficulties in the area of consent is that there may be a substantial difference between the appearance of consent and the reality. Too often patients are presented with a consent form to sign and are not given the requisite information and explanations that would enable the patient to make an informed choice prior to signature. Doctors may be liable for breach of duty if they fail to make a full disclosure of all the factors that a reasonable person would wish to consider before deciding to consent. This potential exposure to liability should encourage doctors to enquire more of their patients and listen to their concerns before the patient commits to a choice. If the patient suffers complications from the procedure, responsibility for the outcome is shared between doctor and patient as long as the patient has been sufficiently informed about the risk of complications arising and has made an informed choice to proceed.

199. One of the fundamental issues that arises in the area of informed consent is the extent of the obligation to disclose risk. As a general rule, the greater the risks to the patient that the doctor knows or should know, but that the patient cannot be expected to know, the greater the duty on the doctor to give the necessary information. A doctor must warn of likely or probable side effects, but there is less clarity about warning of remote possibilities. It is generally accepted that the more questions the patient asks, the more information must be given by the doctor.

200. In *Daniels v. Heskin*[100] the Court considered the duty of a doctor to tell his patient that a broken part of a needle had been left in her body during stitching after childbirth. The doctor had left instructions that the patient should be x-rayed within six weeks if the needle had not been found. When this was done and an examination carried out by a different doctor, an operation was performed to remove the needle.

98. [1989] IR 91.
99. [1989] IR 91 at 108.
100. [1954] IR 53.

The majority of the Supreme Court held that there was no obligation on the doctor to inform the patient or her husband of the presence of the needle. The Court held that if a 'dangerous' operation was planned, then the doctor must disclose the risks involved. However, in other situations the doctor could decide for him- or herself whether or not to make the disclosure. The decision is of limited value in modern terms as it is unclear what was meant by 'dangerous' operations, and the decision is not in keeping with modern developments in the area of patient autonomy and the right to be informed.

201. One of the more important cases in the area of risk disclosure is *Walsh v. Family Planning Services*.[101] In this case the plaintiff had a vasectomy operation carried out. Prior to the operation he had been told that the operation would not negatively affect his sex life and might actually improve it. He was told that there might be some discomfort and swelling after the operation and that, very rarely, some patients experience pain for some years later. The patient suffered a variety of problems after the operation that included severe groin pain, impotence, and eventual removal of his left testicle. Expert evidence showed that he had suffered a rare but known possible consequence of vasectomy called orchialgia. At the time of the operation there was no known practice amongst doctors of disclosing this risk. However, the High Court accepted that the patient had been sufficiently warned.

202. Finlay CJ was the only judge in the Supreme Court who was prepared to adopt the reasonable doctor test put forward in the *Dunne* case,[102] with the caveat that if the nature of the warning given was inherently defective, the Court might be more prepared to judge that the doctor had not fulfilled the duty of disclosure prior to obtaining consent. He also accepted that when the procedure was elective, the courts might more readily decide that there were inherent defects in standard medical procedure such that the patient should have been warned about them. He was satisfied that:

> There is of course, where it is possible to do so, a clear obligation on a medical practitioner carrying out or arranging for the carrying out of an operation, to inform the patient of any possible harmful consequence arising from the operation so as to permit the patient to give an informed consent to subjecting himself to the operation concerned. I am also satisfied that the extent of this obligation must, as a matter of common sense, vary with what might be described as the elective nature of the surgery concerned. The obligation to give a warning of the possible harmful consequences of a surgical procedure which could be said to be elective may be more stringent and onerous.

203. For all the judges in this case, the fact that this was an elective procedure was of importance in deciding the extent of disclosure required. The element of choice meant that the doctor did not have to weigh up the risks of not performing the surgery against the risks involved in the procedure. O'Flaherty J said:

> In the case of elective surgery if there is a risk – however exceptional or remote – of grave consequences involving severe pain stretching for an appreciable time into the future and involving the possibility of further operative procedures, the

101. [1992] IR 496.
102. *Ibid.*

exercise of the duty of care owed by the defendants requires that such possible consequences should be explained in the clearest language to the plaintiff.

204. In *Bolton v. the Blackrock Clinic, Wood and Cumiskey*[103] the plaintiff had sought treatment for a pulmonary condition for which surgery was recommended. She later complained that she had not been given sufficient information regarding the risks involved in this surgery. The High Court held that in relation to disclosure, this is to be determined on ordinary principles of negligence and in this case the risks had been properly disclosed. The Supreme Court agreed on the finding of fact in this case but held that the matter should be determined on the basis of the *Dunne* principles.

205. In *Geoghegan v. Harris*[104] the plaintiff alleged negligence in the carrying out of a dental implant by the defendant dentist, during the course of which a bone graft was taken from the plaintiff's chin. This was alleged to have damaged a nerve in the front of the chin and left the patient with chronic neuropathic pain. It was alleged that the patient had not been informed of the risk that such pain might be a consequence of the procedure.

The defendant accepted that he did not disclose this risk as he was of the view that he had a duty to disclose rare complications only where the risk exceeded 1%. The plaintiff gave evidence that he would not have consented even if the risk was 0.1%. Kearns J held that there is a requirement to give a warning of any material risk that is a known complication of a procedure properly carried out. The test of materiality in elective surgery is to enquire only if there is any risk, however, exceptional or remote, of grave consequences involving pain for an appreciable time into the future; statistical frequency is irrelevant.

206. The judge adopted the reasonable patient test in relation to causation. This involves the patient convincing the court that he or she would not have proceeded with the procedure if the information had been disclosed. The problem this raises for claimants is that, because in the vast majority of cases the risks in a procedure are quite small and the potential benefits are quite large, most claimants cannot convincingly argue that they would have acted any differently even if they had been provided with a full picture. Although not a Supreme Court case, this case was important in firmly upholding the right of the patient to choose his or her treatment with full knowledge of all material facts.

207. The most recent Supreme Court case on the matter of disclosure is *Fitzpatrick v. White*.[105] The facts involved an alleged failure to give a warning to a patient prior to eye surgery. Kearns J reaffirmed the position adopted in *Walsh* that a warning must in every case be given of a risk, however remote, of grave consequences involving severe pain continuing into the future and involving further operative intervention. He went on to say:

> the argument that the giving of an adequate warning, far from being a source of nuisance for doctors, should be seen as an opportunity to ensure they are protected from subsequent litigation at the suit of disappointed patients. I am thus fortified

103. 20 Dec. 1994 (Unrep HC).
104. [2000] IEHC 129.
105. [2007] IESC 51.

> to express in rather more vigorous terms than I did in Goeghegan v. Harris my view that the patient centred test is preferable, and ultimately more satisfactory from the point of view of both doctor and patient alike, than any 'doctor centred' approach favoured by part of this Court in Walsh v. Family Planning Services.

The judge held that a risk may be seen as material if, in the circumstances of the particular case, a reasonable person in the patient's position, if warned of the risk, would be likely to attach significance to it.

208. Another noteworthy point from the judgment of that case is in relation to the timing of seeking informed consent. In this case the plaintiff accepted that a warning had in fact been given but alleged that a warning that was given only shortly before the procedure was carried out was insufficient to discharge the duty of care on the doctor. In this case, the plaintiff had his eyesight fully tested and evaluated four months before his operation and the options for surgical intervention were plain from the orthoptist's report from that time. The plaintiff was seen on three occasions prior to his operation. The judge took the view that the risks associated with squint surgery could have easily been explained to the plaintiff at any of these meetings, or certainly well in advance of the time when they were explained – a mere thirty minutes before his operation. The judge said:

> There are obvious reasons why, in the context of elective surgery, a warning given only shortly before an operation is undesirable. A patient may be stressed, medicated or in pain in this period and may be less likely for one or more of these reasons to make a calm and reasoned decision in such circumstances.

209. In this case, the plaintiff gave no evidence of being unduly stressed or anxious on the day of his operation, he was not in pain, and he had not been sedated prior to his operation. He was facing what could fairly be described as a minor operation only. His evidence suggested he was in a clear and lucid mental state on the day of the operation and well capable of making a decision. He described how his conversation with the doctor was both cordial and relaxed. While the plaintiff said he would have 'walked straight out of the hospital' had he been warned on the day, he did not say he could not deal with a warning given at that point in time. In fact he said the opposite. In the absence of clear evidence that the plaintiff was actually disadvantaged in some material way by the lateness of the warning, the judge held that he would not declare or find the warning given to be invalid because it was given at a late stage. He went on to say that there was nothing in the evidence to suggest the plaintiff could not assimilate or properly understand what he was being told. He said, 'I would make the point strongly however that in other cases where a warning is given late in the day, particularly where the surgery is elective surgery, the outcome might well be different.'

210. Further detailed guidance on information disclosure prior to treatment is available in the HSE National Consent Policy[106] and the Medical Council's Guide to

106. HSE National Consent Policy (2013) http://www.hse.ie/eng/about/Who/qualityandpatientsafety/National_Consent_Policy/.

Professional Conduct and Ethics.[107] Both documents follow the principles set down by the courts in the cases described above but give further advice to health and social care professionals and medical practitioners respectively in relation to the practical application of those principles.

§3. Privacy

211. The right to privacy has been recognized by the Irish courts as an unenumerated personal right under Article 40 of the Constitution. In the case of *McGee v. the Attorney General*,[108] the right to privacy was established in the context of marriage. In *Kennedy and Arnold v. Ireland*,[109] Hamilton J said:

> Though not specifically guaranteed by the Constitution, the right of privacy is one of the fundamental personal rights of the citizen which flow from the Christian and democratic nature of the State … The nature of the right to privacy must be such as to ensure the dignity and freedom of an individual in the type of society envisaged by the Constitution, namely, a sovereign, independent and democratic society.

However, it was stated that the right is not absolute and may be restricted 'by the constitutional rights of others or by the requirements of the common good and it is subject to the requirements of public order and morality'.

212. The right to privacy is not specified in the personal rights set out in the Irish Constitution. However, the courts have recognised a category of rights referred to as unenumerated rights which are implicit in Article 40.3 of the Constitution. These include the right to marry, the right to bodily integrity and the right to earn a living. In *Norris v. Attorney General*,[110] the right to privacy was recognized as another of these unenumerated rights and was described by the court as the right to be let alone, or the right of non-interference in private affairs. However, the court also recognized that the right to privacy can be overridden by competing interests. In this case although an individual constitutional right to privacy was recognized by the Court, it was held that homosexual acts between consenting adult males were not included in the scope of that constitutional protection. This was at a time when homosexuality was illegal in the State. This is no longer the case.[111]

107. At https://www.medicalcouncil.ie/News-and-Publications/Reports/Guide-to-Professional-Conduct-Ethics-8th-Edition.html.
108. [1974] IR 284.
109. [1987] IR 1.
110. [1984] IR 36.
111. In 1988 Norris took a case to the ECHR to argue that by criminalizing homosexuality, Irish law was incompatible with the European Convention on Human Rights. The Court ruled that the criminalization of homosexuality violated Art. 8 of the Convention, which guarantees the right to privacy in personal affairs. The Irish Parliament (*Oireachtas*) decriminalized homosexuality five years later in the Criminal Law (Sexual Offences) Act 1993.

213. The doctor-patient relationship does not feature in the cases on privacy already decided by the Irish courts. However, given the nature of the personal information disclosed to doctors in the expectation that the information will remain private, it may be expected that the ethical principle that provides for medical confidentiality would also be covered by the constitutional principle. Medical practitioners may be seen in the same light as bankers, accountants, journalists, or priests who are bound by a duty that the law respects and upholds to prevent them disclosing information obtained in a professional capacity without the consent of the person who entrusted that information to them.

214. In *Cook v. Carroll* [1945] IR 515, the Court stated that the test as to whether a relationship of confidence existed was as follows:

- the communications must originate in a confidence that they will not be disclosed;
- this element of confidentiality must be essential to the full and satisfactory maintenance of the relation;
- the relation must be one that in the opinion of the community ought to be sedulously fostered; and
- the injury that would enure to the relation by the disclosure of the communication must be greater than the benefit thereby gained for the correct disposal of litigation.

§4. Secrecy

215. Although there is no specific legislation in Ireland setting out the duty of secrecy or confidentiality, it may nonetheless arise in a number of ways. It can arise from the ethical duties imposed on doctors, contractual or other legal obligations, or constitutional rights to privacy. The constitutional right to privacy has been discussed above at paragraph 211.

216. In relation to contractual issues, if an express contract exists between doctor and patient, the obligation to maintain patient confidentiality may be a term of that contract and the extent of the obligation will then depend on the interpretation of the terms used in the contract. However, written contracts between doctors and patients are not usual, and therefore such a term would not commonly be expressly written. The obligation may be incorporated into the relationship between doctor and patient by other means. It may, for example, be argued by the patient that although there was no written contract, it was reasonable for the patient to assume that the doctor would adhere to the ethical principles of the profession, which include the duty of confidentiality, and that this obligation should, therefore, be an implied term of the contract.

217. The ethical duty of medical confidentiality originates from the Hippocratic oath, which requires doctors to undertake that 'what I see or hear in the life of men which ought not to be spoken of abroad, I will not divulge as reckoning that all such should be kept secret'. This has been reaffirmed in the Declaration of Geneva 1947 and most codes of professional conduct worldwide. It is generally understood that the duty of confidence relates not only to information imparted to the doctor by the patient him- or herself but also information about the patient that the doctor learns from other sources such as specialists and family members.

218. The Guide to Professional Conduct and Ethics (8th edn) published by the Irish Medical Council in 2016,[112] states:

> 29.1 Confidentiality is central to the trust you and your patients and a core element of the doctor-patient relationship. However, sharing information, in appropriate circumstances is also important, both for patient care and for the safety of the patient and others.

219. In *House of Spring Gardens v. Point Blank Ltd*,[113] Costello J said that in order for an action for breach of confidence to succeed it must be established that:

- there exists in the relationship between the parties an obligation of confidence regarding the information;
- the information must be properly regarded as confidential;
- the recipient has used the information for a purpose for which it was not intended and to the detriment of the informant.

In the context of medical practise the first two of these criteria would be easily satisfied. The third criteria may give rise to dispute in circumstances where a doctor discloses confidential patient information without the patient's consent. In order to avoid an action for breach of confidence the doctor would have to successfully plead that he or she did so in the best interests of the patient.

I. Exceptions to Medical Confidentiality

220. In certain circumstances the doctor has to weigh competing interests against his or her duty of confidentiality. For example, if maintaining confidentiality results in risk to another person, then the doctor may consider that he or she has an obligation to protect the other person from the risk presented. This may arise in relation to HIV/AIDS or other sexually transmitted diseases where the issue is starkly illustrated.

221. Despite the assurances of confidentiality given in most professional medical codes around the world, it is also commonly stated in those documents that the assurance is not without exception. Apart from situations in which the doctor is legally obliged to divulge information, such as to a court or other legally established tribunal, the other exceptions generally relate to protection of the best interests of the patient or another person, or the public interest.

222. Although the patient's consent to disclosure is always preferable where the doctor intends to disclose confidential information, it is also possible for the doctor to try to justify disclosure in the absence of consent on the grounds that it was necessary to protect the interests of the patient. This may be envisaged, for example, where a doctor communicates information regarding the patient's health to a relative or carer so as to ensure the patient is adequately cared for. The disclosure is done on the basis

112. At https://www.medicalcouncil.ie/News-and-Publications/Reports/Guide-to-Professional-Conduct-Ethics-8th-Edition.html.
113. [1984] IR 611.

that the doctor assumes the patient impliedly consents to such disclosure. However, doctors should be cautious about such a justification as it may not always be assumed that the patient gives consent in such circumstances. If the patient clearly refuses to authorize such disclosure, this must be respected by the doctor even where the doctor is of the opinion that this is contrary to the patient's best interests. The *Medical Council's Ethical Guide*[114] states:

> 31.1 When you disclose information as required by law or in the public interest, you should inform patients of the disclosure, unless this would cause them serious harm, or would undermine the purpose of the disclosure.

223. Apart from specific statutory such as to notify infectious diseases to the appropriate authority, there may also be ethical obligations to disclose information in the public interest such as where there are reasonable grounds for believing that a serious assault or other violence has been committed against a child or other vulnerable person.

224. In the case of patients who present a serious risk of violence a doctor may consider whether he or she is legally and ethically justified in breaching confidentiality in the public interest. While there are no Irish cases directly in point, some English case law in this area is instructive. In *W v. Egdell*[115] a consultant psychiatrist, Dr Egdell, was asked to examine a prisoner, W, who had been convicted of firearms offences in which a number of people had been killed and others wounded and who was in a secure hospital, in order to assess W's application to be transferred to a less secure unit. Dr Egdell examined W and strongly advised against such a move on the grounds that W remained interested in firearms and explosives. As a consequence of this report W withdrew his application for a transfer, with the result that Dr Egdell's report was not seen by anyone other than W's legal team. Dr Egdell sent a copy of his report to the medical director of the hospital where W was housed. The hospital, with the doctor's permission, sent a copy of the report to the Secretary for State who, in turn, sent it to the tribunal dealing with applications for transfer of prisoners.

225. W sought an injunction against the recipients of the report to prevent them from using or disclosing the report further, and damages for breach of confidentiality. The Court was of the opinion that the circumstances of the medical examination did import a duty of confidentiality on Dr Egdell so that, for example, he could not have sold the contents of his report to a newspaper. Stephen Brown P referred to Lord Goff's judgment in the *Spycatcher* case,[116] where he said that:

> Although the basis of the law's protection of confidence is that there is a public interest that confidences should be preserved and protected by the law, nevertheless that public interest may be outweighed by some other counter-vailing public interest which favours disclosure … .It is this limiting principle which may require a court to carry out a balancing operation weighing the public interest in

114. At https://www.medicalcouncil.ie/News-and-Publications/Reports/Guide-to-Professional-Conduct-Ethics-8th-Edition.html.
115. [1990] 1 All ER 835.
116. [1988] 3 All ER 545.

maintaining confidence against a countervailing public interest favouring disclosure.

226. In the circumstances of this case, it was held that Dr Egdell was within the scope of the exception in relation to communicating confidential information to other health professionals involved in W's treatment. There were also broader considerations involved. Although the doctor had been engaged by W's legal team, his duty was not to W alone. Dr Egdell also owed a duty to the public that would require him to place before the appropriate authorities the result of his examination if, in his opinion, the public interest so required. Therefore, Dr Egdell was justified in making the disclosure to those responsible for W's treatment and to the Secretary of State who was responsible for public safety. Bingham J stated:

> Where a man has committed multiple killings under the disability of serious mental illness, decisions which may lead directly or indirectly to his release from hospital should not be made unless a responsible authority is properly able to make an informed judgement that the risk of repetition is so small as to be acceptable. A consultant psychiatrist who becomes aware, even in the course of a confidential relationship, of information which leads him, in the exercise of what the court considers a sound professional judgement, to fear that such decisions may be made on the basis of inadequate information and with a real risk of consequent danger to the public is entitled to take such steps as are reasonable in all the circumstances to communicate the grounds of his concern to the responsible authorities.

227. Disclosure of information may also be made to other healthcare professionals as part of the medical care of the patient or as part of quality assurance systems or education and training. While it is preferable to anonymize such information wherever possible, there may be situations in which it is not possible or appropriate to do so. In such circumstances, the patient should be informed and given the opportunity to object to such disclosure and use of his or her personal information.

§5. Complaints

228. Complaints in respect of individual medical practitioners may be made to the Medical Council, which will investigate whether the doctor has a case to answer on grounds of professional misconduct, unfitness to practise, poor professional performance, and so on. *See* paragraph 137. Similar complaints mechanisms exist for other healthcare professionals within their respective regulatory bodies. There is information available to the public on the internet on how to make a complaint in respect of any practitioner or service in the health system in Ireland.[117]

229. Complaints in respect of services provided by the HSE may be made in accordance with procedures established by Part 9 of the Health Act 2004 which came into operation in January 2007. These regulations include provision for the designation

117. At http://www.healthcomplaints.ie/.

of complaints officers and review officers, timeframes for the management of complaints, and procedures for the management of complaints.

230. The HSE published a feedback policy entitled 'Your Service, Your Say'[118] that sets out a number of mechanisms by which service users can make a complaint in person, writing, email, telephone, through consumer panels, and via other means. Complaints must be made within twelve months and any complaints directed at an identifiable person must be made in writing. The relevant HSE complaints officer will be informed of all verbal complaints that could not be resolved at the first point of contact and will receive a copy of all written complaints. Depending on the nature of the complaint, the complaints officer, with the consent of the people involved, may consider if an informal resolution might be appropriate. As part of the informal resolution the complaints officer may arrange a meeting between the parties concerned or use mediation services. If informal resolution is not appropriate or turns out not to be successful, the complaints officer will start a formal investigation of the complaint.

231. The complaints officer will investigate a complaint within thirty working days of the acknowledgment of the complaint. The officer may call on other staff, witnesses, experts, and so on to assist with the investigation. If the complaint cannot be investigated within thirty days of acknowledging the complaint, the complaints officer will tell the complainant this before this timeframe passes. The officer will also indicate the time it will take to complete the investigation and must then update the complainant every twenty working days until the matter is resolved. On conclusion of the investigation the complaints officer will write a report of the investigation and give a copy of the report to the complainant, the general manager of the hospital or service, and the relevant service manager or staff member who was the subject of the complaint. The final report will include any recommendations needed to resolve the matter. The complaints officer will invite everyone involved to contact him or her with questions about any issues and will advise the complainant of his or her right to a review of the recommendations made by the complaints officer by the HSE's Head of Consumer Affairs.

232. Within thirty working days of receiving the report from the complaints officer, the general manager of the service must put an action plan in place to implement the complaints officer's recommendations. The action plan will outline who will be responsible for implementing the recommendations and the time it will take. If the general manager believes that the recommendations would require material changes to the plan for their service, the manager may amend or reject the recommendations or take other measures to resolve the issue. The general manager must give reasons for the decision. If the complainant is not satisfied with the recommendations made by the complaints officer, he or she has a right to an HSE internal review of the entire complaint and how it has been handled. The Head of Consumer Affairs will appoint an appropriate review officer who will try to conduct and conclude the review process within twenty working days. If the complainant is not satisfied with the outcome of the internal review or the HSE's response, he or she has the right to request a review of the complaint by the Ombudsman who is responsible for ensuring that the public receive good customer care and fair treatment from the government and public bodies.[119]

118. At http://www.hse.ie/eng/services/Publications/Your_Service,_Your_Say_Consumer_Affairs/.
119. At http://www.ombudsman.gov.ie/en/.

233. In some service areas, for example, nursing homes or disability services, there are specific laws in place for managing complaints. There are also some complaints that the HSE policy cannot cover. If a complaint falls into one of these categories, the HSE will refer the complainant to the appropriate service or authority. Under Part 9 of the Health Act 2004, a complaint cannot be made on the following topics:

- A matter that is or has been the subject of legal proceedings before a court or tribunal.
- A matter relating solely to the exercise of clinical judgment (a decision about diagnosis or treatment) by a person acting on behalf of either the HSE or a service provider.
- An action taken by the HSE or a service provider solely on the advice of a person exercising clinical judgment.
- A matter relating to the recruitment or appointment of an employee by the HSE or a service provider.
- A matter relating to a contract of employment that the HSE or a service provider proposes to enter into.
- A matter relating to the Social Welfare Act.
- A matter that could be the subject of an appeal under section 60 of the Civil Registration Act 2004.
- A matter that could prejudice an investigation by the *Garda Siochana.*
- A matter that has been brought before any other complaints procedure established under legislation.

However, complaints in these categories can be managed using alternative processes.

§6. Access to Medical Records

234. Doctors have a duty to maintain accurate and up-to-date records of patient care either in manual or electronic form. Doctors have obligations under the Data Protection Acts[120] in relation to secure storage and eventual disposal of such records as well as relevant published Codes of Practice.

235. Patients are entitled to receive a copy of their own medical records, provided it does not put their health (or the health, safety, or privacy of others) at risk. This formal right of access is provided for by law as described below. There are two sets of legislative provisions in operation in Ireland that have relevance in relation to access to medical records.

I. Freedom of Information Acts

236. The Freedom of Information Act 2014 which repealed the earlier 1997 and 2003 Acts cover official information that an individual may seek to have access to and to have amended if inaccurate. The legislation establishes a presumption in favour of

120. At http://www.dataprotection.ie.

access to information in visual, written, or electronic forms. It gives a broad definition of such information and a framework of access. It gives individuals rights to access personal and non-personal information, have personal records amended or deleted where the information is incorrect, incomplete, or misleading, and to seek reasons for decisions affecting them. Personal information is defined generally in the Act as information about an identifiable individual that: (a) would in the ordinary course of events, be known only to the individual or members of the family, or friends, of the individual; or (b) is held by a public body on the understanding that it would be treated as confidential. The Act gives illustrative examples as including information relating to the educational, medical, psychiatric, or psychological history of the individual. Limitations on rights of access are clearly outlined, reasons for refusals of access must be given, and the Office of Information Commissioner has been set up to review decisions by and practices of public bodies as well as the operation of the Act generally.[121]

237. It is important to note that the Act applies only to public bodies.[122] This means that it applies to the Health Service Executive which administers public hospitals in the State and doctors who are employed by the State. However, medical records held by private hospitals or clinics are not accessible under the Act though the obligations under the Data Protection Acts considered below do apply to private as well as public health providers. There are a number of exemptions under the Act that are designed to protect the public interest and the privacy of individuals. There are two broad categories of exemptions:

- class exemptions, where all records in that class or category are exempt – e.g., records to which legal professional privilege attaches; and
- harm-based exemptions, where records that might damage a particular public interest are exempt – e.g., records that reveal the negotiating positions of public bodies.

Examples of exemptions include circumstances in which disclosure of the record would prejudice the privacy of another person, the request is frivolous, vexatious, or voluminous, or the record would disclose deliberations of a public body so that it would be against the public interest to disclose. Many but not all exemptions may contain what is often referred to as a public interest override – i.e., even though a record is exempt under the Freedom of Information (FOI) Act, a public body or the Information Commissioner may decide, on balance, that the overall public interest justifies its release. Some exemptions may provide that a public body may refuse to disclose the very existence of a particular record where to do so might disclose exempt information. Some classes of records may also be excluded from the scope of the FOI Act, for example, records created by the Attorney General, records relating to the President, and the private papers of *Teachta Dàla* (member of Parliament) (TDs) and Senators.

238. An issue which can cause difficulty in practice is in relation to a parent's right of access to the health record of their children. A child under the FOI Act is

121. *See* generally M. McDonagh, *Freedom of Information Law in Ireland* (3rd ed., Round Hall 2015).

122. For list of public bodies under the Act, *see* http://www.oic.gov.ie/en/PrescribedPublicBodies/.

defined as a person under the age of 18. Although as a general rule a person can only seek access to personal records about themselves, family relationships require special consideration. In *McK v. The Information Commissioner*[123] the issue to be decided by the Court was whether a father, a widower who had been separated from his late wife, and who was joint guardian of his children, was entitled under the Freedom of Information Act 1997 to information, in the form of hospital notes, about an illness of his daughter. The circumstances were that there had been an unproven allegation of sexual abuse by the man of his daughter prior to the couple's separation. As part of the separation agreement, the man had supervised access to his children and the parties were working toward a position of unsupervised access at the time of the wife's death. By agreement, the children went to live with the wife's brother. The father, his brother-in-law, and his wife were joint guardians of the children. Following admission of the man's daughter to hospital for an unspecified viral infection, the man sought further information from the hospital, which was not forthcoming. The other joint guardian refused permission for release of the records. On appeal to the Information Commissioner, the Commissioner decided that in any situation in which there is disagreement between parents/guardians regarding the release of records relating to a minor, release will only be directed where there is tangible evidence that such release would actually serve the best interests of the minor.

On appeal to the High Court and subsequently to the Supreme Court it was held that:

> As a matter of Constitutional and family law a parent has rights and duties. In general a parent would expect to be given and would be given medical information about his or her child. It would only be in exceptional circumstances that medical information about a child would not be given to a parent/guardian.

The Supreme Court held that the Commissioner erred in determining that release of the medical information would only be directed where there is tangible evidence that such release would actually serve the best interests of the minor.

The Court held that a parent has rights and duties in relation to a child. It is presumed that his or her actions are in accordance with the best interests of the child. This presumption, while not absolute, is fundamental. The 'tangible evidence' test of the Commissioner reversed the onus of proof. The obverse is the correct approach. The presumption is that the release of such medical information would best serve the interests of the minor. However, evidence may be produced that it would not serve his or her interests, and, in considering the circumstances, his or her welfare is paramount.

239. Access to medical records may be refused if it is prejudicial to the physical or mental well-being of the individual concerned, although access through a nominated health professional may be possible.[124] This serves to reinforce the position that rights of access to medical records are dependent on the decision of either the executive of

123. [2006] IESC 2.

124. Section 26(4) The aim of the provision is to give the individual to whom the information relates indirect access to the information and, as it has been expressed in an Australian report, 'to ensure that people receive 'disturbing' information in a supportive environment'. McDonagh, *supra* n. 121, at 284.

the public body in question (who may not have any medical qualifications with which to assess the request for access) or a nominated health professional who will exercise his or her own medical judgment. Although such refusals are subject to the right of appeal, the individual in this situation does not have a broad right to records of his or her healthcare, which seems to be in conflict with the overall aim of the Act.

II. Data Protection Acts

240. Data protection legislation seeks to protect personal information about individuals that is stored on computer or in a structured manual file by institutions or individuals. Personal information is defined as any data related to a living individual who can be identified by the data. The definition of 'sensitive personal data' includes data relating to the physical or mental health or condition or sexual life of the individual, and therefore is the category into which medical information held by health professionals and healthcare providers would fall.

241. The aim of data protection law is to ensure that data protection principles are complied with. These principles are set out in the Data Protection Acts 1988–2003. They may be summarized as follows:

- personal data must be obtained and processed fairly;
- it must be kept only for one or more specified and lawful purposes;
- it must be processed only in ways that are compatible with the purposes for which the data was given;
- it must be kept securely;
- it must be kept accurate and up-to-date;
- it must be adequate, relevant, and not excessive;
- it must not be retained for longer than is necessary for the specified purpose(s);
- a copy of the data must be given on request to the individual to whom it relates.

Processing data includes almost any use of the data, including:

- obtaining, recording, or keeping the information or data;
- collecting, organizing, storing, altering, or adapting the information or data;
- retrieving, consulting, or using the information or data;
- disclosing the information or data by transmitting, disseminating;
- otherwise making it available; or
- aligning, combining, blocking, erasing, or destroying the information or data.

242. There are a number of requirements in relation to the processing of sensitive personal data. Only one of these must be met before the data may be lawfully processed. They include obtaining patient consent, processing for the discharge of a legal obligation or to protect the vital interests of the patient, or processing by a health professional for 'medical purposes'. Patient consent to the storage of data may be implied from the patient's attendance at a clinic or the doctor's consulting rooms but it is preferable to expressly make it known to patients that their data will be stored or processed in other ways. The Data Protection Commissioner has held that in some circumstances it will not be sufficient to simply display a notice to this effect on the wall in a hospital, as patients who attend a hospital would be expected to be ill, anxious, and stressed, and therefore would not be best placed to take account of notices of this kind at such times.[125]

243. In relation to medical data the Data Protection (Access Modification) (Health) Regulations 1989 provide that health data should not be made available to an individual if the data is likely to cause serious harm to the physical or mental health of the individual. The data may be released to a nominated health professional such as the patient's own doctor. This is similar to the exemption under the Freedom of Information Acts.

244. In terms of which piece of legislation offers most access to the individual, the Freedom of Information Act is subject to a far greater number of exclusions and exemptions than the Data Protection Act. This could lead to the conclusion that applicants for access to personal information would be more successful applying for access under the latter Act. In the context of healthcare information, both pieces of legislation contain exemptions in relation to requests for access to such information. There are significant differences between the two regimes. One difference is that while the refusal of access that, if disclosed, could be damaging to the requester is discretionary under the Freedom of Information Act, it is mandatory under the data protection regulations. There is also a difference in the degree of potential harm to the requester justifying denial of access. Under the data protection regime information shall be denied 'if it would be likely to cause serious harm to the physical or mental health of the requester'. The Freedom of Information Act contains a lower threshold in that the head of the public body to whom a request is made may refuse if 'disclosure of the information concerned to the requester *might be* prejudicial to his or her physical or mental health' (italics added).

125. Case 1/97 Data Protection Commissioner http://www.dataprotection.ie.

Chapter 2. The Physician-Patient Relationship in Specific Terms

§1. The Minor Patient

245. The Non-Fatal Offences Against the Person Act 1997, section 23, provides:

(1) The consent of a minor who has attained the age of 16 years to any surgical, medical, or dental treatment which, in the absence of consent, would constitute a trespass to his or her person, shall be as effective as it would be if he or she were of full age; and where a minor has by virtue of this section given an effective consent to any treatment it shall not be necessary to obtain any consent for it from his or her parent or guardian.
(2) In this section 'surgical, medical, or dental treatment' includes any procedure undertaken for the purposes of diagnosis, and this section applies to any procedure (including, in particular, the administration of an anaesthetic) which is ancillary to any treatment as it applies to that treatment.

246. Although this section is contained in a criminal law statute and its wording simply provides a defence to a charge of assault, it has generally been interpreted in health and social care practise as enabling persons over the age of 16 to give their own consent to surgical, medical, or dental treatment.[126] The section has not been the subject of interpretation by the courts to date. It is not clear from the Act whether persons under the age of 16 years may also give a valid consent, as the language used in the section does not appear to prohibit this. It is also unclear whether a medical intervention such as the prescription of contraception would come within the definition of 'treatment' in the Act.

247. The provisions of the Irish Constitution are also relevant here. The personal rights recognized by the Constitution clearly apply to children as well as adults. In *G v. An Bord Uchtala* [1980] IR 32, Walsh J said:

> The child's natural rights spring primarily from the natural right of every individual to life, to be reared and educated, to liberty, to work, to rest and recreation, to the practise of religion, and to follow his or her conscience.

Therefore, a child has a right to privacy and to bodily integrity that might extend to the right to consent to medical treatment even if the child was under the age of 16

126. *See* HSE National Consent Policy, Part Two http://www.hse.ie/eng/about/Who/qualityandpatientsafety/Advocacy/National_Consent_Advisory_Group/NationalConsentPolicy.pdf. Also the Medical Council's Guide to Professional Conduct and Ethics (8th edn. 2016) https://www.medicalcouncil.ie/News-and-Publications/Reports/Guide-to-Professional-Conduct-Ethics-8th-Edition.html.

years. However, the Constitution also recognizes the special position of the family in Article 41:

> 1. 1 The State recognises the Family as the natural primary and fundamental unit group of Society, and as a moral institution possessing inalienable and imprescriptible rights, antecedent and superior to all positive law.
>
> 2 The State, therefore, guarantees to protect the Family in its constitution and authority, as the necessary basis of social order and as indispensable to the welfare of the Nation and the State.

248. Article 42 provides that the State acknowledges that the primary and natural educator of the child is the family and guarantees to respect the inalienable right and duty of parents to provide, according to their means, for the religious and moral, intellectual, physical and social education of their children. In 2015 the citizens of Ireland voted in a referendum to include in the Constitution a new provision to re-balance the rights of children. This provision, Article 42A, provides that the State recognizes and affirms the natural and imprescriptible rights of all children and shall, as far as practicable, by its law protect and vindicate those rights. Further provisions in the Article deal with circumstances in which the parents fail in their duties towards their children, adoption of children, and hearing the views of the children on such matters.

249. The issue of parental autonomy in respect of medical decisions for a child was considered in *North Western Health Board v. HW and CW* [2001] 3 IR 622. In this case the Supreme Court was asked to decide whether the parents of a 14-month-old child could be required to permit the health board to conduct a medical test on the child to ascertain whether the child was suffering from certain biochemical or metabolic disorders. These disorders are treatable if diagnosed at an early stage but if untreated could have potentially serious consequences for a child, including severe mental disability. The test is commonly carried out within the first few days after the baby's birth, by way of a pinprick to the baby's heel, extracting a small sample of blood that is then tested for the disorders. The risk to the child in taking the blood sample is regarded as minimal and there is no indication of any adverse consequences having arisen as a result of this testing in Ireland.

In this case the parents of the child objected to the invasive nature of the test, which involved puncturing the child's blood vessel. The health authorities argued that it was in the child's best interests to have the test and that the refusal of his parents to consent to the test was a failure on their part to vindicate the child's personal rights.

250. The High Court judge held that while the State had a duty to vindicate the personal rights of citizens, this was not an unlimited or universal obligation. The Court only had jurisdiction to interfere or provide for children where the parents had for physical or moral reasons failed in their duty toward their children. In this case the objective medical evidence clearly indicated that it was in the child's best interests to undergo the test, but the judge also looked at the policy of the State in relation to other procedures, such as infectious disease vaccinations, where the decision is left to the parents. He took the view that the parents in this case, who were regarded as caring and conscientious parents, had made a decision that was contrary to medical opinion but that such a decision could not be said to constitute an exceptional case such that the State could interfere in it. He said:

> If the State were entitled to intervene in every case where professional opinion differed from that of parents, or where the State considered the parents were wrong in a decision, we would be rapidly stepping towards the Brave New World in which the state always knows best. In my view that situation would be totally at variance with both the spirit and the word of the Constitution.

251. The judge said that the rights of the family are in a very special position under the Constitution. When seeking to balance parental rights against a child's rights, where medical opinion was to the effect that it was in the child's best interests to undergo the test, the latter might override parental rights. However, the parents' refusal to consent in this case did not come within the realm of 'exceptional cases' envisaged by the Constitution as it was within the permissible range of risk that did not affect the very life of the child. It is not clear to what extent, if any, the new Article 42A described above will influence future courts in regard to parental decision-making for children.

§2. The Mental Patient

252. The primary legislation in relation to mental health patients for many years in Ireland was the Mental Treatment Act 1945. Under this Act there were two categories of detained patient:

a. the temporary patient who required up to six months of treatment; and
b. 'persons of unsound mind' who could be detained indefinitely.

Under this Act there was a legal duty on hospitals to release patients when they recovered but there was no independent review of patients' situations. The only remedy was to take a habeas corpus application or application under Article 40 of the Constitution for infringement of personal rights.

I. Mental Health Act 2001

253. The Mental Health Act 2001 (which was commenced on 1 November 2006) provides a new legal framework for involuntary detention in compliance with the European Court of Human Rights (ECHR). Article 5(1) of the ECHR provides that no one shall be deprived of his or her liberty save in certain cases and in accordance with a procedure prescribed by law. Article 5(e) provides for the lawful detention of persons for the prevention of the spreading of infectious diseases, of persons of unsound mind, alcoholics or drug addicts, and vagrants.

254. Article 5(2) provides that everyone who is arrested shall be informed promptly, in a language that he or she understands, of the reasons for the arrest and of any charge against him or her. Article 4 provides that everyone who is deprived of his or her liberty by arrest or detention shall be entitled to take proceedings by which the lawfulness of his or her detention shall be decided speedily by a court and his or her release ordered if the detention is not valid. Article 8 provides that all individuals have the right to respect for their private and family life, their home, and their correspondence and prohibits interference by a public authority with this right except in accordance with law as is necessary in a democratic society in the interests of national security, public safety, for the prevention of disorder or crime, for the protection of health or morals, or for the protection of the rights and freedoms of others.

255. The 2001 Act sets out the procedure and process by which involuntary detention must be reviewed and establishes the Mental Health Commission (MHC) to promote, encourage, and foster the establishment and maintenance of high standards and good practices in the delivery of mental health services and to take all reasonable steps to protect the interests of persons detained in approved centres under the Act. The MHC is also responsible for ensuring that the administration of Mental Health Tribunals is done properly.

II. Grounds for Involuntary Admission and Detention

256. The grounds for involuntary admission and detention are that the person is suffering from a mental disorder as defined in section 3 as follows:

> 3. In this Act 'mental disorder' means mental illness, severe dementia or significant intellectual disability where –
>
> (a) because of the illness, disability or dementia, there is a serious likelihood of the person concerned causing immediate and serious harm to himself or herself or to other persons, or
> (b) (i) because of the severity of the illness, disability or dementia, the judgment of the person concerned is so impaired that failure to admit the person to an approved centre would be likely to lead to a serious deterioration in his or her condition or would prevent the administration of appropriate treatment that could be given only by such admission, and
> (c) (ii) the reception, detention and treatment of the person concerned in an approved centre would be likely to benefit or alleviate the condition of that person to a material extent.
>
> 4. 'Mental illness' means a state of mind of a person which affects the person's thinking, perceiving, emotion or judgment and which seriously impairs the mental function of the person to the extent that he or she requires care or medical treatment in his or her own interest or in the interest of other persons; 'Severe dementia' means a deterioration of the brain of a person which significantly impairs the intellectual function of the person thereby affecting thought, comprehension and memory and which includes severe psychiatric or behavioural symptoms such as physical aggression; 'Significant intellectual disability' means

a state of arrested or incomplete development of mind of a person which includes a significant impairment of intelligence and social functioning and abnormally aggressive or seriously irresponsible conduct on the part of the person.

257. It is important to note that detention of a person suffering from a mental disorder must be in accordance with procedures prescribed by law. This is required by both Article 5 of the ECHR referred to above, but also Article 40 of the Irish Constitution 1937, which provides that 'no citizen shall be deprived of his personal liberty save in accordance with law'. It is to ensure that persons suffering from mental disorders are accorded the same rights as other citizens.

258. Section 18(1) of the Act deals with the review of detention by a Mental Health Tribunal:

> S. 18(1) Where an admission order or a renewal order has been referred to a tribunal under section 17, the tribunal shall review the detention of the person concerned and shall either –
>
> (a). if satisfied that the patient is suffering from a mental disorder and
>
> (i) that the provisions of section 9, 10, 12, 14, 15 and 16, where applicable, have been complied with, or
>
> (ii) if there has been a failure to comply with any such provision, that the failure does not affect the substance of the order and does not cause an injustice, affirm the order, or
>
> (b) if not so satisfied, revoke the order and direct that the patient be discharged from the approved centre concerned.

If the procedures set out in the Act are not complied with, the person's detention is not lawful. Compliance will be adjudicated upon in accordance with principles of natural justice.

III. Procedure

259. There are two ways in which a person can be detained involuntarily: (1) where the person needs to be admitted and (2) where the person is already a patient voluntarily.

260. In circumstances where a person is not already in hospital and needs to be admitted, an application on a special form is made by the person concerned to a registered medical practitioner to have the person admitted against his or her will to an approved centre. Section 9 of the Act describes those who may apply. It includes a spouse (other than where the parties are separated, or in respect of whom an application has been made under the Domestic Violence Act 1996), or relative, an authorized officer of a health board, a Garda, or any other person. If a Garda believes that a person is suffering from a mental disorder and is a risk to him- or herself or others, the Garda may enter the premise and take the person into custody (section 12), and complete the application as soon as possible.

261. Those who may not apply include: a person under 18 years, a Garda who is a relative of the person or his or her spouse, a staff or member of the governing body of an approved centre, anyone with an interest in the payments for taking care of the person in the approved centre, a registered medical practitioner at the approved centre, or a spouse, parent, grandparent, sibling, uncle, or aunt of the other disqualified person.

262. On receipt of the application, the doctor examines the person, and if the doctor reaches the opinion that the person is suffering from a mental disorder, he or she may complete a recommendation form to recommend involuntary admission and detention. Under section 10, this examination must take place within twenty-four hours of the receipt of the application. The person must be informed about the reason for the examination unless the doctor believes this may be prejudicial to his or her mental or emotional health or well-being. This recommendation for involuntary admission and detention remains in force only for seven days.

263. Following the recommendation, the person is brought to the approved centre. If there is a serious likelihood that the person may cause immediate and serious harm to him- or herself or others, the Gardai may be asked for assistance. The Gardai may enter premises where they believe the person may be, and take all reasonable measures to remove the person to the approved centre, including detention and restraint if necessary.

264. The person brought to the approved centre may be held for up to twenty-four hours for the purpose of examination by a consultant psychiatrist under section 14(2). Following the examination the consultant, if satisfied that the person is suffering from a mental disorder, makes an involuntary admission order. This authorizes the reception, detention, and treatment of the patient. It lasts for twenty-one days and can be extended following examination by the consultant for three months, then six months, and then twelve months. Such extensions are called renewal orders.

265. Within twenty-four hours of making the admission order the consultant psychiatrist must send a copy of the order to the MHC and give notice in writing of the making of the order to the patient. This notice states whether the person is being detained under an admission order or renewal order, that he or she is entitled to legal representation, a general description of the treatment to be administered to the person, that he or she is entitled to communicate with the mental health inspector, that the Mental Health Tribunal will review the detention, that he or she may appeal the tribunal's findings, and that he or she may be admitted as a voluntary patient.

266. When the MHC receives this order it must refer the matter to a tribunal, assign a legal representative, and organize an independent report by a consultant psychiatrist. The legal representative assigned by the MHC to the patient must within two days consult with the patient, and review the relevant forms and medical records.

IV. Voluntary Admissions

267. Section 2(1) provides that a 'voluntary patient' means a person receiving care and treatment in an approved centre who is not the subject of an admission order or renewal order. Such a person admits him- or herself to an approved centre but may refuse medication. Consent is defined in section 56 of the Act as 'consent obtained freely without threats or inducements', where: (a) the consultant psychiatrist responsible for the care and treatment of the patient is satisfied that the patient is capable of understanding the nature, purpose, and likely effects of the proposed treatment; and (b) the consultant psychiatrist has given the patient adequate information in a form and language that the patient can understand, on the nature, purpose, and likely effects of the proposed treatment.

268. The consent of the patient is required for treatment except where, under section 57, the consultant psychiatrist reaches the opinion that the treatment is necessary to safeguard the life of the patient, to restore his or her health, to alleviate his or her condition, or to relieve his or her suffering, and by reason of his or her mental disorder, the patient is incapable of giving such consent.

269. Where a voluntary patient indicates that he or she wishes to leave, the person can be detained for up to twenty-four hours if a registered nurse working at the centre, or a registered medical practitioner or consultant psychiatrist, believes the person is suffering from a mental disorder (section 23). This holding period allows for a second consultant psychiatrist to examine the person and make a detention order if required (section 24).

270. In *Q v. St Patrick's Hospital, the Mental Health Tribunal and the Mental Health Commission*[127], there was a misunderstanding about the application of section 23. The treating consultant psychiatrist did not use section 23 before making a detention order under section 24, as he said she had not expressed a desire to leave the centre. He could not allow her to continue as a voluntary patient as she would not or could not consent to the administration of treatment. O'Higgins J took the view that section 24 only operates where section 23 is used first. This means that the person must have expressed a wish to leave the hospital or treatment centre. Therefore, in this case the detention of the patient was not in accordance with the Act and the Court ordered the patient's release (despite the fact that it was agreed that the patient was suffering from a mental disorder).

271. This case demonstrates the gap in the 2001 Act in relation to persons who admit themselves for treatment and do not consent to treatment. The doctor may not administer treatment without consent unless persons are held involuntarily, and they may not be held involuntarily unless they express a wish to leave.

V. Review of Detention by Mental Health Tribunal

272. As outlined above, section 18 provides that the Mental Health Tribunal must review the detention of the patient as soon as possible but not later than twenty-one days after the making of a detention order. The tribunal must decide if the patient

127. High Court 21 Dec. 2008.

is suffering from a mental disorder within the meaning of the Act. The hospital must prove that, on a high level of probability, the person is suffering from a mental disorder.[128] Once the tribunal is so satisfied, then compliance with the procedures in the Act will be assessed. If there has been compliance, the tribunal must confirm the detention. If there has not been compliance, the tribunal must decide whether or not to affirm.

273. In *WQ v. Mental Health Commission*,[129] the Court states that the best interests of a person suffering from a mental disorder are secured by faithful compliance with the statutory safeguards in the 2001 Act. This means that only insubstantial failures of compliance that do not cause injustice are likely to be excused by the Mental Health Tribunal.

274. In *TO'D v. Harry Kennedy & Others*,[130] Charlton J held that the tribunal is entitled to look at the substance of the order to see if it is technically valid in terms of the statutory scheme of the Act, and if it is not, whether the substance of the order is sufficiently well justified by the condition of the patient.

275. In *JH v. Professor Brian Lawlor*,[131] Peart J said:

> The Court must have regard to the best interests of the applicant when balancing the nature of the failure to adhere strictly to the procedures and time-limits referred to in the Act, against the need, in the applicant's own best interests, to be detained for care and treatment. It is therefore not every incident of non-compliance which will render the detention of a person to be unlawful, particularly where no injustice has occurred, and where no protection which the applicant is entitled to under the statutory scheme has been denied to him.

276. The tribunal must review the detention within twenty-one days of the making of the admission or renewal order. The patient will attend with his or her legal representative unless the patient does not wish to attend or the tribunal believes it would be prejudicial to his or her health or well-being (section 49(11)). The consultant psychiatrist will also attend the tribunal, which is held in private. The tribunal is comprised of a chairperson who is usually a solicitor or barrister, a consultant psychiatrist, and a layperson. They will consider the medical notes of the patient, hear evidence from the consultant psychiatrist, and review submissions from the patient's legal representative and the patient.

277. In *M v. the Mental Health Commission, the Mental Health Tribunal, the Clinical Director of St Patricks Hospital*,[132] the facts related to a consultant psychiatrist who used a standard MHC form to make a renewal order for 'not more than twelve months'. The Court held that this was not provided for under the 2001 Act (the Act provides for renewal orders of six, three and twelve months of duration) and was, therefore, void for uncertainty and the applicant's detention was unlawful. Judge McMahon said:

---

128. *TO'D v. Harry Kennedy & Others* [2007] 3 IR 689.
129. [2007] 3 IR 755.
130. [2007] 3 IR 689.
131. 25 Jun. 2007 (High Court).
132. [2008] IEHC 441.

> It must be remembered that what is at stake here is the liberty of the individual and while it is true that no constitutional right is absolute, and a person may be deprived of his/her liberty 'in accordance with the law', such statutory provisions which attempt to detain a person or restrict his/her liberty must be narrowly construed. Further, such a renewal order, has consequences for the applicant in that while an order is in existence, the applicant is denied the right to be referred to the tribunal and the right to an independent medical examination by a consultant psychiatrist under section 18.

278. He also considered the interpretation of section 15, which 'purports to restrict a constitutional right to liberty albeit for the patient's own good and safety and the safety of others'. He was of the view that the section should be interpreted in a proportionate way so that the detention is not for longer periods than are necessary to achieve the object of the legislation. He went on:

> The approach to an interpretation of the section should be that which is most favourable to the patient while yet achieving the object of the Act. To accept the arguments advanced by the respondents, that a renewal order for a period 'not exceeding 12 months' is an order for a fixed period of twelve months, would be to adopt an interpretation which is neither in the patient's interest, nor proportionate in the circumstances. On the contrary, one would be restricting the patient's rights in an unnecessarily wide way. To accept the respondent's interpretation would mean that the patient would have an order for the maximum period allowed in every situation when a shorter period might be warranted. This would in turn deprive the patient of a fresh tribunal hearing and an examination by an independent psychiatrist as well as the possibility of a fresh appeal to a Circuit Court (see subsections 17 and 19). Such an interpretation in not justified on the wording of the section, does not advance the intention of the section and results in a greater erosion of the patient's right to liberty than is necessary to attain the objects of the section itself or the Act in general. More significantly, however, such an interpretation would prevent the treating psychiatrist from making shorter orders, in the best interests of the patient, where the consultant psychiatrist deems it appropriate to do so.

279. The judge reached the conclusion that the authorization order made by the psychiatrist in this case did not conform with the requirements of section 15(3) of the Mental Health Act 2001, and accordingly did not provide a legal basis for the detention of the applicant. However, he accepted that the applicant was a very ill young woman requiring medication and supervision on an ongoing basis. Therefore, he did not order the applicant's immediate release from her detention, as to do so would not be in the interests of the applicant herself or other persons with whom she might come in to contact. He made an order for her release with a stay of four weeks to give the relevant parties sufficient time to comply with the provisions of the legislation before determining what, in the opinion of the relevant authorities, including the applicant's treating psychiatrist, is the appropriate order in these circumstances.

280. On the eve of the High Court judgment in the above case, the *Oireachtas* passed the Mental Health Act 2008[133] to deal with the ramifications of the decision. The Act provides that a detention renewal order shall be deemed to be valid notwithstanding either: (a) that the consultant psychiatrist failed to consider that he or she had the discretion to extend the period for a lesser period than the maximum period concerned, or (b) that the order did not specify a period during which the order was to remain in force or a date on which the order was to expire.

§3. The Dying Patient

I. General Principles

281. A doctor who takes a patient under his or her care is obliged to take all possible steps to protect the patient's well-being. The practice in Irish hospitals is to treat the terminally ill patient for pain and provide as much comfort as possible for the patient, or if that pain has gone beyond management, to induce and maintain a coma where death can occur naturally. As a condition worsens, pain-controlling medicines are increased in dosage and frequency. Each step is carefully taken and considered in light of the patient's needs. Where there are prospects for recovery, the medical care provided must have regard to the duty of the doctor not to cause harm or disability. There is no legal obligation on the doctor to provide treatment that is clinically futile.

282. The Medical Council's Guide to Professional Conduct and Ethics (8th edn (2009)) states:

> 46.1 When patients are nearing the end of life, it is your responsibility to make sure they are comfortable, suffer as little as possible and die with dignity. You should treat them with kindness and compassion.
>
> 46.2 Communicating with patients and their families is an essential part of good care. You should be sensitive in presenting information, but make sure that patients and their families have a clear understanding of what can and cannot be achieved. You should offer advice on other treatment or palliative care options that may be available to them. You should make sure that support is given to patients and their families, particularly when the outcome is likely to be distressing for them.
>
> 46.3 Usually you will give treatment that is intended to prolong a patient's life. However, there is no obligation on you to start or continue treatment, including resuscitation, or provide nutrition and hydration by medical intervention, if you judge that the treatment

133. At http://www.irishstatutebook.ie/2008/en/act/pub/0019/index.html.

- is unlikely to work; or
- might cause the patient more harm than benefit; or
- is likely to cause the patient pain, discomfort or distress that will outweigh the benefits it may bring.

> 46.4 You should carefully consider when to start and when to stop attempts to prolong life. You should make sure that patients receive appropriate pain management and relief from distress, whether or not you are continuing active treatment.

283. There is no legislation in Ireland relating to issues that arise in the context of the dying patient, and there has also been very little judicial consideration to date.

II. Right to Privacy and Bodily Integrity

284. One of the questions that has arisen in the context of constitutional law in Ireland in recent years is whether the recognized rights to privacy and bodily integrity encompass the right to be left alone to die in peace. The right to privacy was recognized in *Norris v. AG*[134] as an unenumerated constitutional right, a 'right to be let alone'. However, this right is not absolute and is subject to considerations of the common good. In *Kennedy v. Ireland*, Hamilton P said:[135]

> The nature of the right to privacy must be such as to ensure the dignity and freedom of an individual in the type of society envisaged by the Constitution, namely a sovereign, independent and democratic society.

285. In *In Re a Ward of Court*[136] the Supreme Court had to consider the question of whether life support, in the form of nutrition and medical treatment, could be withdrawn from a woman in a near persistent vegetative state (PVS), at the request of her family. The institution at which the woman was housed was opposed to the withdrawal of treatment and nutrition on ethical grounds. It was accepted that the Court could not make an order that would require a medical institution to contravene its philosophy and code of ethics. The majority of the judges held that the right to life under the Constitution necessarily implies the right to let nature take its course and to die a natural and dignified death and, unless the individual chooses otherwise, not to have life artificially maintained by the provision of nourishment that has no curative effect and merely prolongs life.

---

134. [1984] IR 36.
135. [1987] IR 587.
136. [1996] 2 IR 79.

III. Patients Without Capacity

286. Where a patient has no realistic clinical hope of recovery, the legal position differs between those who have capacity to make their own decisions and those who do not. In the first instance, where an adult who is presumed to have capacity makes an informed decision not to continue with treatment, the legal position respects that decision. This can be extrapolated from the Supreme Court case *In Re a Ward of Court.*[137]

287. Although the case was not directly concerned with the right of a competent adult to refuse medical treatment, each of the judgments in the Supreme Court considered this question before turning to the issue of the incompetent patient. Hamilton CJ said:

> There is no doubt but that the ward, if she were mentally competent, had the right, if she so wished, to forego such treatment or at any time, to direct that it be withdrawn, even though such withdrawal would result in her death.

288. Hamilton CJ supported the view that the dignity and autonomy of the human person oblige the State to recognize that decisions relating to life and death are ones that competent adults should be free to make without undue interference or restraint by the State.[138] Although there might be circumstances in which the State might have a valid interest in restricting such decisions, such as in the case of contagious diseases:

> in the case of the terminally ill, it is very difficult to see what circumstances would justify the interference with a decision by a competent adult of the right to forego or discontinue life saving treatment.

289. O'Flaherty J also clearly took the view that a competent person had the right to refuse medical treatment even if it leads to death, calling it 'an absolute right' and one that he said was not in dispute in this case. He grounded the right in common law as well as the constitutional rights of bodily integrity and privacy.

290. Blayney J said 'where a person who is compos mentis has a condition which, in the absence of medical intervention, will lead to death, such a person has a right in law to refuse such intervention'. Denham J took the same view, saying that medical treatment given without consent may be a trespass, a battery, and a breach of constitutional rights. She continued:

> The consent which is given by an adult of full capacity is a matter of choice. It is not necessarily a decision based on medical considerations. Thus, medical treatment may be refused for other than medical reasons. Such reasons may not be viewed as good medical reasons, or reasons most citizens would regard as rational, but the person of full age and capacity may make the decision for their own reasons.

---

137. [1996] 2 IR 79.
138. D. Costello, *The Terminally Ill – The Law's Concerns*, 21 Ir. Jurist 35 (1986).

291. This case clearly states that a competent adult is entitled to refuse medical treatment for whatever reasons, even though the consequences may be death. It also recognizes the difficulties that arise where the ethical position of those who might be expected to comply with such a refusal is contrary to that position. This issue was also dealt with in *Fitzpatrick v. K and others*[139] where Judge Laffoy said that 'it could not be argued that a competent adult is not free to decline medical treatment.' This matter is also now clearly dealt with by the Assisted Decision-Making (Capacity) Act 2015 which provides in section 8(2) that an adult with capacity is entitled to refuse treatment for any reason (including a reason based on his or her religious beliefs) notwithstanding that the refusal appears to be unwise, not based on sound medical principles, or may result in his or her death. This Act is discussed above at 180184

292. Where a patient lacks capacity to make his or her own decisions, the legal position may be more difficult, as in most cases the patient's wishes are unknown. The Assisted Decision-Making (Capacity) Act 2015 provides a number of solutions to people who anticipate losing capacity and appoint co-decision-makers or decision-making representatives to act either jointly with the relevant person or on his or her behalf. There may still remain some circumstances in which the relevant person has not appointed a decision-maker to act on their behalf. The Act provides that any intervener must consider the relevant person's past and present will and preference, and take into account the relevant person's beliefs and values.

293. For patients in a persistent or permanent vegetative state, deprivation of oxygen from the brain through hypoxia can result in varying degrees of intellectual disability, depending on how quickly the brain is oxygenated. The extent of cognitive ability retained depends on the degree of damage to the cortex. The brain stem can continue to function even if the cortex is destroyed, leading to the PVS. The condition is characterized by an irregular but cyclic state of circadian sleeping and waking unaccompanied by any behaviourally detectable expression of self-awareness, specific recognition of external stimuli, or consistent evidence of attention or inattention or learned responses. Such patients are not immobile and do retain certain reflexes, including those related to auditory and visual stimuli, depending on the degree of damage to the brain. Thus, the patient in PVS is alive, has a beating heart, and can breathe, but cannot have any contact with the outside world. If well managed, a patient in PVS can live for many years.

294. The ethical and legal difficulties that arise in relation to patients in PVS focus on the withdrawal of treatment with fatal consequences, medical futility, and euthanasia, with the lines between them often indistinct. Decision-making in this context has in the past been based on a number of standards, the subjective test, the substituted judgment test, and the best interests test. The subjective test is only applicable in few circumstances, where the patient has at some time expressed his or her wishes as to treatment. The substituted judgment test is based on what it is imagined the patient would have decided had he or she been competent to do so, according to his or her character and stated opinions. The best interests test is based on the court's interpretation of what is preferable to be done for the patient, in line with good medical practice. Of these tests, the one that most closely adheres to principles of autonomy and self-determination is the subjective, or at least, the substituted judgment test that endeavours

139. [2008] IEHC 104.

to treat the patient as he or she would have wished, rather than according to what others might presume for him or her. This appears to be what the 2015 Act is trying to achieve in stating that the intervener must act in accordance with the relevant person's past and present will and preference, and take into account the relevant person's beliefs and values.

295. The only Irish case to consider the issues raised by PVS is *In Re a Ward of Court*,[140] considered above. In this case a 45-year-old woman (referred to as the Ward as a result of wardship proceedings in which her mother was appointed as 'the committee of the ward' to make decisions on her behalf) had suffered irreversible brain damage as a result of cardiac arrest during a minor gynaecological operation in 1972. Since then she had been in an almost PVS.[141] The High Court judge, Lynch J, described her condition as follows:

> She is spastic as a result of brain damage. Both arms and hands are contracted. Both legs and feet are extended. Her jaws are clenched and because she had a tendency to bite the insides of her cheeks and her tongue, her back teeth have been capped to prevent the front teeth from fully closing. She cannot swallow. She cannot speak. She is incontinent.[142]

296. Although she was not fully in PVS and had some minimal cognitive ability to recognize strangers and track people with her eyes, much of this was considered to be reflex from the brain stem, and the judge was of the opinion that 'if such minimal cognition as she has includes an inkling of her catastrophic condition, then I am satisfied that that would be a terrible torment to her and her situation would be worse than it she were fully PVs'.

297. The Ward's family requested that the gastrostomy tube used for feeding the woman be withdrawn but the hospital and healthcare professionals responsible for her care refused, as it was felt that such action would violate their philosophy and code of ethics. In 1995 the Ward's mother, in her capacity as committee of the ward, obtained High Court consent for withdrawal of the feeding tube, Lynch J concluding that the courts should approach such cases from the standpoint of 'a prudent, good and loving parent in deciding what course should be adopted'.[143] The case was appealed to the Supreme Court.

298. By a four-to-one majority the Supreme Court held that the High Court was justified in giving consent to withdrawal of the feeding tube on the grounds that this was in the best interests of the Ward; it was lawful and in pursuance of the Ward's

140. [1996] 2 IR 79.
141. Lynch J in the High Court held that the Ward was not terminally ill, in the sense that she would not, in her present condition, die within a few months. As long as her condition was stabilized, she could live for many more years. In the Supreme Court Hamilton CJ disagreed, stating that the Ward was terminally ill since she was kept alive by artificial means that, if withdrawn, would result in her death. Denham J said the classification was irrelevant since the decision to withhold treatment or not would have to be made irrespective of the classification of the illness.
142. Per Lynch J.
143. [1996] 2 ILRM 401 at 419.

constitutional rights to life, privacy, self-determination, and bodily integrity.[144] In doing so, the Court did not use the 'prudent parent test' applied by Lynch J but came to the same conclusion nonetheless.

299. Egan J, dissenting, decided that the inevitable result of removing the tube would be to kill the Ward, which, in view of the Constitution's protection of life, would require strong justification not present in this case. All of the majority judgments base their decision on the best interests of the Ward, although each one's interpretation of what is meant by that test is slightly different.[145] Hamilton CJ was of the view that the trial judge had decided the matter appropriately, taking into account the Ward's condition and its duration, the intrusiveness of the treatment and its futility, the wishes of the Ward's mother, and the medical evidence.

300. Blayney J seemed to deviate slightly from the language of best interests, saying that the question was whether it was for the 'benefit' of the Ward that her life be prolonged. However, as he approved of the High Court decision that was grounded on best interests, this may have been what he intended. Denham J also seemed to move away from a best interests test in suggesting that, amongst fifteen factors to be taken into account, any wishes expressed by the Ward prior to her incapacity should be considered.[146]

301. It is crucial to the decision that in the context of the right to life some of the judges recognize that the right to life is not absolute and necessarily implies the right to die a natural death. Hamilton CJ stated:

> As the process of dying is part, and an ultimate inevitable consequence, of life, the right to life necessarily implies the right to have nature take its course and to die a natural death and, unless the individual concerned so wishes, not to have life artificially maintained by the provision of nourishment by abnormal artificial means, which have no curative effect and which are intended merely to prolong life.[147]

302. He went on to explain that this does not give a right to terminate one's own life or to have death accelerated. It is confined to the natural process of dying. Loss of mental capacity does not result in the diminution of that person's constitutional rights, and in this case the Ward's right to life necessarily implies a right to die a natural death. The cause of death would not be the withdrawal of food and nutrition, but the original injuries she sustained during the operation in 1972.

303. O'Flaherty J concurred, saying that the present case was not about euthanasia, which involved the termination of life by a positive act. This case concerned 'the

---

144. *See* similar decision in Germany in *OLG Frankfurt, a.M.*, a decision from 15 Jul. 1998 – 20 W. 224/98, N.J.W. 1998, 2749, discussed in M. Aziz, *The Role of Care Assistants in the Withdrawal of Hydration and Nutrition in Germany*, 7 Med. L. Rev. 307–326 (1999).

145. For a general commentary *see* D. Feenan, *Death, Dying and the Law*, 14 ILT 90–94 (1996).

146. The use of best interests has been criticized by Hanafin, who says that as the patient was unconscious and no longer capable of having interests, this was a 'fictional strategy'. *D(en)ying Narratives: Death, Identity and the Body Politic*, 20 Leg. Stud. 393 (2000).

147. [1996] 2 ILRM 401 at 426.

withdrawal of invasive treatment in order to allow nature to take its course'.[148] He was of the opinion that the advances of medical technology now resulted in the rendering a patient a prisoner in a ward from which there may be no release for many years without any enjoyment or quality of life, indeed without any life in the proper meaning of the word. He found it impossible to use the substituted judgment test in the circumstances; as the Ward had never expressed her wishes on this matter before her injuries, it was necessary to use the best interests test to decide the matter.[149] On this basis he was satisfied that the trial judge had made the correct decision and that nature should take its course.[150]

304. Denham J also took the view that the right to life under the Constitution is not absolute, no more than life itself is an absolute. She was of the opinion that the sanctity of life was an intrinsically important part of our society, not from a religious perspective, but in terms of the respect granted to all persons' right to life under the Constitution. Respecting death also gives respect to life – life need not be preserved at all costs as this would not be sanctifying life. She said: 'To care for the dying, to love and cherish them, and to free them from suffering rather than simply to postpone death, is to have fundamental respect for the sanctity of life and its end.'[151] Although the State has an interest in the protection of life in the common good, the State also recognized that respect for the life of an individual also entailed respecting the right to refuse medical treatment for religious or other reasons.

305. Egan J, dissenting, took the view that the right to life is the highest in the hierarchy of rights in the Constitution. It would require a strong and cogent reason to justify the taking of a life, which was, in his view, what was proposed to be done by the removal of a feeding tube. He was concerned about the slippery slope on which the courts might be embarking by accepting the High Court's decision. This was not a case of full PVS, as the Ward had some minimal cognitive function, and Egan J was concerned at the drawing of the line between PVS and cases of minimal consciousness. He said:

> If slightly more cognitive function existed, would a right to withdraw sustenance still be claimed to be permissible? Where would the line be drawn? Cognition in a human being is something which is either present or absent and should, in

148. *Ibid.*, 432.
149. For arguments as to why the best interests test is inapplicable to patients in PVS, *see* D. Harmon, *Falling Off the Vine: Legal Fictions and the Doctrine of Substituted Judgment*, 110 Yale LJ 1 (1990): 1; M. Minow, *Making All the Difference: Inclusion, Exclusion and American Law* 325 (Cornell University Press 1990).
150. Brock is of the view that the use of such language as 'letting nature take its course' and 'stopping prolonging the dying process' is part of the court's way of shifting responsibility from the doctor who stops the life support to the fatal disease itself. There is an unease in the courts with equating treatment withdrawal and killing. By distinguishing between the two, the courts are attempting to distance themselves from death's violent nature, and ultimately serve to confuse the issue. *See* D. Brock, *Life and Death: Philosophical Essays in Biomedical Ethics* 211 (Cambridge University Press 1993).
151. [1996] 2 ILRM 401 at 459.

my opinion, be so recognised and treated. Any effort to measure its value would be dangerous.[152]

He was of the view that, notwithstanding the horrendous situation faced by the Ward's family, any sympathy for their plight did not justify making the orders sought.

306. The right to privacy was also seen as contributing significantly to the Supreme Court's decision, although the Court did not elaborate on the exact meaning of the right. Hamilton CJ and O'Flaherty J both mentioned privacy as one of the Constitutional rights relevant in this case, and both made the point that such rights were not diminished by the Ward's incapacity. In her more detailed judgment, Denham J said that part of the right to privacy is the giving or refusing of consent to medical treatment. She stated that, 'merely because medical treatment becomes necessary to sustain life does not mean that the right to privacy is lost, neither is the right lost by a person becoming insentient'. In such cases the exercise of the right may take place through a different process, but the right exists nonetheless. Part of this right is also concerned with the right to die naturally, with dignity and with minimum suffering.

307. Following the judgment of the Supreme Court in this case, the medical profession continued to follow its previous stance on this issue. The Irish Medical Council and the Irish Nursing Board both issued statements to the effect that it was not ethical for a doctor or nurse to withdraw artificial hydration or nutrition from a patient who is not dying, the argument here being that the Ward could have lived for many more years in her condition and was not facing imminent death.[153] The current position of the Medical Council in relation to withdrawal of nutrition and hydration is contained in paragraph 45 of the 8th edn of the Guide as follows:

45.1Food and drink are basic needs of human beings. All patients are entitled to appropriate food and drink and to assistance from healthcare staff if they need help to eat and drink. You should check with patients and with the healthcare team that your patients are receiving sufficient food and drink along with any help they may need to eat and drink.

45.2 If a patient is unable to take sufficient food or drink orally, you should consider giving nutrition and/or hydration by subcutaneous, intravenous or enteral feeding routes. You should assess whether doing this will be of overall benefit to the patient, taking into account the patient's views, if known, and balancing the benefits, burdens and risks of each form of treatment. You should be sensitive to the emotional impact on the patient and their family of not providing nutrition and/or hydration. If you decide that providing artificial nutrition or hydration through medical intervention will not be of overall benefit to the patient, you must make sure the patient is kept as comfortable as possible and their symptoms

152. *Ibid.*, 437.

153. *See* Irish Medical Council, *Statement of the Council after Their Statutory Meeting on 4th August 1995* (The Medical Council 1995), and Irish Nursing Board, *Guidance of the Irish Nursing Board of 18th August 1995* (The Nursing Board 1995). Both are extracted in (1995) MLJI, 60.

addressed. Where possible, you should tell the patient and/or those close to them of your decision and the reasons for it.[154]

308. .Another difficult case which considered the issue of withdrawal of care was *PP v. Health Service Executive*[155] in which the High Court had to consider whether treatment should be withdrawn from a 26 year old woman who was fifteen weeks pregnant and also the mother of two young children. She had fallen ill very suddenly and suffered brain stem death. Her family was advised that she should not be resuscitated in the event of a cardiac arrest. She was being maintained on a ventilator and fed by nasogastric tube as well as medication for a number of other conditions. The medical team believed that her condition would rapidly deteriorate and would become unsustainable. Her father was of the view that treatment should be discontinued in the circumstances. A question arose as to whether there was an obligation to maintain the woman in this condition to enable the foetus to reach viability so that it could be born alive. The court held that on the extraordinary facts of the case, continuing treatment of the woman would cause distress to the unborn child in circumstances where it has no genuine prospect of being born alive. The court also held that to continue the treatment for the woman would deprive her of dignity in death, which was a hallmark of civilized societies from the dawn of time, and subject her family to unimaginable distress in a futile exercise.

IV. Advance Directives

309. An advance directive is a statement made in advance of an illness about the type and extent of treatment one would want, on the assumption that one may be incapable of participating in decision-making about treatment when the need arises.[156] Directives are usually in written form and may be distinguished on the basis that the typical 'living will' sets out specific treatments that are refused in advance, and others nominate a person – a healthcare surrogate decision maker – to make decisions on behalf of the author of the directive. The latter allows more flexibility, as the specific circumstances and treatments are not restricted to what has been written in the directive.

310. Advance directives began in the United States as a means of addressing the difficult impasse that may occur when a decision has to be made as to whether to continue with treatment of someone who is unable to communicate his or her own views. Family members, doctors, and nurses often find it extremely difficult to make such decisions where the consequence will be the patient's death. Strict application of agency law, under which one person (the principal) appoints another (the agent) to carry out instructions on his or her behalf, would negate the operation of the living will as the agency is deemed to terminate when the principal becomes incompetent. This would mean that 'applied to the medical context, traditional agency law renders instructions in a living will non-binding at the very moment when they are intended

154. Available at http://www.medicalcouncil.ie.
155. [2014] IEHC 622.
156. A. Capron, *Advance Directives*, in *A Companion to Bioethics* 261–271 (H. Kuhse & P. Singer eds., Blackwell 1998).

to go into effect'.[157] Doctors seeking to justify overriding such instructions frequently used the non-binding nature of advance directives in their reasoning.

311. Legislation began to be introduced in the United States following the decision of the New Jersey Supreme Court in *In Re Quinlan*, although there was no advance directive in that case. The plight of Karen Quinlan and her family reinforced in the public perception the horrific scenario of being maintained by machines indefinitely in a hospital room with doctors controlling the time and means of death. Statutes were introduced throughout the United States to authorize the instruction directive and appointment directive, which allow the person to specify what treatments should be given and to nominate a surrogate decision maker, respectively. Issues have arisen in relation to the precision with which the wording of the directive must be drawn so as to specifically deal with the situation that later arises, and the definition of terms often used such as 'terminal illness' or 'heroic measures'.

312. Outside of the United States, legislation on advance directives has not taken hold as firmly, with only a few European jurisdictions enacting laws to cover this situation. There are many possible reasons for this. One is that medical treatment at the end of life has tended to be more aggressive in the United States than in other countries, so the need to resist treatment was more strongly felt. Also, the passing of legislation in many of the US states was as a result of high-profile cases dealing with the issue of life-prolonging treatment and the general move away from medical paternalism toward autonomy and informed consent:[158]

> In other countries, not only were medical heroics less likely to be employed but judges were less inclined to diminish physicians' authority to make decisions on behalf of their patients. Thus, legislatures had less reason to develop means by which persons could extend their autonomous choice into a future in which they had lost the ability to exercise such choice.[159]

313. Both in the United States and in other countries, there are concerns about giving effect to advance directives that, for instance, the person may unwittingly be depriving him- or herself of beneficial advances in medical science that take place after the living will was drafted, and that he or she may not fully understand the nature of the intervention in question. Others argue from a more philosophical perspective that the person in PVS is not the same person that made the advance directive, and therefore that treatment decisions should be made in the best interests of the present patient.[160]

314. In Ireland, the legal position in relation to advance directives was unclear until recently due to the lack of legislation or case law on the matter. The Powers of Attorney Act 1996 provides that a person may appoint another as decision maker in case of the donor's subsequent mental incapacity but does not make explicit reference to advance directives.

157. Capron, 263.
158. Capron, 267.
159. Capron, 267.
160. *See* for example, E. Bernat, *The Living Will: Does an Advance Refusal of Treatment Made with Capacity Always Survive Any Supervening Incapacity?* 4 Med. Law Intl. 1–21 (1999).

315. The Act makes provision in relation to the form and registration of an enduring power of attorney and the protection of those relying on it. The attorney is empowered to make personal care decisions on behalf of the donor, including decisions on:

(a) where the donor should live;
(b) with whom the donor should live;
(c) whom the donor should see and not see;
(d) what training or rehabilitation the donor should get;
(e) the donor's diet and dress;
(f) inspection of the donor's personal papers;
(g) housing, social welfare, and other benefits for the donor.

There is no provision empowering the attorney to make healthcare decisions for the donor, which would not come within these categories. However, the new Assisted Decision-Making (Capacity) Act 2015 provides for an extension of the attorney's powers to healthcare decisions, though it does not allow an attorney to direct the withdrawal of life-sustaining treatment.

316. Part 8 of the 2015 Act provides for advance healthcare directives which are defined in section 82 as 'an advance expression made by the person ...of his or her will and preferences concerning treatment decisions that may arise in respect of him or her if he or she subsequently lacks capacity.' Section 84 sets out the requirements for the making of a valid advance directive and provides that a refusal of treatment in such a directive shall be complied with if three conditions are met:

- At the time in question the directive-maker lacks capacity to give consent to the treatment.
- The treatment to be refused is clearly identified in the directive.
- The circumstances in which the refusal of treatment is intended to apply are clearly identified in the directive.

If these conditions are met, the advance refusal is to be treated as effective as if it were a contemporaneous refusal.

317. The directive must be in writing, signed and witnessed. A request for a specific treatment is not legally binding but must be taken into consideration where relevant. If the request is not complied with, the healthcare professional must record in the person's records the reason why it was not complied with. The directive will not be valid if the person did not make it voluntarily, or if the person had (before losing capacity) done anything clearly inconsistent with the relevant decision in the directive. The directive will not apply if the treatment in question is not materially the same as the treatment refused in the directive or if the circumstances set out in the directive are absent or not materially the same. The directive will not apply to life-sustaining treatment unless this is substantiated by a statement in the directive to the effect that it is to apply even if his or her life is at risk. An advance directive does not apply to the administration of basic care which includes warmth, shelter, oral nutrition, oral hydration, and hygiene measures.

318. There are specific provisions which apply in circumstances where the directive-maker is pregnant. Section 85(6)(a) provides that where a person making an advance directive is pregnant and her directive does not state whether or not she intends her refusal in the directive to apply if she were pregnant, there is a presumption in favour of providing the treatment. Section 85(6)(b) provides that where a person making an advance directive is pregnant and states that she does intend her refusal in the directive to apply if she were pregnant, and the refusal will have a deleterious effect on the unborn child, an application must be made to the High Court to determine whether or not the treatment should be provided. The Court will consider the potential impact of the refusal on the unborn, the invasiveness, and duration of the treatment, and the risk of harm to the woman if the treatment were to be provided.

319. In the context of psychiatric care, an advance refusal poses particular problems. The question that arises in this context is whether a competently executed advance directive by a person with a fluctuating mental disorder, made at a time of full competence, can be binding on a health professional. The example of anorexia nervosa is illustrative, where the patient is usually competent but refuses food to the point of death. What is the situation if such a person makes an advance refusal of food and subsequently becomes unconscious due to very low body weight? The strong autonomy argument states that if the patient is competent at any time and states that in the event of future lack of competence, certain treatments are not to be given, then the professional must observe such refusal. The strong paternalism argument takes the view that the advance refusal should be respected until such point as the patient's life is in danger as a result of mental disorder, and it then becomes acceptable to treat the patient in his or her best interests. The rights-based argument provides that an advance refusal of treatment made by a competent person should be respected except where the person has a mental disorder that requires that he or she be compulsorily detained for treatment under statutory authority.

320. The English case of *Re C (Refusal of Medical Treatment)*[161] is instructive here. In this case a 68-year-old man suffering from paranoid schizophrenia, who had been a long-term patient at a mental institution, developed gangrene in his right foot. Doctors recommended amputation of the leg below the knee in order to save his life. C refused to consent to amputation under any circumstances, now or at any future time. Alternative treatment was provided and the immediate threat to his life receded but there was a chance that it might recur in the future. C was concerned that this might happen at a time when his capacity to refuse consent might be diminished and that the hospital would perform the operation in his 'best interests'. Therefore, he applied to the court for an injunction restraining the hospital from amputating his foot without his express consent. The High Court granted the injunction. Thorpe J held that despite the patient's chronic mental illness, there was a rebuttable presumption that an adult has the capacity to decide whether to consent to medical treatment. This presumption had not been displaced in this case. As well as laying down helpful guidelines for the determination of patient competence, 'by granting the injunction sought…this decision has helped to dispel any lingering doubts that anticipated refusals in the form of a

161. [1994] 1 FLR 31. *See* commentary by A. Grubb, *Treatment Without Consent: Adult: Re C (Refusal of Medical Treatment)*, 2 Med LR 92 (1994).

living will or otherwise are only directory in nature and not binding'.[162] In Ireland a directive made be a person whose treatment is regulated by Part 4 of the Mental Health Act 2001 or who is the subject of a conditional discharge order under section 13A of the Criminal Law (Insanity) Act 2006 is not legally binding unless the directive relates to an unrelated physical illness rather than a mental disorder.

321. In terms of the kind of action that may be taken if an advance directive exists and is disregarded by the medical team, the most likely is negligence. In order to succeed in establishing negligence in the medical context, the patient would have to prove that the doctor owed him or her a duty of care, which is usually unproblematic; that the doctor breached that duty, which is determined according to the level of skill employed by the doctor as compared to that which might be expected of a reasonable doctor; and that the breach of duty caused harm to the patient. It is this last aspect that may prove difficult for a patient who sues his or her doctor in negligence for not complying with an advance directive refusing life-saving measures. The harm inflicted in this case is the saving of the patient's life. Section 86 of the 2015 Act provides that nothing in the Act imposes any civil or criminal liability on a healthcare professional who complies with an advance directive believing on reasonable grounds that it was valid and applicable. Therefore, the family of a deceased person would not be able to take legal action against a doctor who acted on the basis of a patient's wishes. The Act also provides that nothing in the Act imposes any civil or criminal liability on a healthcare professional who has not complied with an advance directive believing on reasonable grounds that it was invalid or inapplicable. The Act also specifically states that it does not affect the law relating to murder or manslaughter, or assisted suicide.

V. Do Not Attempt Resuscitation Orders

322. There has been a growing trend in some countries toward laws dealing with Do Not Attempt Resuscitation (DNAR) orders. A DNAR order is a doctor's written order not to attempt cardiopulmonary resuscitation (CPR) on a particular patient. CPR was originally designed to treat unexpected cardiac and respiratory arrests after surgery or accidents, but is now commonly used to treat any patient who arrests. It has been argued that in the large majority of cases the procedure is not employed to long-term effect. Routine use of CPR will not always be in the patient's best interests, and therefore the practice has developed of making a DNAR order to indicate that CPR is inappropriate. This does not mean that other medical treatment, such as antibiotics, will not be given.

323. In Ireland DNAR orders are made in hospitals, although there is no legislative authority or judicial precedent upholding their legality. Guidance is available to practitioners in the HSE's National Consent Policy (2013).[163] The Policy states that DNAR orders must be made in the context of the likelihood of success and the potential risks as well as the individual's overall goals and preferences for his or her treatment. This requires discussion with the individual who may choose to have his or her family present. DNAR orders should be clearly documented in the individual's medical record

162. Grubb, at 93.

163. Available at http://www.hse.ie.

along with how the decision was made, the rationale for it, and who was involved in making the decision. The order should be reviewed if the individual's clinical condition changes, their preferences regarding CPR change, an individual who previously lacked capacity regains capacity, or clinical responsibility for the individual changes such as when the person is transferred or discharged.

Chapter 3. Specific Activities

§1. Abortion

324. Abortion has been a very contentious issue in Irish society over the last three decades. The legal position on abortion in Ireland can be divided broadly into two areas: the statutory provisions and the Constitutional interventions, together with interventions by the European Court of Justice (ECJ) and the ECHR.

I. Statutory Provisions on Abortion

325. Sections 58 and 59 of the Offences against the Person Act 1861 state:

> S.58 Every woman, being with child, who, with intent to procure her won miscarriage, shall unlawfully administer to herself any poison or other noxious thing, or shall unlawfully use any instrument or other means whatsoever with the like intent, and whosoever, with intent to procure the miscarriage of any woman, whether she be or be not with child, shall unlawfully administer to her or cause to be taken by her any poison or other noxious thing, or shall unlawfully use any instrument or other means whatsoever with the like intent, shall be guilty of felony, and being convicted thereof shall be liable … to be kept in penal servitude for live.

> S.59 Whosoever shall unlawfully supply or procure any poison or other noxious thing, or any instrument or thing whatsoever, knowing that the same is intended to be unlawfully used or employed with the intent to procure the miscarriage of any woman, whether she be or be not with child, shall be guilty of a misdemeanour, and being convicted thereof shall be liable … to be kept in penal servitude.

326. The continued application of these laws was confirmed in section 10(b) of the Health (Family Planning) Act 1979. In addition, the traditional prolife stance of the Irish Government can also be seen in section 58 of the Civil Liability Act 1961.[164]

327. When considering the operation of these statutes, it must be noted that the full offence consists of the use of any instrument or poison with intent to procure a miscarriage, regardless of whether the woman is pregnant or not, and regardless of whether the foetus is alive or not. This was probably due to the fact that medical science was far less advanced at the time of the 1861 Act, and so the legislative intent to prevent

164. 'For the avoidance of doubt it is hereby declared that the law relating to wrongs shall apply to an unborn child for his protection in like manner as if the child were born, provided the child is subsequently born alive.'

abortions in most circumstances had to be broadly framed to include cases where pregnancy was uncertain.

328. These statutes only criminalize *unlawful* abortions and were never interpreted as criminalizing abortion in cases where it was considered sound medical practice. This was confirmed in the United Kingdom in *R v. Bourne*[165] and, in the absence of pertinent case law in this jurisdiction, can be confirmed in Ireland by the teaching of surgical abortion procedure to doctors in Ireland in the 1940s and 1950s. In recent times in Ireland, these provisions have, in practice, been rarely used to prosecute abortions.[166] Charges of murder, however, have been brought where women died as a consequence of an abortion.[167] Parliamentary records note that, in the twenty years prior to the first Constitutional Amendment relating to abortion, only four such prosecutions were brought with no convictions.[168]

329. Due to perceived uncertainty in the statutory position in the early 1980s, it was also thought that a constitutional attack could be mounted on the state's unenforced and outdated abortion laws.

II. Constitutional Provisions on Abortion

330. Even before the right to life of the unborn was explicitly recognized by the Constitution, the courts had interpreted Article 40.3 as it then was, to recognize the right to life of the unborn and to suggest that the Constitution implicitly prohibited abortion: *McGee v. Attorney General*,[169] *G v. An Bord Uchtála*,[170] *Finn v. Attorney General*[171] and *Norris v. Attorney General*.[172]

331. A right to marital privacy (overturning a prohibition on the sale and importation of contraceptives) had already been recognized as a right deriving from the 'imprescriptible rights, antecedent and superior to all positive law' of the family under Article 41 of the Constitution in the case of *McGee v. A.G.*,[173] and it was thought that this could be interpreted to encompass a right to personal privacy in the context of abortion. This would parallel developments in the United States, where, after the recognition of personal privacy struck down a ban on contraceptives in *Griswold v. Connecticut*,[174] the landmark case of *Roe v. Wade*[175] extended this right to include abortion.

332. The Irish Government was subjected to vigorous lobbying calling for a constitutional amendment to prevent this development. This amendment was the Eighth

165. [1938] 3 ALL ER 615.
166. J. Casey, *Constitutional Law in Ireland* 434 (Roundhall 2000) suggests none since Independence.
167. *People AG v. Cadden* [1956] 91 ILTR 97.
168. Dáil Éireann – Volume 340 – 16 Feb. 1983 Written Answers – Prosecutions under Offences against the Person Act 1861.
169. [1974] IR 284.
170. [1980] IR 32.
171. [1983] IR 154.
172. [1984] IR 36.
173. [1974] IR 284.
174. [1965] 381 U.S. 479.
175. [1973] 410 U.S. 113.

Amendment to the Constitution, which was approved by popular referendum and inserted the following new article, Article 40.3.3, into the Constitution:

> The State acknowledges the right to life of the unborn and, with due regard to the equal right to life of the mother, guarantees in its laws to respect, and, as far as practicable, by its laws to defend and vindicate that right.

This goes far beyond imposing a negative duty on the State to simply prevent the recognition of a personal right to abortion by respecting a right to life of the unborn, and instead imposes a positive duty on the State to intervene legislatively to 'defend and vindicate' this right.

333. This Article has since been subject to four subsequent amendments, in addition to several interpretations in case law. First, in the cases of *A.G. (SPUC (Ireland) Ltd) v. Open Door Counselling Ltd*[176] and *SPUC (Ireland) v. Grogan,*[177] the positive duty to defend and vindicate was interpreted to include an obligation on the State to prevent the publication in Ireland of information detailing abortion services lawfully available in another jurisdiction, the United Kingdom.

334. In *SPUC v. Open Door Counselling*, the Supreme Court held that Article 40.3.3 was self-executing, and that the positive duty was imposed as a general duty on the courts even where no particular pregnant woman had been offered abortion information.[178] A defence based on an unenumerated constitutional right to receive and impart information was rejected by the Court as to accept such a right would, in this case, 'defeat the constitutional right to life of the unborn child'.[179] The High Court injunction restraining the defendants from distributing abortion advice was, therefore, upheld. The ECHR later held that women's rights had been breached under Article 10 of the Convention by the injunction.[180]

335. In *SPUC v. Grogan*, the conveying of information on abortion was again restrained by injunction, following the precedent of *SPUC v. Open Door Counselling*. However, a significant development occurred here when a preliminary ruling on a point of EC law by the ECJ was sought. Although the injunction was granted, the ruling from the ECJ that abortion, performed in accordance with the law of a Member State, constituted a service within the meaning of Article 60 (now 50) of the EC Treaty meant that even though the defendants' claim that they had a right to disseminate information about such services under Article 59 (now 49) was rejected on the ground that the defendants were not linked to the providers of the service in another Member State, it might be possible for an abortion clinic to commercially advertise and publish information in Ireland under this provision. If this occurred, under Article 29.4.7 of

176. [1988] IR 593.
177. [1989] IR 753.
178. Per Finlay CJ at 623: 'If the jurisdiction of the courts is invoked … for the protection of the constitutionally guaranteed right to life of the unborn, the courts, as the judicial organ of government of the State, would be failing in their duty as far as practicable to vindicate and defend that right if they were to refuse relief upon the grounds that no particular pregnant woman who might be affected by the making of an order was represented before the court.'
179. Per Finlay CJ at 625.
180. *Open Door and Dublin Wellwoman v. Ireland* [1992] 15 EHRR 244.

the Irish Constitution, no provision of the Constitution (such as Article 40.3.3) could be invoked to defeat the application of Community Law on this point. This has not happened to date.

336. The next significant development in Irish abortion law was in the case of *Attorney General v. X*,[181] which involved a 14-year-old girl who had become pregnant as a result of rape. In this case the right to life of the unborn was in conflict with the right to life of the mother, as there was a real and substantial risk that if her pregnancy continued she would commit suicide. In the High Court Costello J granted an injunction restraining her from travelling to the United Kingdom for an abortion, as the risk of her death from suicide was held to be less certain than the certain death of her unborn child by abortion. However, the Supreme Court on appeal held that her risk of suicide was real and substantial, and reversed the High Court decision.

337. This was a significant decision as it extended the State's positive duty to intervene to prevent women travelling for abortions where there was no risk to their own lives. This duty, as noted by McCarthy J, would apply regardless of the woman's nationality or the place of conception. This case also suggested that an exception would exist to the prohibition on the publication of abortion information where this was sought in relation to a lawful abortion, as defined in *X*.

338. In response to the judgment in these cases the government proposed three further amendments to the Constitution in 1992. The Twelfth Amendment, if passed, would have confirmed the *X* case ruling that abortion is only lawful where it is necessary to save the *life* of the mother, but, significantly, would have removed the risk of suicide as a justification for abortion. This proposed amendment was not passed.

339. The Thirteenth Amendment removed the State's obligation, recognized in the *X* case, to prevent women from travelling abroad for an abortion.[182] The Fourteenth Amendment removed the State's obligation to prohibit the publication of abortion information, while allowing the State to regulate such information by law. The two amendments that were approved significantly limited the State's positive duty to intervene to vindicate the right to life of the unborn, and left Article 40.3.3 as little more than an article imposing a negative right on the State to not legislate to introduce abortion on anything other than the strict grounds imposed by the *X* case. The legislation passed on foot of the Fourteenth Amendment was the subject of a Presidential referral to the Supreme Court.[183]

340. In *In Re Article 26 and the Regulation of Information (Services outside the State for Termination of Pregnancies) Bill 1995*,[184] Hamilton CJ confirmed that the exception where information was sought in relation to a lawful abortion must have applied prior to the passing of the Fourteenth Amendment.[185] The Bill itself was upheld

181. [1992] IR 1.

182. Text of the Thirteenth Amendment: 'This subsection shall not limit freedom to travel between the State and another state.'

183. Article 26 of the Constitution provides that 'the President may, after consultation with the Council of State, refer any Bill to which this Article applies to the Supreme Court for a decision on the question as to whether such Bill or any specified provision or provisions of such Bill is or are repugnant to this Constitution or to any provision thereof'.

184. [1995] 1 IR 1.

185. At 34–35.

and passed into law that year. It remains the primary legislation on abortion information in Ireland, and it strictly regulates the provision of information on abortion services available abroad. Under the Act, public advertisements and the distribution of unsolicited publications are prohibited.[186] Information providers cannot promote or advocate abortion,[187] and any economic links between the information giver and the abortion service provider are prohibited,[188] as is any financial or other benefit for supplying the information.[189] Section 6, preventing any economic link between the information giver and the provider, may be questionable under Article 49 of the EC Treaty, which may recognize a right to disseminate information in relation to abortion services where there is a commercial link between the provider and the information giver. However, such a case has yet to arise.

341. In 2002 a further constitutional amendment was proposed to remove the risk of suicide as grounds for an abortion. This was defeated by an extremely narrow margin. The next case to consider the issue of abortion in Irish law was *D v. Ireland.*[190] Ms D, who was pregnant with twins, travelled to the United Kingdom for an abortion upon learning that one of her twins had died, and the other suffered from a severe foetal abnormality, Edward's Syndrome. She alleged that Ireland was in breach of the ECHR by:

- violating her right to be free from inhumane and degrading treatment under Article 3;
- violating her right to privacy under Article 8;
- violating her right to receive information under Article 10;
- by discriminating against her as a pregnant woman or as a pregnant woman whose child suffered from a lethal abnormality; and
- by failing to provide an effective domestic remedy for breaches of these Convention rights under Article 13.

342. Ms D further argued that though she had not sought relief in the Irish courts, she had, in effect, exhausted all possible domestic remedies as none were available to her under the strict grounds on which abortion is lawful in Ireland, as established in the *X* case. She argued that this had a 'strong negative impact on her physical or mental health'. She argued that had she taken legal advice and gone through the Irish courts, 'it would have confirmed that she had no effective remedy and the doctrine of exhaustion did not require a litigant to embark on exceptionally hazardous and uncertain litigation'.[191]

343. However, the Irish Government argued, and the Court agreed,[192] that Ms D could have potentially succeeded in having a new exception to Article 40.3.3 recognized by the courts by arguing that the right to life envisioned in Article 40.3.3

---

186. Section 4.
187. Section 5.
188. Section 6.
189. Section 7.
190. *D v. Ireland*, App. No. 26499/02, ECHR 1 [2006].
191. At 32.
192. At 36.

may not vest in a foetus that is almost certain to die shortly after birth. In this regard, the Court was impressed by the innovation of the Supreme Court in the *X* case in recognizing an exception to Article 40.3.3 on grounds of a mother's risk of suicide. Consequently, the Court rejected her application on the ground that she had failed to exhaust domestic remedies.[193]

344. Though this case marked a defeat for Ms D, it could be argued that it outlined that the next significant development in Irish abortion law might come if and when the Irish courts consider a case where abortion of a foetus with a severe abnormality is sought. In addition, it is clear that the ECtHR will leave this issue to the national courts. This development would, the Court noted, enjoy the support of a significant part of the medical profession in Ireland also.[194] While this would create some definitional difficulties for the courts in determining what constitutes a sufficiently severe risk of foetal abnormality, such a legal development would at least be a further clarification of Ireland's abortion law.

345. In the landmark case of *A, B and C v. Ireland*,[195] the ECtHR upheld the case of one of three women who argued that the State's abortion laws were in breach of their Convention rights under Articles 3 and 8, as in the *D* case above, and additionally as a breach of their right to life under Article 2 because of the State's failure to legislate for the exception recognized by the *X* case. Finally, they alleged discrimination on grounds of gender and financial status under Article 14. The first plaintiff (A) was a woman living in poverty with four children who were in care. She became pregnant accidentally. At that time, she was attempting to reunite her family, and felt unable to cope with a fifth child. She travelled to the UK for an abortion. The second plaintiff (B) was a single woman who became pregnant when emergency contraception failed. She did not consider that she could care for a child at that time in her life, and travelled to the UK for an abortion. The third woman (C) had been treated for cancer for three years. When she became unintentionally pregnant she was in remission, and being unaware of this fact, went for a series of follow-up tests related to her illness which were contraindicated during early pregnancy. She was unable to obtain clear medical advice as to the effect of the pregnancy on her health/life or as to the effect of the medical treatment on the foetus, and feared the possibility that the pregnancy might lead to a recurrence of the cancer. She decided to have an abortion and travelled to the UK for the procedure.

346. Unlike in the *D* case above, the three plaintiffs put forward a strong argument that the national courts failed to provide them with an adequate remedy as they sought to overturn the accepted constitutional position on abortion as enunciated repeatedly by the courts, rather than to have a further, likely, exception recognized, as in *D*. In the past, the European Court has been reluctant to pronounce on the issue of the right to life of the unborn, preferring to resolve abortion cases with reference to other rights, such as the State's right to set and enforce a public morality in *Open Door and Dublin*

193. Under Art. 26.

194. The Masters of the three Dublin obstetric hospitals, which together account for approximately 40% of all births in Ireland, supported such an exception in a 2002 press conference on the proposed amendment to the Constitution removing the threat of suicide as a justification for abortion.

195. Application No. 25579/5.

Well Woman v. Ireland[196] or by determining in *Vo v. France*[197] that the issue of the right to life of the unborn lay within the Member States' margin of appreciation. The ECtHR held that Article 40.3.3 of the Constitution is not inconsistent with the European Convention on Human Rights. The Court accepted that Article 40.3.3 of the Irish Constitution, as interpreted by the Supreme Court in the X case, provides that it is lawful to terminate a pregnancy in Ireland if it is established as a matter of probability that there is a real and substantial risk to the life, as distinct from the health, of the mother, which can only be avoided by a termination of the pregnancy. This has not been altered by this judgment. The Court dismissed the applications of A and B finding that there had been no violation of their rights under the Convention.[198]

In the case of C, the Court found that Ireland had failed to respect the applicant's private life contrary to Article 8 of the Convention, as there was no accessible and effective procedure to enable her to establish whether she qualified for a lawful termination of pregnancy in accordance with Irish law. The Court ruled that 'no criteria or procedures have been ... laid down in Irish law ... by which that risk is to be measured or determined, leading to uncertainty ... ' and held that further legal clarity was required. Since Ireland has signed and ratified the European Convention on Human Rights, Article 46 of which states that signatories agree to abide by any judgment of the Court in any case to which they are parties, Ireland was, therefore, under a legal obligation to implement the judgment of the European Court of Human Rights in *A, B and C v. Ireland.*

Following the judgment the Government established an expert group to advise it of the options on how to implement the judgment taking into account the constitutional, legal, medical, and ethical considerations involved in the formulation of public policy in this area. The Report of the Expert Group was published in November 2012[199] Following publication of the Report, the Government subsequently decided to implement the ABC judgment by the introduction of legislation and regulations. The legislation, entitled the Protection of Life during Pregnancy Act 2013 was passed by Parliament and signed into law on the 30 July 2013. The Act gives effect in statutory law to the terms of the Constitution as interpreted by the Supreme Court in the 1992 judgment Attorney *General v. X* (the 'X case') discussed above. That judgment allowed for abortion where pregnancy endangers a woman's life, including through a risk of suicide. The provisions relating to suicidality have been the most contentious part of the passage of the bill through Parliament as a number of politicians were of the view that there is no sound evidence base for the provision of an abortion as a treatment for suicidality of a pregnant woman.

The Act specifies the number and specialty of medical practitioners who must concur that a termination of pregnancy is necessary to prevent a risk of death. These criteria differ in three scenarios:

- Risk of loss of life from physical illness: Two physicians, one an obstetrician and the other a specialist in the field of the relevant condition, must concur. For

196. [1993] 15 EHRR 244.
197. *Vo v. France*, App. No. 53924/00, ECHR [2004].
198. *A, B, C v. Ireland* [2010] ECHR 2032.
199. At http://www.dohc.ie/publications/Judgement_ABC.html.

example, if the woman has cancer, the two physicians would be an obstetrician and an oncologist. Where relevant, the specialists must also consult the woman's General Practitioner (GP). The termination would be an elective procedure performed at an appropriate institution.

- Risk of loss of life from physical illness in emergency: In a medical emergency, a single physician must both provide the diagnosis and perform the termination.
- Risk of loss of life from suicide: Three physicians must concur; an obstetrician, a psychiatrist with experience treating women during or after pregnancy, and another psychiatrist. At least one of them should consult the woman's GP with her consent. The termination would be an elective procedure performed at an appropriate institution.

The physicians' diagnosis must be 'an opinion formed in good faith which has regard to the need to preserve unborn human life as far as practicable'. Normal informed consent is required. Medical personnel with conscientious objections to abortion will not be required to participate in terminations, but must transfer care of a patient in such cases. Where a termination is requested but refused, a woman may appeal to the Health Service Executive (HSE) which will establish a panel of at least ten physicians, from whom a committee of two or three will review any application within three days. The committee members' specialties will depend on whether the condition is physical or mental, in the same way as for the initial assessment. The Act creates a new offence of 'destruction of unborn human life', with a maximum penalty of fourteen years' imprisonment. As required by the Constitution, the right to travel abroad for abortion (13th amendment), and to provide information about foreign abortion (14th amendment), are protected.

III. Legislative Provisions on Provision of Abortion Information

347. The primary piece of legislation dealing with the provision of information about abortion services outside the State is the Regulation of Information (Services Outside the State for Termination of Pregnancies) Act 1995,[200] which is discussed above at paragraph 332.

IV. Ethical Guidelines

348. The most recent *Guide to Professional Conduct and Ethics* (8th edn 2016) from the Medical Council provides as follows:

> 48.1 You have an ethical duty to make every reasonable effort to protect the life and health of pregnant women and their unborn babies.

200. At http://www.irishstatutebook.ie/1995/en/act/pub/0005/index.html.

48.2 During pregnancy, rare complications can arise where a therapeutic intervention is required which may result in there being little or no hope of the baby surviving. In these exceptional circumstances, it may be necessary to terminate the pregnancy to protect the life of the mother while making every effort to preserve the life of the baby.

48.3 Abortion is legally permissible where there is a real and substantial risk to the life of the woman which cannot be prevented by other means. This risk, while substantial, may not be immediate or inevitable in all cases. This risk should be assessed in light of current evidence-based best practice.

48.3 With regard to abortion abroad, it is lawful to give information in Ireland subject to strict conditions. However, it is not lawful to promote or advocate an abortion in such cases.

48.5 You have a duty to provide care, support and follow up for women who have had an abortion.

§2. Sterilization

349. Sterilization became widely available in Ireland in the early 1980s, amid considerable controversy. Its non-availability prior to this time in certain institutions was largely for religious and ethical reasons.

350. Both male (vasectomies) and female (tubal ligation) sterilization procedures have been available in Ireland for many years. There appears to have been a dramatic decline in laparoscopic sterilization in Ireland in recent years. This decline has coincided with the introduction of progestogen-loaded contraceptive devices, particularly the levonorgestrel releasing intra-uterine contraceptive device (LNG-IUS), which has seen a huge increase in sales over the same period.

351. The swiftness of the change in medical practice probably suggests that this has been physician led, rather than patient-demand led, from the outset. It may reflect that doctors, particularly gynaecologists, were not very enthusiastic about laparoscopic sterilization and were eager to adopt potentially safer and reversible alternatives.

352. No remarkable decline in non-laparoscopic sterilizations (which are almost all performed at the time of caesarean section) was observed. This suggests that there is no aversion to sterilization per se among obstetricians or patients but rather to the method involved. Issues likely to have been responsible for the change in medical practice include reversibility, safety, and the availability of reliable alternatives.

§3. In Vitro Fertilization

353. Assisted Human Reproduction (AHR) is not provided for by legislation in Ireland, although AHR services have been available since 1987. Clinics provide ovarian stimulation treatments, artificial insemination, *in vitro* fertilization (IVF), and Intra-Cytoplasmic Sperm Injection (ICSI). There is currently no sperm bank facility in Ireland for donor sperm, though one hospital provides a sperm storage facility for men undergoing cancer treatment. Sperm is sometimes imported by clinics on behalf of patients seeking this facility.

354. Treatments in Ireland are only available privately. Some clinics state that in the absence of relevant legislation in Ireland governing assisted reproduction, they voluntarily use the standards imposed in the United Kingdom by the Human Fertilization and Embryology Authority as a guide for this purpose. Due to the absence of any central regulatory body with the task of collecting statistics as well as monitoring quality of service, the number of people being treated in Ireland is difficult to ascertain. It is estimated by support groups and by those working in this clinical area that over 2,000 couples are treated annually in Irish clinics. There is a tax refund scheme in existence for the cost of the treatment and a drug refund scheme currently operated by the HSE for the cost of the necessary drugs involved in IVF.

I. Ethical Guidelines

355. In the absence of legislation, the only guidance for the profession is the ethical guidelines published by the Medical Council. These guidelines act as a self-imposed disciplinary code for registered medical practitioners, sanction for the contravention of which includes striking off the register. Although they do not carry the force of law, the guidelines must inevitably form an important part of the medical practitioner's approach to his or her practice due to this possibility of loss of his or her livelihood. The most recent edition of the Guide (8th edn 2016) states:

> 47.1 Assisted human reproduction treatments, such as In Vitro Fertilisation (IVF), should only be used after thorough investigation has shown that no other treatment is likely to be effective. You should make sure that patients have been offered appropriate counselling and have had enough time to consider the information before giving informed consent to any treatment.
>
> 47.2 Assisted reproduction services should only be provided by suitably qualified professionals, in appropriately accredited facilities, and in line with international best practice. You should do regular clinical audits and follow-up of outcomes.
>
> 47.3 If you offer donor programmes to patients, you must have strong governance procedures and keep accurate records so that the identity of the donor can be

traced. Donor programmes should be altruistic and non-commercial. You should also comply with industry accreditation standards for donation programmes.

47.4 You must not take part in the creation of new forms of human life solely for experimental purposes. You must not engage in human reproductive cloning.

II. Tissue and Cell Regulations (2006)

356. The EU Tissue and Cells Directive 2004/23/EC was transposed into law in Ireland by the European Communities (Quality and Safety of Human Tissues and Cells) Regulations (No. 158 of 2006) in 2006. These Regulations apply to reproductive cells and tissue, and therefore IVF clinics must comply with the Regulations and be licensed by the competent authority in Ireland. The Health Products Regulatory Authority is the competent authority under the Irish Regulations.[201]

357. The purpose of the Directive is to introduce high common safety and quality standards across the European Union concerning the exchange of tissues and cells between states, and to secure protection for patients receiving tissue and cell treatments. Basic requirements introduced in the Regulations include an inspection and licensing scheme, an adverse incident reporting scheme, and a documented quality assurance scheme. Tissue and cells used for industrially manufactured products and medical devices are covered by the directive only as far as donation, procurement, and testing are concerned. The Directive and Regulations apply to tissues and cells, including umbilical cord and bone-marrow cells, reproductive cells (sperm and eggs), foetal tissues, and stem cells (adult and embryonic). It excludes blood and blood products, human organs, and cells of animal origin. Autologous grafting, that is, when tissues are removed and later transplanted to the same patient, is not covered.

358. The Regulations do not cover research using tissue and cells unless applied in clinical trials to the human body. It does not interfere with Member States' decisions as to use of stem cells, or to decisions as to meaning of 'person' or 'individual'. The donation of cells from a living body must be preceded by a medical examination to ensure that the donor's health will not be affected. Donation from deceased persons must respect the dignity of the deceased, particularly by reconstruction of the body. Donation should be based on voluntariness, altruism, and anonymity. Donors must be given assurances regarding confidentiality of their donation and any related test results, and traceability of their donation. The Data Protection Directive applies to personal data processed in application of this directive.

359. States must organize inspections and control measures to ensure that tissue establishments comply with the directive. Personnel involved in tissue establishments must be appropriately qualified and provided with relevant training. Adequate tracing of tissue must be established through identification procedures, record maintenance, and an appropriate labelling system. As a general rule, the identity of recipients should not be disclosed to the donor and vice versa. However, Member States may provide for the lifting of anonymity in exceptional cases such as in gamete donation.

201. At http://www.hpra.ie.

III. Commission on Assisted Human Reproduction (2005)

360. In March 2000 the Minister for Health established the Commission on Assisted Human Reproduction (CAHR) 'to prepare a report on the possible approaches to the regulation of all aspects of AHR and the social, ethical and legal factors to be taken into account in determining public policy in the area'. The Commission reported to the Minister in March 2005.[202] The Commission made a range of recommendations relating to the area of assisted reproduction, including that legislation should be introduced to establish a regulatory body to issue licences to service providers. This regulatory body should publish guidelines to govern superovulation and egg harvesting, fertilization, embryo transfer, embryo freezing, and other related procedures. Other recommendations (not exhaustive) include:

- The embryo formed by IVF should not attract legal protection until placed in the human body, at which stage it should attract the same level of protection as the embryo formed *in vivo*.
- Services should be available without discrimination on the grounds of gender, marital status, or sexual orientation subject to consideration of the best interests of any children that may be born.
- Donation of sperm, ova, and embryos should be permitted and should be subject to regulation.
- Any child born through use of donated gametes should, on maturity, be able to identify the donors involved in his or her conception.
- Donors should not be paid nor should recipients be charged for donations per se.
- The intent of all parties involved – that donors will not have any legal relationship with the child – should be the basis for assignment of legal parentage.
- Surrogacy should be permitted subject to regulation.
- The child born through surrogacy should be presumed to be that of the commissioning couple.
- Embryo research, including embryonic stem cell research, for specific purposes only and under stringently controlled conditions, should be permitted on embryos donated specifically for research up to fourteen days post-fertilization.
- Reproductive cloning should be prohibited.
- Pre-implantation Genetic Diagnosis (PGD) should be permitted to reduce the risk of serious genetic disorders and for tissue typing for serious diseases that cannot otherwise be treated.

The CAHR Report was referred by the Minister for Health to the Joint Oireachtas Committee on Health and Children in 2005 for its consideration. Some of the recommendations in relation to the legal recognition of families created by assisted reproduction have been incorporated in the Children and Family Relationships Act 2015.

202. At http://www.dohc.ie/publications/cahr.html.

IV. Family Law Issues

361. In the absence of legislation relating to the status and parentage of children born through AHR techniques, it was until recently difficult to ascertain what the legal rights and responsibilities of parents in these circumstances are with any degree of certainty. Given the precedent from other jurisdictions as well as the constitutional background against which family law matters are adjudicated, that in relation to the issue of legal maternity in cases where there is separation of function between the genetic mother (egg donor) and the gestational or birth mother, it was always likely that an Irish court faced with such a question would decide that the woman who has given birth to a child is its legal mother. This issue was finally addressed by the Supreme Court in a case called *MR and others v. an t-Ard Chlaratheoir, Ireland and the Attorney General.*[203] In this case a married couple made an altruistic surrogacy arrangement with the woman's sister who agreed to carry a pregnancy for the couple. An embryo was created from the gametes of the couple and transferred to the sister. Twins were subsequently born and there was no dispute the twins would be raised by the couple. An issue arose when the couple tried to register the twins in their name as parents. The Registrar of Births (an t-Ard Chlaratheoir) refused to register the married woman as the mother as she had not given birth to the children. The couple took a judicial review action against this decision so the Supreme Court had to decide for the first time the question of who is the legal mother in Irish law in circumstances of surrogacy.

362. The Supreme Court held that the gestational mother (the sister in this case) should be regarded as the legal mother unless and until the legislature provided otherwise. The court interpreted the word 'mother' for birth registration purposes as the birth mother and any change to this position would have to come from legislation. All of the judges made strong statements about the need for legislation to deal with the issues raised by this case and assisted reproduction generally. No legislation dealing with surrogacy has been enacted to date.

363. Another case to come before the Supreme Court on the issue of assisted reproduction related to the rights of natural fathers in the context of sperm donation. In *McD v. L and Another*,[204] a gay man applied for guardianship of a child born through his donation of sperm to a lesbian couple with whom he had a friendship at the time of the conception. The parties all agreed that he would have no parental role in relation to the child, would be regarded as a 'favourite uncle', would not bear any financial responsibilities toward the child, and would see the child only at the discretion of the couple. After the child's birth, the relationship between them became strained, with the man increasingly seeking to develop more of a parental role in relation to the child than had been agreed. The couple decided to move to Australia with the baby and the plaintiff applied for an order allowing him access to the child and to be appointed as a guardian of the child. As explained above, as an unmarried biological father the plaintiff did not enjoy any automatic rights to guardianship or access and was obliged to apply under the Guardianship of Infants Act 1964 (as amended by the Status of Children Act 1987) for such rights as may be granted in the best interests of the child.

203. [2014] IESC 60.

204. High Court [2008] IEHC 96, Supreme Court [2009] IESC 81.

In light of the acrimonious relationship and the lack of trust between the parties, the Court considered that it was not in the best interests of the child to make such orders.

364. The applicant also claimed rights under Article 8 of the European Convention on Human Rights, stating that there existed between him and the child ties of a close personal nature that give rise to family rights under the article. He cited the case of *M. v. Netherlands*,[205] which is a decision of the former European Commission on Human Rights. In this case, the Commission found that a sperm donation does not of itself give rise to respect for family life with a child born thereby. The specific circumstances must be examined to determine if in fact there exist 'close personal ties' that give rise to the same.

365. The facts of M were somewhat similar to those of this case, although in that case there was no agreement waiving his parental rights. The applicant attempted to distinguish the case from his own by claiming an 'intertwining' of his life with that of the couple prior to the birth of the child. The judge held that this was not borne out by the evidence. In reality, it seemed on the evidence that in M the relationship with the child was closer; for example, M had at least weekly contact with the child on his own as a babysitter. The Commission did not find these ties to be sufficient. The ties that emerged in the evidence in this case did not seem to the Court to support the existence of close personal ties between the plaintiff and the child such as would, in addition to the biological link, give rise to family rights under Article 8.

366. As to the applicability of Article 8 in respect of the relationship between the lesbian couple and the child, it was clear from the evidence that they had lived together in a loving, committed, and supportive relationship for thirteen years. They had decided to try to have a child within this relationship and embarked upon a long and arduous path toward that end. The High Court held that this relationship clearly complied with the requirements of the ECHR as set out in *X, Y, and Z v. UK*[206] and was, therefore, a de facto family within the meaning of Article 8 of the European Convention on Human Rights.

The judge held that there was nothing in Irish law to suggest that a family composed of two women and a child has any lesser right to be recognized as a de facto family than a family composed of a man and a woman unmarried to each other and a child. The Court also noted the absence of any provisions in Irish law taking account of the existence of same-sex couples and securing their rights under Article 8 of the European Convention on Human Rights and recommended urgent consideration by the legislature.

367. On appeal to the Supreme Court, the Court did not grant guardianship to the appellant but did grant him access rights. The Court was of the view that the High Court had erred in not giving sufficient weight to the status of the man as the father of the child and to other factors relevant to the welfare of the child. The Court held that the agreement between the parties in relation to his role in the child's life was not an enforceable contract but it was relevant insofar as it showed the intent of the parties at the time. It was intended that the child would know the identity of his father and that there would be some level of contact. Denham J said in this regard that 'clearly the parties had the best interests of the child at heart' and that 'these are admirable

205. (App. 16911/90) (judgment of 8 Feb. 1993).
206. [1997] 24 EHRR 143.

aspirations'. She also said that in general there is benefit to a child to have the society of his or her father.

368. The Court disagreed with the High Court judge in relation to his finding that the lesbian couple and child constituted a de facto family. Under the Irish Constitution the family is given a special status as a social unit. Although not expressly defined in the Constitution, it has been interpreted by the courts as the family based on marriage between a man and a woman. There is no institution of a de facto family in Ireland, and although there have been some movements toward recognition of such family units by virtue of Article 8 of the ECHR, the European Court has not yet itself recognized such units as a de facto family. Even if the ECHR did provide for such a situation, it would be in conflict with the Irish Constitution and in such circumstances the provisions of the Constitution would take precedence.

The Children and Family Relationships Act 2015

In 2015 the Government introduced the Children and Family Relationships Act[207] to provide legal clarity to new and diverse family forms including those formed through assisted reproduction. Parts 2 and 3 (which have not been commenced yet) deal with donor assisted reproduction. Part 2 provides that the parents of a donor-conceived child are the mother and the mother's husband, civil partner or cohabitant as long as that person has consented. A cohabitant is one of two adults (whether of the same or opposite sex) who live together as a couple in an intimate and committed relationship and who are not related to each other or married to each other. Couples who do not live together are not covered by the Act. These parentage provisions will only apply where the donor insemination has been performed in a recognized facility. The Act requires the operator of the facility to give information on parenthood to the relevant parties prior to the giving of informed consent. The donor is not the legal parent of a child born as a result of the use of his or her gametes. Donors are entitled to be paid reasonable expenses including travel costs, medical expenses, legal, and counselling costs. Clinics can only use gametes from identifiable donors (other than for existing siblings). The Act provides for the establishment of a new national donor-conceived persons' registry which will record information on donor-conceived children, donors, and parents for the purpose of enabling a donor-conceived child to trace his or her identity from the age of 18. The clinic must provide relevant information relating to the birth of a donor-conceived child to this new registry. When an entry is made in this donor-conceived persons' registry, a corresponding note must be made to the General Register of Births. Therefore, when a person over 18 applies for a birth certificate, the Registrar of Births will be able to notify him/her that additional information relating to the person is available from the donor-conceived persons' register. This means that it is possible that the first time that a person discovers that they were donor-conceived may be when they apply for their birth certificate. In reality this will impose a mandatory obligation on parents to tell their donor-conceived child of the method of the child's conception rather than have the child discover this fact from the Registrar of Births. As mentioned above, these provisions have not been commenced yet and there is no indication as to when commencement will occur.

207. At http://www.irishstatutebook.ie/eli/2015/act/9/enacted/en/html.

V. Right to Procreate

369. The Department of Health is currently considering the introduction of legislation for assisted reproduction more generally. One of the questions that may arise in the discussion around what assisted reproduction procedures should be provided in the State is the extent to which citizens have a constitutional right to reproduce using medical assistance and the basis on which the State may justifiably interfere or regulate in this area. The right to procreate is not specifically provided for by the Constitution, but the right to privacy has sometimes been seen as a means of including procreation in the realms of constitutional protection. This has most commonly been seen in relation to the availability of contraceptives, which is the enforcement of a negative right against State interference with reproductive choices.

370. Marital privacy was the first area to be significantly considered as part of the right to privacy. In *McGee v. Attorney General*,[208] which considered the constitutionality of a statutory provision that effectively deprived the plaintiff, a married woman, of access to contraceptives, the Court recognized that necessity of the marital relationship having the protection of a right to privacy.[209] Walsh J said:

> The sexual life of a husband and wife is of necessity and by its nature, an area of particular privacy. If the husband and wife decide to limit their family, or to avoid having children, by use of contraceptives, it is a matter peculiarly within the joint decision of the husband and wife and one into which the State cannot intrude unless its intrusion can be justified by the exigencies of the common good.

Walsh J went on to explain that public morality does not of itself justify State intervention, as this would be seeking to impose on a married couple a code of private morality that they did not desire. However, unlike the other judges in the Supreme Court, Walsh J did not base the right to marital privacy on Article 40.3.1, but on Article 41 of the Constitution, which seeks to protect the family. Since it is 'a matter exclusively for the husband and wife to decide how many children they wish to have' and since the

208. [1974] IR 284.

209. During the 1970s there was an apparent tension between Church leaders and politicians. The Church was anxious that the liberal moral trends it perceived in other jurisdictions would not take hold in Ireland through rights decisions in the courts. Contraception proved to be a contentious issue at this time, with bills being raised by backbenchers to relax the prohibition on contraceptives, Church leaders opposed to any such move, and party leaders not wanting to hold the 'hot potato'. After *McGee v. Attorney General* in 1974 a number of measures were attempted to provide for access to contraceptives, some restrictive and unworkable measures that tried to yield a little to pressure from the Church. Eventually in 1985 the Family Planning (Amendment) Act was passed, which was seen as 'the triumph of pluralist politicians over the Church. Although the hostility of the Church was made very clear, the official stance of the Hierarchy conformed to the 1973 principles: it was for the clergy to give guidance to Catholics and for the politicians to decide. However, some bishops and many other clergy did not adhere to that line, and by adopting a harder and more traditional stance heightened the impression of a confrontation between the Church and the state which the Church lost'. B. Chubb, *The Politics of the Irish Constitution* 53 (Institute of Public Administration 1991).

State cannot dictate that they shall have a certain number of children, 'the husband and wife had a correlative right to have no children'.[210] While the Court agreed that, wherever the right was based, the intimacy of married life was possibly the most fundamental situation in which the right to privacy necessarily operated, Budd J took the view that if the State is entitled to prevent people from determining the number of children they shall have, then the constitutional guarantees are virtually meaningless:

> The State guarantees as far as practicable by its laws to vindicate the personal rights of the citizen. What more important personal right could there be in a citizen than the right to determine in marriage his attitude and resolve his mode of life concerning the procreation of children?[211]

371. Henchy J was of the opinion that the violation by the State of Mrs McGee's right to privacy was in frustrating and making criminal any efforts by her to effectuate a decision taken, on medical advice, by herself and her husband, to use contraceptives so as to ensure her health and the security of her family. Thus, in this decision, the Supreme Court recognized that a right to privacy is constitutionally guaranteed, whether through Article 40.3.1 or Article 41. This applies to the broad area of personal marital relations and control of reproduction within the marital relationship. In this sense, then, it might be used to establish a right of a married couple to make positive decisions regarding the medical treatment of their infertility. Thus, a married couple could argue that they have a constitutional right of access to IVF treatment (within the limits set down by the medical profession regarding medical indications and so on), without interference from the State.

VI. The Common Good Justification in Ireland

372. Despite a judgment in favour of the existence of the right to privacy, the Court in *McGee* agreed that there remained the possibility of State intervention in the interests of the common good, although no such State interest existed in the circumstances of this particular case. Such reliance on the 'common good' might enable the State to resist attempts to make public funding available, for example, for egg donation services for post-menopausal women, or for surrogacy arrangements. Unfortunately, very little useful definition of this expression 'the common good' may be taken from the judgment, as the judges tended to refrain from any general discussion of the law and morality question. Walsh J did draw a distinction between public and private morality, although he did not clarify how public morality was to be ascertained:

> It is undoubtedly true that among those persons who are subject to a particular moral code no one has a right to be in breach of that moral code. But when this is a code governing private morality and where the breach of it is not one which injures the common good then it is not the State's business to intervene.[212]

210. [1974] IR 284 at 311.
211. *Ibid.*, 322.
212. *Ibid.*, 313.

373. In *Norris v. Attorney General*,[213] which challenged the constitutionality of laws penalizing homosexual acts between males, the plaintiff asserted that the State had no business in the area of private morality and for the State to legislate in relation to private sexual conduct between consenting adults was, as O'Higgins CJ put it, 'to shatter that area of privacy which the dignity and liberty of human persons require to be kept apart as the haven for each citizen'. The Court accepted, however, that as a general proposition concerning the purpose of law and with particular reference to the constitutional right to privacy, the State must have an interest in the general moral well-being of society and must be entitled to discourage conduct that is contrary to the values of society.

374. O'Higgins CJ was of the view that there are certain acts that may take place in private that, although they do not harm any other individual, must be condemned by the State on the basis that they are morally wrong. He gave the examples of abortion, incest, suicide attempts, suicide pacts, and euthanasia or mercy killing, though saying nothing directly relevant to the present context. A right of privacy, the Court held, can never be absolute.

McCarthy J (dissenting) said 'the right to privacy is not in issue – it is the extent of that right – the extent of the right to be let alone'. He referred to the compelling State interest that is necessary in order to justify intrusion into areas within the realm of the right and stated that a 'very great burden lies upon those who would question such personal right'. The examples of justifiable interference that he gave included the protection of minors or incapacitated persons, and public decency. If none of these obvious justifications exists, then he was of the view that State interference would be of a most grievous kind.

Henchy J (also dissenting) recognized that there were many aspects to the right to privacy that are as yet judicially undeveloped and that they all seemed to fall:

> within a secluded area of activity or non-activity, which may be claimed as necessary for the expression of an individual personality, for purposes not always necessarily moral or commendable, but meriting recognition in circumstances which do not endanger considerations such as State security, public order or morality, or other essential components of the common good.

He, therefore, recognized that there are activities that may be carried out in private, and that do not contravene policy considerations of the State, that are neither moral nor commendable, but yet should not be condemned by law. The extent of the justification of State policy, particularly in the area of morality, was unfortunately not elaborated on here.

213. [1984] IR 36.

375. On the basis of the consideration of the right to privacy by the Irish Courts[214] it can be said that the right is seen as worthy of constitutional protection but not in any absolute form. It is seen as necessarily subject to State interference in the interests of the common good, which is itself a general and undefined term. As Walsh J stated in an academic article:[215]

> Various justifications are offered for invasions of privacy such as the public interest and these are to some extent recognised by the European Convention of Human Rights in Article 8 … . The State's rights as such, can only be upheld if they can be equated with the common good and again a delicate balance has to be preserved between the power of the Oireachtas to decide what is in the common good and the powers of the judge to so decide … . What is, I think, universally acceptable is that the requirements of the public good must depend upon the needs and conditions which exist at any given moment.

376. The argument might be made that the right to procreate, which it is thought would come within the realms of the right to privacy, would also be similarly susceptible to State interference along those principles.[216] The phrase 'common good' seems to import notions of public morality, social justice, and perhaps good government. It is thought that the 'common good' or 'social justice' cannot be regarded as being of a constant quality, as what is good for citizens of one State may not be considered good in another State. The courts have not expressed clearly what is intended by the use of the phrase 'common good' and seem to use it as an all-encompassing formula for principles of public morality and social justice.

377. In the context of procreational choices, it is perhaps difficult to see how the 'common good' could be used in any way other than imposing a set of *moral* principles on a private individual or couple without having to demonstrate harm to

214. *See also Kennedy & Arnold v. Ireland* [1987] IR 587, which involved the interception of telephone conversations of two journalists by order of the Minister for Justice, wherein Hamilton P recognized the general right of privacy and held that the plaintiffs' constitutional rights had been violated. He also held that the right to privacy was not absolute and was open to exceptions such as the common good, public order, and morality, and the constitutional rights of others. In *Attorney-General (Society for the Protection of the Unborn Child) v. Open Door Counselling Ltd* [1987] ILRM 477, Hamilton P held that the right to privacy could not be invoked to interfere with such a fundamental right as the right to life of the unborn. Although this was because of the express protection of the unborn under Art. 40.3.3, the case broadly demonstrates again the limited development and use of the right to privacy in Ireland when faced with competing claims.

215. Brian Walsh, *The Judicial Power and the Protection of the Right to Privacy*, Dublin U. L. J. 3 (1977).

216. In *Murray v. Ireland* [1991] 1 ILRM 465 the right to reproduce was seen as necessarily subject to the exigencies of the provision of State security, in the context of a refusal to grant conjugal rights to prisoners in order that they might conceive a child. This was a case in which the Court gave insufficient weight to the couple's reproductive rights and too much weight to the State's claims of administrative inconvenience, but it is submitted that due to the special circumstances of the case, that is to say, the special setting of a prison, it is not a strong precedent for limiting procreative freedom in non-prison settings.

any specified person/group of persons. The State should have to show a pressing and substantial concern that must be of such sufficient importance to justify overriding a constitutional right, and the infringement on the right ought to be proportionate to the concern to be safeguarded. It may be argued that there are very few circumstances in which such a substantial concern might be demonstrated to be sufficiently weighty so as to justify State intervention here.

VII. Constitutional Protection of the Unborn: Article 40.3.3

378. Article 40.3.3 of the Irish Constitution 1937 states:[217]

> The State acknowledges the right to life of the unborn and, with due regard to the equal right of life of the mother, guarantees in its laws to respect, and, as far as practicable, by its laws to defend and vindicate that right.[218]

The most important word, from the perspective of IVF, is the word 'unborn'. For the purposes of IVF if the 'unborn' means the fertilized egg then it could be argued that freezing may not be permissible, at least unless there was a guarantee that the embryo would subsequently be transferred to a receptive uterus. This would be due to the interpretation of the 'right to life' as meaning the right to have the opportunity to grow and develop in the uterus and be born. This is evident from *G. v. An Bord Uchtala*,[219] in which Walsh J stated:

> [A child] has the right to life itself and the right to be guarded against all threats directed to its existence whether before or after birth ... The right to life necessarily implies the right to be born, the right to preserve and defend, and to have preserved and defended, that life.

379. The use of the word 'unborn' in the Constitution is unfortunate because it introduces uncertainty into the law regarding the presumed intention of the People that is reflected in that document. If the 'unborn' means 'not yet born' or 'with the potential to be born' then, in the light of the biological development of the early embryo and the absence of potential in the pre-implantation embryo, it is arguable that the embryo in the laboratory does not qualify for this constitutional protection.

380. In its report the Constitutional Review Committee said in relation to Article 40.3.3:

> There is no definition of 'unborn' which, used as a noun, is at least odd. One would expect 'unborn human' or 'unborn human being'. Presumably the term 'unborn child' was not chosen because of uncertainty as to when a fetus might properly be so described. Definition is needed as to when the 'unborn' acquires the protection of the law. Philosophers and scientists may continue to debate

217. Discussed in the context of abortion at paras 332 et seq.
218. Inserted by the Eighth Amendment of the Constitution in 1983.
219. [1980] IR 32.

when human life begins but the law must define what it intends to protect. 'Unborn' seems to imply 'on the way to being born' or 'capable of being born'. Whether this condition obtains from fertilisation of the ovum, implantation of the fertilised ovum in the womb, or some other point, has not been defined.[220]

381. In *Attorney-General (Society for the Protection of Unborn Children (Ireland) Ltd) v. Open Door Counselling Ltd,*[221] Hamilton P held that the Offences against the Person Act 1861 protects the foetus in the womb, and that protection dates from conception. However, the Court appears to have confused fertilization with implantation in ruling that the right to life of the unborn applied from the moment of conception.

382. In the case of *Attorney General v. X.* in 1992[222] the Supreme Court considered Article 40.3.3 in the context of whether a young girl who was at risk of suicide could travel abroad to obtain an abortion. The Court held that the interpretation of the provision required that the termination of pregnancy was permissible only when it was established as a matter of probability that there was a real and substantial risk to the life of the mother if such termination were not affected.

383. For the purposes of a consideration of the meaning of the provision in relation to the pre-implantation embryo, the judgment of the Court is not of great assistance. It must be borne in mind that the Court, in referring to the 'unborn' in the course of the judgment, was doing so in light of the facts of the case that involved a pregnancy already begun, an embryo *on the way to being born.* For this reason much of the judgment of the Court is not applicable to the pre-embryo outside the body that is not *on the way to being born* unless implantation takes place. In instances where the meaning of 'unborn' is indirectly averted to, it is spoken of in relation to 'the life of the infant in the womb'. This has no application to the embryo *outside* the womb.[223]

According to Hederman J (dissenting), the objective of the constitutional provision is the protection of human life. He states:

---

220. Report of the Constitution Review Group (1996) Dublin, at 275.

221. [1988] IR 593.

222. [1992] 1 IR 1. This case appears to have been followed by the Court in a case in which a pregnant 13-year-old girl, who had allegedly been raped, was allowed to travel to the United Kingdom for an abortion on the grounds that she would commit suicide if she had to continue with the pregnancy. The facts were seen as coming within the precedent set by the *X* case and therefore it was unnecessary to go into the meaning of 'unborn' or the protection given by the Constitution. An unusual aspect of this case was the fact that this girl was in the care of the health board at the time of the application and subsequent journey to the United Kingdom, and therefore the abortion was carried out at the expense of the State. *See A. and B. v. Eastern Health Board* [1998] 1 IR 464.

223. In *Abortion and the Law: an Irish Perspective* (Round Hall, 1997), J. Kingston, J. Whelan & I. Bacik are of the view that the Supreme Court would have the ultimate say in determining when the right to life begins. They note that Hamilton P indicated *obiter* in *Attorney-General (Society for Protection of Unborn Children (Ireland) Ltd v. Open Door Counselling Ltd and Dublin Well Woman Clinic Ltd* [1988] IR 593, that the right to life of the unborn was protected by the criminal law from the moment of conception and he appeared to 'assume that the protection afforded the unborn by the Constitution dates from the same moment. However, as the issue has not been squarely addressed, it cannot be said definitively that the Supreme Court would share Hamilton P's assumption'. 31.

> The Eighth Amendment establishes beyond any dispute that the constitutional guarantee of the vindication and protection of life is not qualified by the condition that the life must be one which has achieved an independent existence after birth. The right of life is guaranteed to every life born or unborn. One cannot make distinctions between individual phases of the unborn life before birth, or between unborn and born life.[224]

384. As might be expected, academic commentators differed on the possible interpretation of Article 40.3.3 in this context. For example, Kingston, Whelan, and Bacik stated that 'it cannot be said with certainty whether the protection afforded by Article 40.3.3 to the 'unborn' applies from the moment of fertilization, the moment of implantation, or from some later date'.[225] Sherlock argued that it was likely that the courts would hold the *in vitro* embryo to come within the protection of the Constitution and, if this were the case, it would rule out embryo research and embryo destruction. 'It would also have implications for infertility treatments Involving In Vitro Fertilisation (IVF) as it would undoubtedly require that all embryos produced would have to be placed in the woman's uterus.'[226] However, Madden argued in 2002 that if the *unborn* means *not yet born* or *with the potential to be born*, then, in the light of the biological development of the early embryo and the absence of potential in the pre-implantation embryo, it was arguable that the embryo in the laboratory did not qualify for this constitutional protection.[227]

385. In the absence of clarification in relation to the interpretation of Article 40.3.3 in the context of IVF and the protection, if any, to be afforded to embryos created by IVF, clinics and health professionals worked in a legal vacuum in this regard for many years. The view appears to have been taken that in the absence of clarity, clinics would not be prepared to accede to the wishes of couples whose embryos were stored by them to remove such embryos from storage without transfer to the uterus. This resulted in clinics perceiving themselves as being obliged to continue to store embryos on behalf of couples for many years, even in the absence of consent to such continued storage by the couple concerned.

386. The uncertainty in relation to the constitutional status of the IVF embryo has also had a consequent effect on embryonic stem cell research (hESC). Such research may be carried out in some other jurisdictions, generally subject to strict compliance with legal conditions and ethical oversight, through the donation of embryos for research by couples who have chosen not to transfer their embryos for reproductive purposes. In some jurisdictions, cell lines have been created from these embryos that are available to researchers. In the Irish context, there is no legislative provision dealing with hESC research, either through the importation of cell lines for research or through the donation of IVF embryos for research purposes.

---

224. *X v. Attorney General*[1992] 1 IR 1.

225. J. Kingston, J. Whelan, & I. Bacik, *Abortion and the Law: An Irish Perspective* 32 (Round Hall 1997).

226. A. Sherlock, *The Right to Life of the Unborn and the Irish Constitution*, XXIV Irish Jurist 13, 24 (1989).

227. D. Madden, *Medicine, Ethics and the Law* para. 6.116 (Butterworths 2002).

387. In 2006 an important opportunity arose for judicial consideration of the interpretation of Article 40.3.3 in the specific context of IVF. This case drew much public and media attention as it was the first case of its kind in Ireland –*MR v. TR & Ors*.[228] The facts of this case were that MR and TR were married in 1992 and sought fertility advice from their GP in 1994. They were referred to the National Maternity Hospital for specialist treatment and subsequently had a son in 1997. Shortly after the birth of the child, MR underwent ovarian surgery as a result of which she sought fertility treatment at an IVF clinic in 2001.

388. In January 2002, the couple attended the clinic and signed a number of documents covering consent to treatment and the cryopreservation of the embryos. TR signed a form in which he acknowledged that he was MR's husband and consented to the fertilization of her eggs and the transfer of three embryos to her uterus. He also acknowledged that he would become the legal father of any resulting child. As a result of the treatment, six viable embryos were created. Three were transferred to MR's uterus and the remaining three were frozen. MR became pregnant and gave birth to a daughter in October 2002. Marital difficulties arose between the couple and they subsequently separated. The present case arose as a result of the fact that MR wished to have the three frozen embryos transferred to her uterus whereas TR did not wish this to happen nor to become the father of any child that might be born as a result of such a treatment.

389. There were a number of issues before McGovern J in this case. The first related to the extent to which TR could be held to have agreed to the transfer of the embryos to MR and whether such an agreement was binding on the parties in the circumstances of their marital separation. The second issue related to whether the embryos enjoyed the protection of Article 40.3.3 of the Constitution.

390. On the first issue, McGovern J held that there was no agreement between the parties as to what would happen to the frozen embryos if the first embryo transfer was successful and resulted in pregnancy. The Court held that TR did not give his consent, either express or implied, to the transfer of the frozen embryos and acknowledged that the clinic was unwilling to release the embryos into the custody of MR in the absence of such consent.

391. In relation to the second issue, the Court heard from a number of witnesses who gave their view as to when life begins. Some argued that 'from the moment of fertilization of the ovum by the sperm a new human life begins'. Others argued that 'it was only when the embryo became implanted in the uterus that the potential to be born existed and that human life began at that point'. Yet other witnesses stated that 'human life began at the formation of the primitive streak' and others took the view that it was impossible to say when human life begins. In this regard McGovern J stated that:

> It is possible for scientists and embryologists to describe in detail the process of development from the ovum to the embryo and on to the stage when it becomes a foetus after implantation of the embryo in the wall of the uterus, but in my opinion, it is not possible for this Court to stat when human life begins.

228. [2006] IEHC 359.

392. The judge went on to acknowledge that the point at which people ascribe human characteristics to genetic material depends on other issues besides science and medicine and is dependent upon one's own moral or religious beliefs. He stressed that it was not the function of the Court to choose between competing moral beliefs and that the only issue that he had to decide was whether the three frozen embryos in this case were 'unborn' within the meaning of Article 40.3.3 of the Constitution.

393. In deciding upon this important point McGovern J first stated that in considering the words in Article 40.3.3 the Court could have regard to the legislative history of the constitutional amendment but not to debates in the *Oireachtas* in order to clarify what was in the contemplation of the People in passing the amendment. He referred to a number of cases mentioned above –*McGee v. Attorney General, G v. An Bord Uchtala, Attorney General v. X*, as well as section 58 of the Civil Liability Act 1961, which provides that the law relating to wrongs 'shall apply to an unborn child for his protection in like manner as if the child were born, provided the child is subsequently born alive'.

394. He also referred to the Medical Council's *Guide to Ethical Conduct and Behaviour*, the Report of the Constitution Review Group, and the Report of the CAHR, also mentioned above. McGovern J concluded that there had been:

> no evidence adduced that it was ever in the mind of the people voting on the Eighth Amendment to the Constitution that 'unborn' meant anything other than a foetus or child within the womb. To infer that it was in the mind of the people that 'unborn' included embryos outside the womb or embryos in vitro would be to completely ignore the circumstances in which the amendment giving rise to Article 40.3.3 arose. While I accept that Article 40.3.3 is not to be taken in isolation from its historical background and should be considered as but one provision of the whole Constitution, this does not mean that the word 'unborn' can be given a meaning which was not contemplated by the people at the time of the passing of the Eighth Amendment and which takes it outside the scope and purpose of the amendment.

395. Consequently, the Court held that the word 'unborn' within Article 40.3.3 does not include embryos *in vitro,* and therefore did not include the three frozen embryos in this case. McGovern J stated that in the absence of any regulation in this country 'embryos outside the womb have a very precarious existence' and that 'until the law or the Constitution is changed this issue remains within the sphere of ethics and morality'.

396. On appeal to the Supreme Court, the Court unanimously upheld the decision of the High Court that the husband had not given consent, either expressly or impliedly, to the transfer of embryos to his wife, and that the constitutional provision in relation to the unborn does not apply to the pre-implantation embryo. On the first issue in relation to consent, the Court held that the forms signed by the husband were not contractually binding and were simply medical consent forms. The husband had not consented to the use by his wife of the surplus embryos. An argument put to the Court that the husband was estopped from withholding consent to embryo transfer after the creation of the embryos and the use of some of them in an earlier successful IVF cycle was not upheld by the Court. Denham J stated that even if the husband had entered an agreement on this issue, it would not necessarily be irrevocable and that the Court would have to take all the circumstances into account, including whether the use of the embryos at issue represented the last opportunity for either party to have a biological child of their own.

397. Denham J also briefly discussed the right to procreate, which was recognized in *Murray v. Ireland*.[229] She said that:

> There is an equal and opposite right not to procreate. In the circumstances of this case, while the plaintiff and her husband have family rights, the exercise of a right not to procreate by the husband is a proportionate interference in all the circumstances of the case to the right of the plaintiff to procreate.

398. The judges all took the view that decisions in relation to the definition of life or adjudications on matters of science, theology, or ethics were not appropriately made by a court of law. The Court's function was to make a legal decision on the interpretation of an article of the Constitution and it was a matter for the legislature to make policy choices in relation to the regulation of AHR and the protection of the embryo.

399. The Court said that the provision had been inserted into the Constitution to deal with termination of pregnancy and the balancing of rights between the foetus and the mother. The language and intent of the article envisages a specific constitutional and legal relationship between the unborn and the mother that only exists by virtue of a physical connection between them. This only happens after implantation, and therefore an 'unborn' under Article 40.3.3 is established when an embryo implants in the womb. Denham J also said that the concept of unborn envisages a state of being born, the potential to be born, or the capacity to be born, which occurs only after implantation. She said that if embryos were considered to be 'unborn' within the Constitution, the State would have an obligation to protect all embryos in the State in every clinic and hospital and would have to intervene to facilitate their implantation irrespective of the parents' wishes, and this would be inconsistent with the rights of the family. A similar point was made by Hardiman J, who expressed concern that if respect for the embryo were carried to the point of equating it to a life in being, that view would lead to the outlawing of one of the most widely used methods of contraception, which operates by prevention of implantation. All five judges said that legislation should be introduced to deal with the legal issues arising in AHR and that it was disturbing that four years after the report of the CAHR the government had still not enacted legislation on these issues.

Following the judgment of the Court, the Minister for Health stated that the government accepted that it had a responsibility to introduce legislation in relation to AHR and that a legislative proposal would be brought before the Cabinet in 2010. No Bill has yet been published on this issue.

229. [1991] 1 ILRM 465.

§4. PRENATAL DIAGNOSIS AND GENETICS

400. Advances in medical testing now allow many genetic disorders and diseases to be detected during pregnancy in the foetus. These include foetal aneuploidy, such as Down syndrome, trisomy eighteen, or the exceptionally rare Turner's syndrome. Neural Tube Defects (NTDs) such as spina bifida can also be detected. This is a particularly important treatment in Ireland, as Ireland has one of the highest incidences of NTDs in the world, at 0.1% of live births (between fifty and ninety births per annum). Tests performed include maternal blood sample testing and examination of ultrasound scans, amniocentesis, and chorionic villus sampling.

401. Testing before birth can be beneficial as it reassures the vast majority of pregnant women whose pregnancies are normal, gives time for parental counselling and education in preparation for the birth of a baby with a genetic disorder, and also allows medical teams to prepare in advance for sub-speciality paediatric consultation, in-utero therapy where this is possible, and optimizing the delivery setting in advance of any medical complications arising at birth due to the genetic disorder, including the emergency heart surgery soon after birth that many babies born with Down syndrome require.[230] However, because increasingly accurate testing is now possible at the earlier stages of pregnancy, even in the first trimester, there is also the possibility that pregnancies where genetic disorders have been detected will be terminated at this stage.[231] This creates an ethical question about such testing in the Irish context of the State's duty to preserve and vindicate the right to life of the unborn under the Irish Constitution. Furthermore, highly accurate testing using amniocentesis carries a risk of miscarriage, which may also create legal difficulties, though no cases have yet been brought before the Irish courts in this regard.

402. Preimplantation Genetic Diagnosis of embryos is now possible in IVF treatment and is an important technique in reducing the miscarriage rate of older women who use IVF treatment. Methods include polar body analysis of unfertilized egg chromosomes and embryo biopsy through fluorescent in situ hybridization (FISH).[232] The use of PGD creates certain ethical difficulties as embryos identified with chromosomal abnormalities are not implanted. PGD is now offered in Ireland, since the decision of the Supreme Court in *MR v. TR* described above in paragraph 387 in which the court held that pre-implantation embryos do not qualify for constitutional protection.

403. Ireland does not have a national policy on prenatal screening, a fact that has been criticized by a report on antenatal hepatitis B screening.[233] In practice, an indication-based approach to prenatal testing is adopted; that is, only women whose babies are in high-risk categories, based on family history, are tested, rather than the

230. C. Lynch & F. Malone, *Survey on Prenatal Screening and Diagnosis*, 100 Irish Med. J. (2007).
231. This is common in the United Kingdom, where approximately 90% of foetuses that test positive for Down syndrome are aborted.
232. At http://www.reproductivegenetics.com/aneuploidy.html and http://www.reproductivegenetics.com/docs/ aneuploidy_pamphlet.pdf. This testing is approximately 95% accurate. The Reproductive Genetics Institute pioneered polar body analysis and has used PGD since it was first developed in 1990.
233. *Antenatal Hepatitis B Screening – Is There a Need for a National Policy?* http://www.ncbi.nlm. nih.gov/pubmed/11440046, 2001.

internationally preferred method of routine ultrasound for all pregnancies. The latter would be the preferred best practice method in other jurisdictions as 'the majority of malformations occur in pregnancies without obvious risk factors'.[234] Internationally, the importance of prenatal diagnosis has been recognized by the WHO.[235]

404. The ethical problems of prenatal diagnosis and the potential constitutional difficulties are reflected in the attitude of a majority of Irish doctors. In a 2007 study,[236] a clear majority of doctors and a significant percentage of consultants and specialist registrars recognized that there are ethical difficulties for patients undergoing prenatal screening and diagnosis.[237] It was also noted that Ireland's constitutional ban on abortion other than in very limited circumstances may be in part responsible for the opinion that prenatal screening is unnecessary where the benefits of this screening, irrespective of whether it results in the termination of a pregnancy or not, are not recognized.

405. Genetic disorders or other disabilities are not grounds for an abortion under Irish law.

406. Another potentially difficult ethical question relates to amniocentesis. This is a more accurate test that is usually performed to confirm the diagnosis of, and eliminate false positives from, the less accurate and less invasive prenatal tests, such as maternal blood tests. Amniocentesis involves extracting amniotic fluid and may carry a 0.5% risk of miscarriage, that is, 1 out of 200 tests will result in a miscarriage. This could affect foetuses with genetic abnormalities or healthy false positives. This risk may be sufficient to constitute an attack on the right to life of the unborn, which the State has a duty to vindicate under Article 40.3.3. However, recent research suggests that the risk of miscarriage may now be as low as 1 in 1,600.[238] Nevertheless, the benefits of this test are minimal, and its main function is as the most accurate test (at 95% accuracy) that can be performed at a sufficiently early stage of pregnancy (even at eleven to thirteen weeks) to allow a safe termination of a foetus with a genetic abnormality. Safe tests such as ultrasounds and maternal serum screens for alfa-fetoprotein can also be performed at a later stage of pregnancy with higher accuracy rates, and therefore it might be argued that amniocentesis presents an unacceptable risk to the life of the foetus.

407. The same arguments could also apply to chorionic villus sampling, which carries an even higher risk of miscarriage (1 in 100) and which offers accurate diagnosis

---

234. C. Lynch & F. Malone, *Survey on Prenatal Screening and Diagnosis*, 100 Irish Med. J. (2007).
235. Prenatal testing: 'Prenatal diagnosis should be offered to those who need it, but there must be no pressure on couples to accept such testing, nor to use the results of the test to compel either continuing or terminating a pregnancy when the fetus is affected with a genetic disorder. (…) Prenatal diagnosis should be done only to give parents and physicians information about the health of the fetus.' *World Health Organization Proposed International Guidelines on Ethical Issues in Medical Genetics and the Provision of Genetic Services* (Geneva: WHO, 1997), http://www.live.who.ch/ncd/hgn/hgnethic.htm.
236. C. Lynch & F. Malone, *Survey on Prenatal Screening and Diagnosis*, 100 Irish Med. J. (2007).
237. Over 70% of doctors, and 38% and 52%, respectively, of consultants and specialist registrars. C. Lynch & F. Malone, *Survey on Prenatal Screening and Diagnosis*, 100 Irish Med. J. (2007).
238. At http://www.webmd.com/baby/news/20061101/amniocentesis-risk-overrated, quoting the study by Edelman in *Obstetrics & Gynaecology*.

at an even earlier stage of pregnancy.[239] In addition, it is also possible, though unlikely, that parents could request prenatal testing under the aegis of the recognition given to parental autonomy in deciding on the welfare of the child by the Irish Constitution.

§5. Genetics

408. Ireland has no legislation specifically dealing with human genetics, and Ireland has not signed the 1997 Oviedo Bioethics Convention. Clinical genetics is a specialty recognized by the Irish Medical Council, and clinical practice is subject to Medical Council guidelines.

§6. Psychosurgical Interventions

409. The Mental Health Act 2001 provides for the carrying out of psycho-surgery (defined as any surgical operation that destroys brain tissue or the functioning of brain tissue and that is performed for the purposes of ameliorating a mental disorder) in section 58:

(1) Psycho-surgery shall not be performed on a patient unless –

(a) the patient gives his or her consent in writing to the psycho-surgery; and
(b) the psycho-surgery is authorized by a tribunal.

(2) Where it is proposed to perform psycho-surgery on a patient and the consent of the patient has been obtained, the consultant psychiatrist responsible for the care and treatment of the patient shall notify in writing the Commission of the proposal and the Commission shall refer the matter to a tribunal.
(3) Where such a proposal is referred to a tribunal under this section, the tribunal shall review the proposal and shall either:

(a) if it is satisfied that it is in the best interests of the health of the patient concerned, authorize the performance of the psycho-surgery; or
(b) if it is not so satisfied, refuse to authorize it.

§7. Organ Transplantation

410. Organ donation and transplantation is not currently dealt with by legislation in Ireland, nor have there been any court decisions on transplantation. Donation from living donors is facilitated in respect of kidneys, tissues such as skin (for treating burns) and bone, and so on. Other organs may only be donated after death (i.e., heart, lungs,

239. Rhodes, Jackson, et al., *The Safety and Efficacy of Chorionic Villus Sampling for Early Prenatal Diagnosis of Cytogenetic Abnormalities*, 320 NEJM 609–617 (9 Mar. 1989), http://content.nejm.org/cgi/content/abstract/320/10/609.

eyes, etc.). Living donors will be asked to give informed consent to donate their organs for transplant.

411. Removal of organs from a deceased donor for transplant purposes is not covered by legislation. Many people carry signed donor cards that indicate their willingness to have their organs used for transplant. However, carrying a donor card does not necessarily mean that the organs will be used. There are various medical and other conditions that must be met before the organs will be deemed suitable for transplantation. Irish law is not clear in relation to the validity of donor cards, but it seems that the deceased's next of kin are not bound by the wishes of the deceased.

412. In some cases, the medical team may request the next of kin to donate the organs of a deceased person. There is no law dealing with the issue of consent to such a procedure. In practice, the consent of the next of kin is accepted as valid and a refusal by the next of kin is not contested. In 2009 the Department of Health published a public consultation document on proposals for a new Human Tissue Bill. This was drawn up principally to deal with the aftermath of the organ retention controversy that led to the publication of the Madden Report on Post-Mortem Practice and Procedure. This report recommends that no hospital post-mortem examination should be carried out and no tissue retained without authorization. It specifically recommends the introduction of legislation to implement the recommendations in relation to post-mortem practice.

413. Another aim of the proposal is to establish a legal framework for organ donation that can benefit patients through transplantation of organs. This part sets out the requirements that are specific to the donation of organs and tissues for transplantation, including the prohibition on the commercialization of organs and tissues for transplantation. It also addresses the issue of consent for donation of organs for transplantation. While the current proposals are drafted on the basis of the 'opt-in' model of consent, four possible models of consent (i.e., opt-in, opt-out, mandated choice, and required request) are under active consideration by the Department. The final bill will be drafted on the basis of either the opt-in or opt-out models, since they are mutually exclusive, but either option may be combined with mandated choice and/or required request. There is no indication from government as to when this legislation might be introduced.

§8. Experiments on Human Beings

414. In Ireland clinical trials involving medicinal products are covered by the European Communities (Clinical Trials on Medicinal Products for Human Use) Regulations (SI 190 of 2004), which implement the EU Clinical Trials Directive (2001/20/EC). The Regulations came into force on 1 May 2004. The Regulations set out measures relating to the conduct of clinical trials on medicinal products for human use. They replace those controls that previously applied to such trials under the Control of Clinical Trials Acts, 1987 and 1990. Aspects dealt with in the Regulations include:

– procedures for obtaining a favourable ethics committee opinion (a single ethics committee opinion is required in the case of multi-centre trials);

- procedures for obtaining authorizations for the conduct of clinical trials from the Irish Medicines Board;
- controls that are to apply to the manufacture, supply, and importation of investigational medicinal products;
- obligations for the reporting of various adverse events encountered in subjects participating in clinical trials, including the recording, reporting, and notifying of such events;
- obligations for compliance with standards of Good Clinical Practice (GCP) and Good Manufacturing Practice (GMP).

415. The Regulations contain provisions for the establishment of, recognition of, and operation of ethics committees. These committees are required to be independent, consisting of healthcare professionals and lay members, and to have responsibility to protect the rights, safety, and well-being of human subjects involved in a trial. They are also required to provide a public assurance of that protection by, among other things, expressing an opinion on the trial protocol; on the suitability of the investigators; on the adequacy of the facilities; on the availability of insurance, indemnity, or compensation; and on the methods and documents to be used to inform trial subjects and to obtain their informed consent.

I. Recognition of Ethics Committees

416. Since 1 May 2004 (with the exception of those trials that are covered by the transitional arrangements), ethics committees have had to comply with criteria set out in the Regulations before being entitled to approve clinical trials for medicinal products. All such committees are required to be established and recognized by the Ethics Committee Supervisory Body under Part 2 of the Regulations.

Under the Regulations, it will also be a matter for the appointing authority to collect fees (as set out in the Regulations) and to provide an appropriate administrative structure and premises to enable the committees to carry out their functions within the strict timelines imposed by the Directive.

417. The implementation of the Directive only imposes controls in relation to clinical trials for medicinal products and does not affect activities that have traditionally been carried out by other ethics committees (including trials not involving medicines).

II. Composition of Ethics Committees

418. The Regulations provide, in Schedule 2, for ethics committees to have a membership of not more than twenty-one members, of which at least one-third are to be lay members and at least half of those are to be persons that have never been healthcare professionals. There is also provision for the appointment of two vice-chairpersons and for the appointment of deputies who may attend in the absence of a member.

The framework for these committees has been designed in such a way as to provide maximum flexibility for their operation as ethics committees and to enable them to properly discharge their functions under the Regulations in a timely manner.

III. Single Ethics Committee Opinion

419. It is obligatory under the Directive (and the Regulations) that, in the case of multi-centre clinical trials, a single ethics committee opinion be given for each Member State. This means that once an ethics committee opinion is given by a recognized ethics committee for a clinical trial in this country, that opinion must prevail at all centres where the trial is to be conducted. This does not mean that such a trial must be carried out at a particular centre. Obviously a local centre may decide, on a case-by-case basis, whether or not it would permit a particular trial to be carried out at its site.

In the context of the single ethics committee opinion, it is necessary that the ethics committee takes into account the suitability of the investigator and supporting staff and the quality and adequacy of the facilities available at each of the proposed trial sites. Any subsequent decisions that may be taken locally at these trial sites can only be taken on a yes/no basis.

IV. Ethics Committee Supervisory Body

420. The DOHC is currently the Ethics Committee Supervisory Body under the Regulations but it is expected that this responsibility will be transferred to the Health Information and Quality Authority (HIQA).

V. Indemnity for Ethics Committees

421. An ethics committee established by an agency covered by the Clinical Indemnity Scheme (CIS) which provides indemnity for all public hospitals in the state will also be covered by the CIS. This cover extends to individual committee members whether or not they are employees of the agency concerned. The same situation would prevail if an ethics committee were to be established by a number of agencies covered by the CIS, acting conjointly. In view of the nature of the CIS, no particular provision has been included in the Regulations in respect of indemnity.

VI. Responsibility for Consideration of Insurance

422. Responsibility for considering the availability of insurance, indemnity, or compensation in the context of clinical trials for medicinal products will be carried out by the ethics committees.

VII. Exemption for Academic Research

423. The Regulations require that investigational medicinal products and the devices for the administration of such products should be made available free of charge by sponsors. An exemption has been incorporated in Regulation 24(3) for academic researchers whereby this requirement will not apply to non-commercial clinical trials that are conducted by investigator-sponsors, without the participation of the pharmaceutical industry, in circumstances where the investigator-sponsors have no commercial or financial interest in the outcome of the trial insofar as such products or devices have not been obtained free of charge by the investigator-sponsor.

VIII. Research Not Covered by Clinical Trials Regulations

424. Other medical research that does not involve clinical trials is not covered by specific legislation. However, the Data Protection Acts do make provision for the protection of personal data collected during the conduct of medical research and the Office of the Data Protection Commissioner has published guidelines on research in the health sector.[240]

IX. Ethical Guidelines

425. There are also professional guidelines on research available for health professionals, including nurses and doctors. For example, the *Medical Council's Guide to Professional Conduct and Ethics* (8th edn) states:

> 25.1 If you are involved in any form of medical research, you have a duty to make sure that the highest ethical standards are followed when conducting the research.
>
> 25.2 In particular, you must make sure that all research participants are fully informed about all aspects of the study and understand the nature of the proposed intervention or treatment, especially if the intervention may not be of benefit to them, for example if they receive a placebo.
>
> 25.3 You must make sure that patients have given their consent voluntarily. If you are the patient's treating physician, you should consider asking someone else associated with the research to get consent from the patient. If a patient refuses to take part in the research, this must not influence your care of that patient in any way.

240. At http://www.dataprotection.ie/documents/guidance/Health_research.pdf.

> 25.4 You must comply with the Data Protection Acts and you should be aware of the guidelines published by the Office of the Data Protection Commissioner in relation to medical research. See also the section on confidentiality, paragraph 29.
>
> 25.5 You must not claim authorship of work you have not written or contributed to. You have a responsibility to make sure any publication you are involved in is accurate.
>
> 25.6 If you are paid, directly or indirectly, by pharmaceutical, medical device or other commercial companies or organisations to conduct medical research, you must make sure that the payment does not influence your study design or interpretation of research data.
>
> 25.7 If you are paid, directly or indirectly, by pharmaceutical, medical device or other commercial companies or organisations in connection with medical research, you must address any potential conflict of interest and disclose the payment in any publication of research results. You should also follow the guidance on conflict of interests in paragraph 62.

§9. Euthanasia

426. While it is generally accepted in most jurisdictions, including Ireland, that doctors must respect their patients' decisions to be allowed to die, killing is regarded as morally and legally different.[241] The most common distinction drawn between killing and allowing to die is based on the difference between acts and omissions resulting in death: A person kills if he or she does something that causes another to die, who otherwise would not have died. A person allows someone to die if he or she has the ability and opportunity to prevent someone from dying, but does not act to prevent the death. Another distinction often drawn is that between active and passive euthanasia:

> In active euthanasia, the physician directly and intentionally kills the patient. In passive euthanasia, he does not commence, or else discontinues a particular treatment which is likely to result in the patient dying, naturally.[242]

The distinction between voluntary and involuntary euthanasia is based on whether the act has been requested by the patient or performed by the doctor without request. The

241. M. Otlowski argues that this alleged distinction reveals an element of self-deception that may assist doctors in justifying their conduct in permitting patients to die. *Voluntary Euthanasia and the Common Law* 192 (Oxford University Press 1997).

242. M. Kelleher, *Euthanasia and Physical Assisted Suicide*, 2 MLJI 77–79 at 77 (1996).

former is the subject of much debate whereas the latter is clearly homicide and generally universally condemned.

427. There is no legislation in Ireland dealing with euthanasia. The Medical Council's Guide *to Professional Conduct and Ethics* (8th edn) states:

> 46.9 You must not take part in the deliberate killing of a patient.

428. In the treatment of certain illnesses, such as cancer, it sometimes becomes necessary to administer large doses of pain-killing drugs to ease the patient's suffering. These drugs may carry higher risks of causing respiratory depression and hastening the patient's death.[243] Most would agree that not to administer such drugs would result in unacceptable pain for the dying patient and justify the actions of the doctor on the basis of his or her intention to relieve suffering as opposed to bringing on the patient's death. The doctrine of double effect is invoked here to substantiate the argument. The doctrine distinguishes between the consequences a person intends and those that are unintended but foreseen. It holds that an action with a bad consequence, such as the patient's death, is justifiable if that consequence is not intended and is necessary to achieve a proportionately good effect, here, the relief of the patient's pain. Of course, there are cases in which the distinction between foresight and intention is blurred, but in relation to pain control it seems clear that the death of the patient is an unintended but foreseen side effect, and therefore morally permissible. If, however, the doctor gave the patient a lethal injection, this would be a deliberate act causing death, and would be morally prohibited. Some argue that in the latter case, euthanasia, the doctor's intention may also be the relief of suffering, at the request of the patient, and therefore the use of intention in this context is not sufficient to distinguish between permissible and impermissible killing.

429. As an alternative to pain-relieving drugs that shorten life, terminal sedation of a patient may be performed[244] to produce unconsciousness before withdrawal of a ventilator or to relieve pain where other options have failed. The intention of the doctor here is only to sedate, not to kill, in order to relieve suffering. However, this has been criticized as a smokescreen for euthanasia.[245] Some argue that inducing unconsciousness crosses the line between making the patient's suffering tolerable and terminating the patient's conscious existence. Terminal sedation was recognized in the US Supreme Court decision *Washington v. Glucksberg*[246] as one of the situations in which doctors are already involved in making decisions that hasten the death of terminally ill patients.

430. In the context of whether terminal sedation can be justified under the doctrine of double effect, it would appear that, of itself, the terminal sedation satisfies

---

243. The WHO states 'If shortening of life results from the use of adequate doses of an analgesic drug, this is not the same as intentionally terminating life by overdose.' WHO, *Cancer Pain Relief and Palliative Care* (WHO 1990).

244. There seems to be disagreement as to whether this is a common, widely accepted practice or an exceptional event. *See* G. Williams, *The Principle of Double Effect and Terminal Sedation*, 9 Med. L. Rev. 41–53 at 48–49 (2001).

245. Berde Truog et al., *Barbiturates in the Care of the Terminally Ill*, 327 New Eng. J. Med. 1678 at 1680 (1991).

246. [1997] 138 L.Ed. 2d 772 at 805 per Stevens J.

the requirement that the treatment is beneficial to the patient, and that the doctor does not intend death but the relief of the patient's pain. However, it is also the case that the sedation usually precedes the withdrawal of nutrition and hydration from the patient, a procedure that is not a method of relieving pain. The British Medical Association justifies this on the basis that although the doctor may foresee that withdrawing artificial nutrition and hydration will result in the patient's death, this is 'fundamentally different from action taken with the purpose or objective of ending the patient's life'.[247] However, while the withdrawal of nutrition and hydration may satisfy the doctrine of double effect in that the death is not intended, merely foreseen, it may be argued that it does not satisfy the other prerequisites of the doctrine, namely that the nature of the act must be morally good, such as the relief of pain, and that the bad effect (death) is not a means of achieving the good effect (relief of pain). If the patient does not die from the underlying disease or the medication, he or she will die from starvation or dehydration. Accordingly, withdrawing food and water from a terminally sedated patient cannot be justified under the principle of double effect.

§10. Suicide and Assisted Suicide

431. At common law, a person who committed suicide was regarded as a self-murderer.[248] Consequently, anyone who instigated or aided another to commit suicide was guilty of murder as an accomplice. In Ireland the Criminal Law (Suicide) Act 1993 was enacted to decriminalize suicide but provides for the criminalization of assisted suicide in section 2, subsection (2):

> A person who aids, abets, counsels or procures the suicide of another, or an attempt by another to commit suicide, shall be guilty of an offence and shall be liable on conviction on indictment to imprisonment for a term not exceeding fourteen years.

247. BMA, *Withholding and Withdrawing Life-Prolonging Medical Treatment. Guidance for Decision-Making* 50 (BMJ Books 1999).

248. For a discussion of the history of suicide and its prohibition, *see* H. Trowell, *The Unfinished Debate on Euthanasia* 1–11 (SCM Press 1973).

A prosecution under this section may only be instigated with the consent of the DPP. Similar measures exist in the United Kingdom,[249] Canada,[250] Australia,[251] New Zealand,[252] and in most US states.[253]

432. It had been speculated that when the European Convention on Human Rights was incorporated into English law, there would be a flood of litigation on issues such as assisted suicide. The Human Rights Act 1998 came into force in the United Kingdom in October 2000 and has in fact been considered in the context of an application for assisted suicide in the recent case of *R (On the Application of Pretty) v. DPP.*[254] In this widely publicized case, P, a 42-year-old married woman, was diagnosed with motor neurone disease, a progressive neuro-degenerative disease of the central nervous system. The disease causes muscle weakness and difficulty in swallowing and speaking. Death usually occurs as a result of weakness in the breathing muscles, leading to respiratory failure and pneumonia. P's condition had deteriorated rapidly since the diagnosis; she no longer had any movement in her arms or legs and was fed by a tube:

> Essentially she is paralysed from the neck downwards. She has virtually no decipherable speech. The disorder is now at an advanced stage and the prognosis, in particular in relation to her life expectancy, is very poor. Her intellect, however, and her capacity to make decisions are unimpaired.[255]

433. P sought to be able to control the time and method of her death but, because of the nature of her illness, was unable to take her own life, an action that would not have constituted a criminal offence. She wanted her husband to be able to carry out some of the steps leading to her death, although she stated that the last acts directly leading to her death would be carried out by herself. She sought an undertaking from the DPP that her husband would not be prosecuted if he provided such assistance. The DPP refused to give such an undertaking and P sought judicial review of that decision.

434. The Court agreed with the DPP that it was not within his power to give an undertaking regarding future criminal conduct. In relation to the human rights argument, the Court recognized the conflict that arose here between the right to life and the right to decide what will and will not be done with one's own body. Both English law and the Convention give greater priority to the first of these rights. 'English law curtails a person's right to bodily autonomy in the interest of protecting that persons' life even against her own wishes. Thus, deliberate killing, even with consent and in the most

249. Suicide Act 1961, s. 2(1).
250. Criminal Code 1985, s. 241.
251. ACT Crimes (Amendment) Ordinance (No. 2) 1990 s. 17(1) and (2), NSW Crimes Act 1900 s. 31 C (1) and (2), NT Criminal Code 1983 s. 168, Qld. Criminal Code 1995 s. 108, SA Criminal Law Consolidation Act 1935 s. 13(a)(5), Tas. Criminal Code 1924 s. 163, Vic. Crimes Act 1958 s. 6B(2), WA Criminal Code 1913 s. 228.
252. Crimes Act 1961 s. 179.
253. *See* New York Task Force on Life and the Law, *When Death Is Sought: Assisted Suicide and Euthanasia in the Medical Context* (New York Task Force on Life and the Law 1994), http://www.health.state.ny.us/nysdoh/provider/death.htm. C. Smith, *What about Legalised Assisted Suicide?* 8 Issues in Law & Med. 505 (1993).
254. [2001] EWHC Admin 788, 63 BMLR 1.
255. Per Tuckey LJ.

pitiable of circumstances, is murder.'[256] Tuckey LJ went on to say that the person's own wishes are not determinative of what can or must be done and that the crucial distinction was between 'killing and letting die'. English law puts helping someone to take his or her own life on the wrong side of the line because, as Hoffmann LJ said in *Bland*, 'the sanctity of life entails its inviolability by an outsider'.[257] The question for the Court was whether this position was in breach of that person's human rights under the Convention.

435. Article 2 of the ECHR provides that everyone's right to life shall be protected by law and has been interpreted as requiring the State to take adequate measures to safeguard lives from attack. But it does not require the State to prohibit suicide or force treatment on those who refuse it. Nor does it require the State to prohibit passive euthanasia as such. The Court concluded that Article 2 might permit the State to allow assisted suicide, but could not oblige the State to do so. If the contrary were the case, people attempting suicide could not be saved by medical intervention for fear that they would have a claim for wrongful life, and that outcome was contrary to public policy.

436. Article 3 of the ECHR provides that no one shall be subjected to torture or to inhumane or degrading treatment or punishment. This is an unqualified right that permits no derogation. As with Article 2, the State is obliged not only to refrain from such treatment itself, but also to take reasonable steps to ensure that people are not subjected to such treatment by others.[258] It was argued before the Court that Article 3 confers the right to die with dignity. By permitting her to receive the necessary help by which to end her suffering, the State would be protecting her from the degrading effects of her disease. Tuckey LJ did not accept this interpretation of the article. He held that the right to human dignity enshrined in the article was not the right to die with dignity, but the right to live with as much dignity as possible, until life reaches its natural end.[259] 'This may well mean not taking futile and undignified steps to prolong life beyond its natural death … . But that is very different from allowing people to take active steps to bring life to a premature end.'[260]

437. This decision was appealed to the ECHR on the basis that the decision of the DPP not to grant immunity from prosecution to the applicant's husband if he assisted her in committing suicide was contrary to P's rights under Articles 2, 3, 8, 9, and 14 of the Convention.[261] The Court was not persuaded by P's argument that the right to life enshrined in Article 2 of the Convention also inferred a negative right to end that life: Article 2 cannot, without a distortion of language, be interpreted as

256. Per Tuckey LJ.
257. [1993] AC 798 at 831.
258. *Costello-Roberts v. UK*[1995] 19 EHRR 112; *A v. UK*[1998] 27 EHRR 611; *Z v. UK* E Ct HR 29392/95, 10 May 2001.
259. He referred here to *D v. UK*[1997] 42 BMLR 149 [1997] 24 EHRR 423, where it was held that deporting a person dying of AIDS to a country where he will receive no treatment or proper care amounts to inhumane or degrading treatment. This was the right to live with dignity until natural death.
260. Arguments were also put to the Court on the basis of the right to privacy in Art. 8; freedom of thought, conscience, and religion in Art. 9; and the prohibition on discrimination under Art. 14, but all were unsuccessful.
261. *Pretty v. the United Kingdom*, Application No. 2346/02, Strasbourg 29 Apr. 2002.

conferring the diametrically opposite right, namely a right to die; nor can it create a right to self-determination in the sense of conferring on an individual the entitlement to choose death rather than life.

438. Article 3 was described by the Court as imposing a primarily negative obligation on states to refrain from inflicting serious harm on persons within their jurisdictions, although the article was flexible enough to address other situations that might arise. In this case the State had not inflicted any ill treatment on P, nor had there been any complaint regarding the medical care that P was receiving. In that sense the case was distinguishable from *D v. UK*, where the State's act in removing the applicant to a jurisdiction where he would not have received appropriate medical treatment was impugned. P's argument was that by refusing to grant immunity to her husband, the State was failing to protect her from the inevitable suffering she would endure at the end of her illness, and that this constituted inhumane treatment. The Court was of the opinion that this would place a new meaning on the word 'treatment' that was not in accordance with the fundamental objectives of the Convention. An obligation to sanction steps intended to terminate life could, therefore, not be derived from Article 3.

The Court, while expressing sympathy for P's situation, similarly dismissed arguments under Articles 8, 9, and 14 of the Convention.

439. In *R (on the Application of Purdy) v. Director of Public Prosecutions*,[262] Ms Purdy was suffering from multiple sclerosis. She needed an electric wheelchair, and she had lost the ability to carry out many basic tasks for herself. She had problems in swallowing and suffered choking fits when drinking. Further deterioration in her condition was inevitable. She stated that she expected that there would come a time when her continuing existence would become unbearable. When that happens she wished to end her life while still physically able to do so. But by that stage she would be unable to do this without assistance. So she wanted to travel to a country where assisted suicide is lawful, probably Switzerland. Her husband was willing to help her to make this journey.

440. Ms Purdy sought clarification of the legal position regarding her husband's potential prosecution for assisting her suicide. She did not seek immunity from prosecution for her husband but rather information from the DPP as to what factors would be taken into account in deciding whether or not to prosecute. The House of Lords took the view that:

> On one view the law, as it stands, could not be clearer. It is an offence to assist someone to travel to Switzerland or anywhere else where assisted suicide is lawful. Anyone who does that is liable to be prosecuted. He is in the same position as anyone else who offends against section 2(1) of the 1961 Act. As with any other crime, the test that will be applied is that which the Crown Prosecution Service code lays down. He may be prosecuted if there is enough evidence to sustain a prosecution and it is in the public interest that this step should be taken. But the practice that will be followed in cases where compassionate assistance of the kind that Ms Purdy seeks from her husband is far less certain.

262. [2009] UKHL 45.

441. The Court stated that the law should be formulated with sufficient precision to enable the individual, if need be with appropriate advice, to regulate his or her conduct. The Court, therefore, required the DPP to promulgate an offence-specific policy identifying the facts and circumstances that he will take into account in deciding, in a case such as that which Ms Purdy's case exemplifies, whether or not to consent to a prosecution under section 2(1) of the 1961 Act. An interim prosecution policy was published in September 2009 and a consultation process was launched by the DPP to assist in finalization of the policy.

442. The interim policy suggests a number of factors to be taken into account by the DPP in deciding whether or not to prosecute an individual who is alleged to have assisted another person to commit suicide. The public interest factors in favour of prosecution are:

(1) The victim was under 18 years of age.
(2) The victim's capacity to reach an informed decision was adversely affected by a recognized mental illness or learning difficulty.
(3) The victim did not have a clear, settled, and informed wish to commit suicide; for example, the victim's history suggests that his or her wish to commit suicide was temporary or subject to change.
(4) The victim did not indicate unequivocally to the suspect that he or she wished to commit suicide.
(5) The victim did not ask personally on his or her own initiative for the assistance of the suspect.
(6) The victim did not have:

   (a) a terminal illness; or
   (b) a severe and incurable physical disability; or
   (c) a severe degenerative physical condition; from which there was no possibility of recovery.

(7) The suspect was not wholly motivated by compassion; for example, the suspect was motivated by the prospect that he or she or a person closely connected to them stood to gain in some way from the death of the victim.
(8) The suspect persuaded, pressured, or maliciously encouraged the victim to commit suicide, or exercised improper influence in the victim's decision to do so, and did not take reasonable steps to ensure that any other person did not do so.
(9) The victim was physically able to undertake the act that constituted the assistance him- or herself.
(10) The suspect was not the spouse, partner, or a close relative or a close personal friend of the victim.
(11) The suspect was unknown to the victim and assisted by providing specific information via, for example, a website or publication, to the victim to assist him or her in committing suicide.
(12) The suspect gave assistance to more than one victim who were not known to each other.

(13) The suspect was paid by the victim or those close to the victim for his or her assistance.
(14) The suspect was paid to care for the victim in a care/nursing home environment.
(15) The suspect was aware that the victim intended to commit suicide in a public place where it was reasonable to think that members of the public may be present.
(16) The suspect was a member of an organization or group, the principal purpose of which is to provide a physical environment (whether for payment or not) in which to allow another to commit suicide.

In most cases, factors (1)–(8) above will carry more weight than the other factors in deciding that a prosecution is needed in the public interest.

The public interest factors against prosecution are:

(1) The victim had a clear, settled, and informed wish to commit suicide.
(2) The victim indicated unequivocally to the suspect that he or she wished to commit suicide.
(3) The victim asked personally on his or her own initiative for the assistance of the suspect.
(4) The victim had:

    (a) a terminal illness; or
    (b) a severe and incurable physical disability; or
    (c) a severe degenerative physical condition; from which there was no possibility of recovery.

(5) The suspect was wholly motivated by compassion.
(6) The suspect was the spouse, partner, or a close relative or a close personal friend of the victim, within the context of a long-term and supportive relationship.
(7) The actions of the suspect, although sufficient to come within the definition of the offence, were of only minor assistance or influence, or the assistance that the suspect provided was as a consequence of his or her usual lawful employment.
(8) The victim was physically unable to undertake the act that constituted the assistance him- or herself.
(9) The suspect had sought to dissuade the victim from taking the course of action that resulted in his or her suicide.
(10) The victim has considered and pursued to a reasonable extent recognized treatment and care options.
(11) The victim had previously attempted to commit suicide and was likely to try to do so again.
(12) The actions of the suspect may be characterized as reluctant assistance in the face of a determined wish on the part of the victim to commit suicide.
(13) The suspect fully assisted the police in their enquiries into the circumstances of the suicide or the attempt and his or her part in providing assistance.

In most cases, factors (1)–(7) above will carry more weight than the other factors in deciding that a prosecution is not needed in the public interest.

In Ireland similar arguments were also unsuccessful in the case of *Fleming v. Ireland*[263] The facts of the Fleming case involved a woman in the final stages of multiple sclerosis who wished her partner to be able to assist her if and when she decided that she wanted to die. The Plaintiff claimed that the blanket ban on assisted suicide breached her constitutional rights and her rights under the European Convention on Human Rights. The High Court rejected her claim finding that it was not possible to relax the ban on assisted suicide without very profound consequences for the law in general, and that ultimately the Oireachtas (Parliament) was justified in keeping an absolute ban in place. The Plaintiff sought prosecuting guidelines from the DPP, similar to the Purdy case discussed above but such an approach was rejected by the High Court. However, somewhat unusually, the court said that it felt that the DPP, 'in this of all cases, would exercise her discretion in a humane and sensitive fashion', while still retaining the full ambit of her discretion to decide whether to prosecute or not.

The Plaintiff appealed to the Supreme Court which held that although suicide is no longer a crime in Ireland, this does not mean that there is 'a constitutional right to commit suicide or to determine the time of one's death'.[264] However Denham J. also said that there was nothing in the judgment to imply that it would not be open to the legislature to deal with such cases bearing in mind legitimate concerns and appropriate safeguards, any competing interests and the practicability of any measures introduced. The Court also ruled on the Article 40.1 equality ground that insofar as there was no right to commit suicide or to choose to terminate one's life, issues such as discrimination did not arise. It also found that there does not exist a constitutional right for a limited class of persons as such rights must be the entitlement of all persons. The Plaintiff did not appeal the High Court's ruling in relation to prosecuting guidelines.

I. Physician-Assisted Suicide

443. As Irish law currently stands, a doctor who actively assists a patient to commit suicide will incur criminal liability. In order to prosecute such a case, it would be necessary to show that the doctor intentionally assisted or encouraged the commission of the act in question or that he or she was at least ready to assist, if required to do so. An argument could be made that a doctor who provides medication merely provides the patient with the option of committing suicide, rather than directly assists in the commission of the suicide itself. However, given the stigma attached to such conduct, it is more likely that it would be held to be, at the very least, counselling or procuring suicide. It would most likely be irrelevant that the patient was suffering from a terminal disease, and that death was imminent anyway.

§11. Others (Transsexual Interventions)

444. There is no law on transsexual interventions in Ireland.

263. [2013] IESC 19.
264. Denham J. para. 98.

Part III. The Physician in Relation to the Healthcare System

Chapter 1. Relations with Other Healthcare Providers

§1. Pharmacists

445. The practice of pharmacy is regulated by the Pharmacy Acts 1875–2007 as well as provisions contained in the Misuse of Drugs Acts. Under the Pharmacy Act 2007, all pharmacies operating in the State must be registered in the Retail Pharmacy Businesses' register kept by the PSI in order to legally operate.

In addition, all pharmacists and pharmaceutical assistants must be registered in the registers kept by the PSI in order to practise. The new registers under the Act were established on 1 January 2009.

446. The PSI Council was established under the Pharmacy Act 2007 as the pharmacy regulator and has a statutory function to protect patient safety. The Council is appointed by the Minister for Health and Children and consists of a majority of non-pharmacists. Of the twenty-one-member Council, nine are registered pharmacists who are elected by registered pharmacists and subsequently appointed by the Minister. In addition, a registered pharmacist representative of the Schools of Pharmacy is appointed. The other members of Council include:

- a nominee of the Irish Medicines Board as representative of the management of the regulation of medicinal products;
- a nominee of the HSE as representative of the management of the public health sector;
- a person representative of the provision of CPD in relation to pharmacy;
- three persons with such qualifications, expertise, interest, or experience to make a substantial contribution to the performance of PSI functions.

The PSI (Council) Rules 2008 (SI No. 492 of 2008) outline the general administration, management, and governance of the Council and its Committees.

447. The principal functions of the PSI are set out in section 7(1) of the 2007 Act:

- to regulate the profession of pharmacy in the State, having regard to the need to protect, maintain, and promote the health and safety of the public;
- to promote and ensure a high standard of education and training for persons seeking to become pharmacists;
- to ensure that those persons and pharmacists obtain appropriate experience;
- to ensure that pharmacists undertake appropriate CPD, including the acquisition of specialization; and
- otherwise to supervise compliance with the Act.

448. The PSI must also, *inter alia*, maintain a register of pharmacists, determine and apply criteria for registration, draw up a code of conduct for pharmacists, approve relevant programmes of education and training, and act as the competent authority for the mutual recognition of pharmacy qualifications obtained in EU Member States. The Society may conduct inquiries into the qualifications and fitness of persons to practise as pharmacists and impose sanctions where appropriate.

449. A person who wishes to become a pharmacist in Ireland must:

- Register with the PSI on commencing a pharmacy degree course.
- Complete a four-year accredited pharmacy degree course in a school of pharmacy in Ireland and obtain a pharmacy degree.
- Complete a period of one year's practical training, approved by the PSI, under the supervision of a practising tutor pharmacist. This is referred to as 'pre-registration training'.
- Pass the Pharmaceutical Licence Examination.
- On completing all four requirements above, the person is entitled to apply to become registered as a pharmacist in Ireland.

§2. Nurses

450. The statutory regulatory body for the nursing profession in Ireland is the Nursing and Midwifery Board which was first established by the Nurses Act 1950 to take over the functions of two bodies, the Central Midwives Board and the General Nursing Council that had been established in 1918 and 1919, respectively. The Board was re-constituted and its functions were redefined and expanded by the Nurses Act 1985 and later by the Nurses and Midwives Act 2011. The Board consists of twenty-three non-executive members, with a lay majority of twelve. Of the remaining eleven members, eight are registered nurses and midwives elected by the profession to represent the general, children's, psychiatric, intellectual disability, public health, and midwifery disciplines. A further three members are appointed by the Minister for Health. The Board's main functions are:

- to establish and maintain a register of nurses;
- to provide for the education and training of nurses and student nurses;

- to inquire into the conduct of a registered nurse on the grounds of alleged professional misconduct or alleged unfitness to engage in such practice by reason of physical or mental disability;
- to give guidance to the profession;
- to manage the Nursing Careers Centre, which was set up in 1998 to facilitate a centralized system of processing and selection of applicants wishing to enter nursing; promote and market nursing as a career; and provide careers information to registered nurses and midwives.

451. Registration with the Board is mandatory in order to practise as a Registered Nurse or Registered Midwife in Ireland. The main function of the Registration Section of the Board is to maintain the Register of Nurses in accordance with the Nurses and Midwives Act 2011

452. Any person may apply to the FTPC of the Board for an inquiry into the fitness of a nurse to practise nursing on the grounds of misconduct, lack of competence, a conviction or caution, physical or mental ill health, a finding by any other health or social care regulator or licensing body that a registrant's fitness to practise is impaired, or fraudulent or incorrect entry in the Register. Once a complaint has been received, the Board will identify the named person to ensure that the nurse/midwife is a registered nurse/ midwife with the Board, as complaints can only be made against registered nurses/ midwives. The Board requests that confirmation be received from the complainants of the grounds upon which they wish to make the complaint, professional misconduct or unfitness to engage in the practice of nursing by reason of physical or mental disability, or both.

453. Once the complainant has identified the grounds upon which the complaint is being made the complainant becomes the applicant. Following this, the letter of complaint is sent to the nurse/midwife for his or her comments in relation to the complaint. When all the correspondence is received, the documentation is forwarded to the FTPC to consider whether or not there is a prima facie case for holding an inquiry.

If the FTPC decides that there is a prima facie case for holding an inquiry, the nurse/midwife is informed of this decision and the inquiry process is started. The inquiry process follows the same procedures as that of the Medical Council, described at paragraphs 137 et seq. If the FTPC decides that there is not a prima facie case for holding an inquiry, the nurse/midwife is informed of this decision and the file is closed.

§3. Dentists

454. The practice of dentistry in Ireland is regulated by the Dentists Act 1985. This Act provides for the establishment of the Dental Council with a remit to promote high standards of professional education and conduct among dentists. The main functions assigned to the Council under the Act are:

- To establish, maintain, and publish a Register of Dentists and a Register of Dental Specialists and to provide for the registration and the retention of dentists names in these registers.
- To satisfy itself as to the adequacy and suitability of the dental education and training provided in the State's dental schools and to the standards required at examinations for primary qualifications.
- To inquire into the fitness of a registered dentist to practise dentistry on the grounds of his or her alleged professional misconduct or his or her alleged unfitness to practise by reason of physical or mental disability and to take appropriate action. The Council has power, subject in some instances to confirmation by the High Court, to advise, admonish, censure, suspend, attach conditions to registration, or erase a dentist's name from the Register of Dentists.
- To make, with the consent of the Minister, schemes for the establishment of classes of auxiliary dental workers.
- To discharge the duties assigned to the Council pursuant to the provisions of EU dental directives.
- To advise the dental profession and the public on all matters relating to dental ethics and professional behaviour.
- To advise the Minister on all matters relating to the functions of the Council under the Act.

455. The Council has a membership of nineteen made up as follows:

- two persons appointed by the University College Cork;
- two persons appointed by the University of Dublin;
- two persons appointed by the Medical Council;
- one person appointed by the Royal College of Surgeons in Ireland – one person appointed by the Minister for Education and Science;
- seven dentists appointed by election by registered dentists;
- four persons appointed by the Minister for Health and Children, of whom at least two must not be registered dentists and who will represent the interest of the public as consumers of dental services.

456. The Act provides for the registration of dentists and it is an offence for a person who is not a registered dentist to use the title of a registered dentist or to practise dentistry. There are two types of registration available, full and temporary. Full registration in the Register of Dentists for Ireland is available to the following:

- graduates in dentistry from a university in Ireland;
- nationals of EEA Member States who graduate within the EEA with a scheduled dental degree/diploma;
- nationals of EEA Member States who qualify for registration under the provisions of the Directive 2001/19/EC;
- dentists, not otherwise entitled to registration, who pass a special Dental Council examination.

457. Temporary registration is available to persons, not eligible for full registration, provided they meet the following conditions:

- they must hold a dental qualification obtained after completing an acceptable undergraduate dental course;
- they must be in Ireland for the purpose of further training, which training must be undertaken under Consultant supervision in an approved training post; or
- they must be in Ireland to take up a teaching appointment or to give a course.

Temporary registration is granted for up to one year in the first instance but it may be extended for further periods provided that the aggregate of periods of temporary registration does not exceed five years.

§4. Coroners

458. A coroner in Ireland is an independent official with legal responsibility for the investigation of sudden and unexplained deaths. The history of the coroner in Ireland probably begins sometime in the late twelfth or early thirteenth centuries, though the exact date is impossible to ascertain with certainty.[265] The modern office of coroner was established by the Coroners (Ireland) Act 1846, which provided for the division of each county into districts, the election and appointment of coroners, and their remuneration. The Coroners Act 1881 required a coroner to be qualified as a medical practitioner, a barrister, or a solicitor. The executive functions of the coroner and his duties to safeguard the financial interests of the Crown changed over time, with increased importance being placed instead on investigation of the cause of death and judicial functions. Coroners Acts were introduced in the 1920s, based in large part on similar provisions in England at that time. However, the principal legislation dealing with coroners in Ireland is the Coroners Act 1962, which remains the primary Act at the present day.

459. A Working Group was established in 1998 to examine the role of the coronial service and how it might be developed. This Group reported in 2000 with over 100 recommendations, including the necessity for a new Coroners Act.[266] It also recommended that the concept of regulation-based Coroners Rules should be an essential element of a new legislative environment for the new Coroner Service. These rules 'should be established by statutory regulation and be capable of being amended. They should cover the various options and procedures available to coroners throughout the cycle of their functions from death reporting right through to the carrying out of formal inquests'. The report recommended the establishment of a Rules Committee to devise these rules. A Rules Committee was subsequently established, and Coroners Rules published in 2003 following discussion between appointed experts and consultation with interested parties and the public.

460. Responsibility for the coroner service lies across a number of government departments at the present time. The Department of Justice, Equality, and Law Reform

265. B. Farrell, *Coroners: Practice and Procedure* Ch. 1 (Round Hall Limited 2000).
266. Report of the Working Group (2000), *Review of the Coroner Service*.

deals with legislation and policy relating to the office of coroner. The Department of the Environment, Heritage, and Local Government has responsibility, through the local authorities, for the appointment and remuneration of coroners and in some areas the maintenance of mortuary facilities. The Department of Health has responsibility to fund pathology services and post-mortem facilities used by coroners.

461. There are forty-eight coronial districts in the State, with a coroner and deputy coroner in each district. Approximately half of the coroners currently in office are doctors, and the remainder are solicitors or barristers. They are paid a basic set fee depending on the size of the district and additional fees for various duties they perform.

462. The coroner is indemnified by the State in respect of an award of damages made against him or her, and/or costs, in relation to performance of his or her duties. The coroner is traditionally given immunity and absolute privilege, in the same way as a judge, while performing the duties of the office. The High Court is empowered to judicially review the acts of coroners. The principal relevant duties of the coroner include the following:[267]

- To be available at all times to receive notification of deaths, to make preliminary inquiries, and to direct post-mortem examinations to be undertaken. Under the 1962 Act, section 18(5), particular persons are obliged to notify the coroner of a death. This duty is discharged if notification is made to a member of the Garda Síochána, not below the rank of sergeant. A medical practitioner in the hospital or place where the body is located pronounces death before the body is removed to the mortuary. The Garda notifies the coroner under section 18(3), usually by telephone or fax to the coroner's office or home. This is recorded on a telephone report form. A form is sent to the coroner with demographic information, a description of the circumstances of the death, confirmation of the identity of the deceased, and the identity of the doctor who pronounced the death.
- To direct the performance of a post-mortem examination. Where a coroner is informed that a body is lying within his or her district and that the circumstances of death require investigation, he or she must make a preliminary inquiry as to whether the death had occurred with no apparent unnatural cause and whether a medical practitioner is in a position to sign a medical certificate as to the cause of death. This may be the deceased's GP or a hospital doctor. A doctor signing the medical certificate of the cause of death must have seen and treated the patient within one calendar month before death. The doctor must know the cause of death, and death must be due to natural causes. If this is not the case, the doctor must report the death to the coroner, who will arrange for a post-mortem examination to be carried out on the body. If, having discussed the circumstances of the death with the doctor, the coroner is satisfied that despite not having seen the deceased for more than one month prior to death, the cause of death is clear, he or she may direct the doctor to certify the death. This may occur, for example, where a person has been chronically ill for some time and was expected to die. Where a person is dead on arrival at hospital or dies shortly after admission (usually within twenty-four hours), the hospital doctor will not usually be in a position to give a medical certificate as to cause of death and will notify the coroner.

267. Farrell, *supra* n. 265, at Ch. 2.

- To inform certain persons. The coroner or his or her officer (usually a member of the Garda Síochána) will inform family or next of kin of the deceased of the time and place of the post-mortem examination. A family member will usually be asked to formally identify the deceased to the Garda, who in turn will identify the body to the pathologist prior to commencing the post-mortem examination.
- To release the body. The coroner will authorize the release of the body following the post-mortem examination. In cases of suspicious deaths, this will be done in consultation with the State pathologist who will usually have performed the autopsy and may take a number of days. The body is released to the family for burial only after the coroner is satisfied that no further examination is necessary.
- To hold an inquest. Section 17 of the 1962 Act provides:

> Subject to the provisions of this Act, where a coroner is informed that the body of a deceased person is lying within his district, it shall be the duty of the coroner to hold an inquest in relation to the death of that person if he is of opinion that the death may have occurred in a violent of unnatural manner, or suddenly and from unknown causes or in a place or in circumstances which, under provisions in that behalf contained in any other enactment, require that an inquest should be held.

This means that if the coroner has reasonable cause to believe that death occurred within the criteria set out in the Act, he or she must hold an inquest.

- To send a certificate to the Registrar of Births and Deaths. When the coroner has completed the inquiry or inquest, he or she must furnish a certificate as to the cause of death to the Registrar, to enable the death to be registered.

463. Certain deaths must be reported to the coroner, either under legal rules or rules of practice that have evolved in the coronial system.[268] These include the following:

- Sudden, unexpected, or unexplained deaths.
- Where a medical certificate as to cause of death cannot be obtained because the deceased had not seen a doctor within the previous month.
- Where the deceased's doctor is not satisfied as to the cause of death even where the deceased was treated within one month prior to death.
- Sudden infant death syndrome (SIDS), also known as cot death.
- Where a death was directly or indirectly due to unnatural causes such as a road traffic accident or any other accident, any physical injury, drug abuse, burns, starvation, neglect, exposure, poisoning, drowning, hanging, firearms.
- Where the death resulted from an industrial disease or accident.
- Where the death may be attributable to any surgical or medical procedure regardless of the lapse of time between the procedure and death.
- Where there is any allegation of medical negligence or misconduct.
- Septicaemia, which may be caused by an injury.

268. Farrell, *supra* n. 265, at Ch. 7.

- Death occurring during a surgical procedure or anaesthesia.
- Abortions and certain stillbirths.
- Acute alcoholism/alcohol poisoning.
- Deaths connected with suspected criminal activity.
- Where death may be due to homicide or suspicious circumstances.
- Death of a person in custody.
- Death of a person connected with a pensionable disability.
- Death of a patient in a mental hospital.
- Death of a child in care.
- Where a person is found dead.
- Where the cause of death is unknown.
- Where the body is to be removed outside of Ireland.

464. Deaths reportable under rules of practice include the following:

- Where a person is brought in dead to a hospital.
- Where a person dies in the casualty department of a hospital.
- Where death occurs within twenty-four hours of admission to a hospital.
- Where death occurs after the administration of an anaesthetic, for a surgical or other procedure.
- Certain deaths that occur in a hospital department such as radiology, or out-patients.
- Where a person dies in a hospital having recently been transferred from a nursing home or other residential institution, including a prison.
- Where there is any doubt as to the cause of death.

I. Powers of the Coroner

465. A coroner has legal possession of the body of the deceased from the moment his or her jurisdiction arises. This occurs on notification that the body of a deceased person lies within his or her district. The coroner then commences the inquiry into the cause of death. The right of the coroner to possession of the body pending investigation of the cause of death means that no other person has prior rights in respect of the body. This may be difficult for family members or next of kin to understand at the time of bereavement, particularly if they are unhappy at the concept of a post-mortem examination being carried out. However, the coroner is obliged by law to investigate the cause of death and to do so must have prior rights in relation to possession of the body for examination.

466. Subject to the coroner's powers in relation to possession of the body in order to carry out his or her functions under the Act, the personal representatives of the deceased (as opposed to family members) have the right to possession of the body, once the coroner has released it for burial purposes. The personal representatives of the deceased are either the executor of the deceased's estate, as identified in the deceased's will, or the administrator of the estate in cases where the deceased dies intestate or without having made a will. The personal representatives are entitled to act in relation to the affairs of the deceased from the moment of death.

II. Inquests

467. An inquest in Ireland is an official, public enquiry, presided over by the coroner (and in some cases involving a jury), into the cause of a sudden, unexplained, or violent death. If a death cannot be explained, an inquest may be held to establish the facts of the death, such as where and how death occurred. An inquest would not normally be held if a post-mortem examination of the body could explain the cause of death. Section 17 of the Coroners Act 1962 makes provision in law in Ireland for the holding of an inquest into a death. The inquest is inquisitorial by nature, as opposed to adversarial. The focus is on a finding of fact, not on apportionment of blame. When the proceedings have been completed, a verdict is returned in relation to the identity of the deceased, and how, when, and where the death occurred. The range of verdicts open to the coroner or jury (in jury cases, it is the jury that returns the verdict) includes accidental death, misadventure, suicide, open verdict, natural causes, and unlawful killing.

Reform of the coronial jurisdiction has been discussed extensively in recent years and a new Coroners Bill was published in 2007 but has not yet been passed through the Oireachtas.

§5. Paramedical Professionals

468. A system of statutory registration for health and social care professionals in Ireland was introduced by the Health and Social Care Professionals Act 2005. The purpose of establishing this system is to ensure that members of the public are protected and informed so that they can be confident that the professional providing the service is properly qualified, competent, and of good standing. The system will also ensure professional conduct and the promotion of high standards of professional education and training among healthcare and social care professionals.

469. The system of statutory registration applies to the following twelve healthcare and social care professions, regardless of whether they work in the public/private sector or are self-employed:

(1) Clinical biochemists.
(2) Medical scientists.
(3) Psychologists.
(4) Chiropodists/podiatrists.
(5) Dieticians.
(6) Orthoptists.
(7) Physiotherapists.
(8) Radiographers.
(9) Speech and language therapists.
(10) Occupational therapists.
(11) Social care workers.
(12) Social workers.

While the system of statutory registration applies initially to twelve healthcare and social care professions, the law allows the Minister for Health and Children to include additional professions in the system.

470. The main elements of the system of statutory registration are a Health and Social Care Professionals Council[269] for the system overall with a Registration Board for each of the professions to be registered. The Act 2005 also provides for the establishment of a fitness to practise structure to deal with complaints and other disciplinary matters. The Council has established three statutory committees common to all the registered professions within the system:

- PPC: following notification of a complaint, this Committee will give an opinion as to whether there is sufficient cause to warrant further action being taken.
- A health committee: will deal with cases where a registered practitioner's ability to practise is impaired by reason of a physical or mental illness, an emotional disturbance, or an addiction to alcohol or drugs.
- A professional conduct committee: will investigate complaints against registered practitioners in relation to professional misconduct or poor professional performance.

471. Hearings of the professional conduct committee will generally be heard in public. Hearings of the health committee will generally be held in private. During the course of a hearing, a committee of inquiry will be allowed to receive evidence, can enforce the attendance and examination of witnesses, and can compel the production of records.

472. The law also provides that in urgent situations, the Council may apply to the High Court to suspend a practitioner pending completion of an inquiry where it is in the public interest to do so. After an inquiry and following confirmation by the High Court, the Council may apply one or more of the following sanctions on a registered practitioner:

- suspension for specified period;
- cancellation of registration;
- prohibited from applying for a particular period to be restored on the register;
- admonishment or censure;
- attachment of conditions to registration.

269. At http://www.coru.ie.

Chapter 2. Relations with Other Healthcare Institutions

§1. Hospitals

473. There are three different types of hospital in Ireland but there is very little difference in practice between the first two types:

- HSE (public) hospitals, owned and funded by the HSE.
- Voluntary public hospitals, most of whose income comes directly from the government. Voluntary public hospitals are sometimes owned by private bodies, such as religious orders. Other voluntary public hospitals are incorporated by charter or statute and are run by boards often appointed by the Minister for Health and Children.
- Private hospitals, which receive no State funding.

474. Public health services are provided in what can broadly be termed the public hospitals, HSE hospitals, and public voluntary hospitals. Most of these hospitals also provide private healthcare but they must clearly distinguish between public and private beds.

475. Acute hospital services in Ireland exist to diagnose, treat, and care for seriously ill or injured patients. Acute hospital services are provided in HSE hospitals, public voluntary hospitals, and private hospitals. Some hospitals are specialist, for example, maternity hospitals, psychiatric hospitals, and cancer hospitals, while others are general. Designated national specialist services incorporate areas of care such as heart, lung, and liver transplants, bone-marrow transplants, spinal injuries, paediatric cardiac services, medical genetics, renal transplantation, and haemophilia. Supra-regional services include neurosurgery and cardiac surgery, as well as complex cancer treatments and radiotherapy.

476. HIQA, which was established in 2007, has a core function in setting standards on safety and quality of services delivered in public hospitals and in monitoring enforcement of those standards in an open and transparent way. HIQA also undertakes national quality assurance reviews of priority service areas such as symptomatic breast disease and hygiene.[270]

477. In 2007 the Commission on Patient Safety and Quality Assurance was established by the Minister for Health to develop proposals for a health-service-wide (encompassing both the public and private sectors) system of governance based on corporate accountability for the safety and quality of health services. The Commission was asked to provide a framework, including mechanisms and arrangements to enable the verifiable implementation of nationally agreed-upon managerial and clinical

270. At http://www.hiqa.ie.

standards. The Commission's report, entitled *Building a Culture of Patient Safety*, was published in August 2008.[271]

One of the Commission's recommendations was for the introduction of a statutory system of licensing for all public and private healthcare providers and services.

Draft legislation is currently under preparation by the Department of Health to implement this recommendation.

478. The National Treatment Purchase Fund (NTPF)[272] was set up in Ireland to take public patients who have been waiting longest for procedures in public hospitals off waiting lists. The NTPF arranges for patients who have been waiting longest on public hospital waiting lists to be treated in private hospitals in Ireland, private hospitals in the United Kingdom, or, if necessary, private hospitals in other countries. Treatments available under the NTPF range from cardiac surgery to hip replacements to treatment for varicose veins and cataracts. The first treatments under the NTPF took place in a number of private Dublin hospitals at the end of June 2002.

§2. Nursing Homes

479. Long-term institutional care for older people in Ireland may be provided in publicly owned and financed institutions or in private and voluntary nursing homes. The HSE owns and runs a number of long-term care institutions. They may be called welfare homes, continuing care units, geriatric hospitals, community nursing units, or public nursing homes.

480. Section 52 of the Health Act 1970 (as amended by the Health [Amendment] Act 1991) obliges the HSE to provide in-patient services for everyone. In-patient services are 'institutional services provided for people while maintained in a hospital, convalescent home, or home for persons suffering from physical or mental disability or in accommodation ancillary thereto'. In theory, therefore, everyone is eligible for a place in a public nursing home but there are not enough places for everyone who needs them.

481. The situation in respect of entitlement to public long-term care is unclear. Virtually everyone who gets a place in a public nursing home is liable for long stay charges. The HSE has contracted beds in private nursing homes and the financial arrangements for these places are similar to those for public nursing homes. Private nursing homes charge fees. A nursing home subvention may be available from the HSE toward the costs of a private nursing home subject to criteria in relation to need and financial means. Private nursing homes are subject to regulation. That is, they must be registered and adhere to minimum standards of care. The law in this area is implemented at present by the HSE.

482. The Health Act 2007 set up an independent Social Services Inspectorate (within HIQA) that is responsible for implementing and monitoring the regulation of both public and private nursing homes. The work of the Inspectorate includes the inspection and registration of residential services in the public, private, and voluntary

271. At http://health.gov.ie/blog/publications/building-a-culture-of-patient-safety-report-of-the-commission-on-patient-safety-and-quality-assurance/.

272. At http://www.ntpf.ie.

sectors for older people and people with a disability. The HSE also currently inspects and registers private and voluntary residential services for older people.

483. Nursing home services have to be registered every three years (to ensure they are able to provide such services in the first instance) and inspected (in order to ensure they are maintaining standards required to operate and are continuously upholding high standards) by the Social Services Inspectorate. As outlined in the Health Act 2007, HIQA has the power to take legal action in the event of non-compliance. If HIQA believes during a registration or following an inspection that the nursing home (residential care centre) is not safe or the standards are not being met, there are a number of actions that can be taken in the interests of the residents. These include the following:

- refusing to allow it to open until it complies with the law and shows how it intends to meet the standards;
- making a recommendation for changes to be made and checking that these are carried out;
- prosecuting for offences under the Health Act 2007, for example, failure to comply with a condition of registration;
- if inspectors come across a situation that poses an urgent risk to residents, which the owner is unwilling or unable to correct urgently, they can take emergency action to close a residential care centre.

484. HIQA published the National Quality Standards for Residential Care Settings for Older People in Ireland. The standards are a significant milestone for the protection of the rights of older people in residential care settings across the country. They will guide and assist service providers in the provision of the highest quality of care to their residents. The purpose of the standards is to promote best practice in residential care settings for older people and improve the quality of life of residents in these settings.[273]

485. The quality standards clearly outline what is expected of a provider of services and what a resident, his or her family, a carer, or the public can expect to receive in residential care settings. They deal with the areas of rights of older people, protection, healthcare and social care needs, quality of life, staffing, the care environment, and management and governance. In addition, the standards include supplementary criteria that apply to units that specialize in the care of people with dementia.

§3. Health Insurance

486. A number of companies offer voluntary private health insurance in Ireland. There are also a number of long-established health insurance providers that deal only with particular groups of employees; membership is confined to employees and retired employees and their dependents. These schemes are known as restricted membership schemes. Examples include the police force, prison officers, and employees of certain

273. At http://www.hiqa.ie.

semi-State bodies. The rules governing health insurance apply equally to all providers, with some limited exceptions for the restricted membership schemes.

487. Health insurance is used to pay for private care in hospitals or from various health professionals in hospitals or in their practices. The arrangements vary from one company to another but most companies have agreements with hospitals that the company will pay the hospital directly.

488. The Health Insurance Authority[274] is the independent statutory regulator for the private health insurance market in Ireland. The Authority monitors the operation of health insurance businesses in Ireland and advises the Minister for Health in this regard, including assessing the effect of any regulations or new legislation on consumers. The Authority aims to ensure that consumers are aware of their rights; that policies and publicity material describe coverage in a fair and comparable way, and that community rating, open enrolment, and lifetime coverage are protected and maintained. The Authority also reviews the appropriateness of the procedures used by insurers in their dealings with consumers.

489. One of the Health Insurance Authority's functions relates to the operation of a Risk Equalization Scheme. Risk equalization is a process that aims to equitably neutralize differences in insurers' costs that arise due to variations in the health status of their members. The Minister for Health and Children determined that risk equalization would commence from 1 January 2006, having considered the recommendation and the supporting evidence submitted by the Health Insurance Authority, and having considered subsequent representations submitted by insurers.

490. Health insurance companies that offer coverage for in-patient hospital services must offer a minimum level of benefits. They must provide a minimum level of coverage in respect of:

- Day care/in-patient treatment.
- Hospital out-patient treatment.
- Maternity benefits.
- Convalescence.
- Psychiatric treatment and substance abuse.
- The minimum accommodation level is semi-private in a public hospital.

491. Companies are allowed to offer contracts limited to certain health services, for example, dental and optical services, without being subject to the general requirements about community rating, open enrolment, and lifetime coverage. They may also offer contracts in relation to GP and out-patient services without having to meet minimum benefit requirements.

492. At present, health insurance companies must accept anyone who wishes to join, subject to any applicable waiting periods before coverage takes effect, regardless of age, sex, or health status – this is known as 'open enrolment'. Restricted membership schemes must accept everyone who is qualified to join.

274. At http://www.hia.ie.

Selected Bibliography

Barrington, R. *Health, Medicine & Politics in Ireland 1900–1970*. Dublin: Institute of Public Administration, 1987.

Commission on Assisted Human Reproduction. *The Report of the Commission on Assisted Human Reproduction*. http://health.gov.ie/wp-content/uploads/2014/03/Report-of-The-Commission-on-Assisted-Human-Reproduction.pdf.

Commission on Patient Safety and Quality Assurance. *Building a Culture of Patient Safety.* It is available at http://health.gov.ie/blog/publications/building-a-culture-of-patient-safety-report-of-the-commission-on-patient-safety-and-quality-assurance/.

Donnelly, M. 'Legislating for Incapacity: Developing a Rights-Based Framework'. *Dublin University Law Journal* 30 (2008): 394.

Donnelly, M. *Consent: Bridging the Gap Between Doctor and Patient*. Cork: Cork University Press, 2002.

Horgan, R., J.R. Higgins, & G. Burke. 'The Decline of Laparoscopic Sterilisation.' *Irish Medical Journal* 101, no. 2 (February 2008).

Kingston, J., J. Whelan & I. Bacik. *Abortion and the Law: An Irish Perspective*. Dublin: Round Hall, 1997.

Law Reform Consultation Paper on Vulnerable Adults and the Law. LRC 83-2006.

Leahy, A. & M. Wiley (eds). *The Irish Health System in the 21st Century*. Dublin: Oak Tree Press, 1998.

Madden, D. *Medicine Ethics and the Law*. 3rd edn. Dublin: Bloomsbury, 2016.

Madden, D. *Report on Post Mortem Practice and Procedure*. Dublin: Department of Health, 2006.

McAuliffe, E. & L. Joyce. *A Healthier Future? Managing Healthcare in Ireland*. Dublin: Institute of Public Administration, 1998.

McDonagh, M. *Freedom of Information Law in Ireland*. 3rd edn. Dublin: Round Hall, 2015.

Medical Council. *Guide to Ethical Conduct and Behaviour*. 8th edn. Dublin: The Medical Council, 2016, https://www.medicalcouncil.ie/News-and-Publications/Reports/Guide-to-Professional-Conduct-and-Ethics-8th-Edition-2016-.pdf.

Mills, S. *Clinical Practice and the Law*. Dublin: Tottel Publishing, 2007.

Schweppe, J. *The Unborn Child, Article 40.3.3 and Abortion in Ireland*. Dublin: Liffey Press, 2008.

Selected Bibliography

§1. WEBSITES

Department of Health http://health.gov.ie/ Health Service Executive www.hse.ie.
Health Information and Quality Authority www.hiqa.ie.

Index

The numbers here refer to paragraph numbers.

Index

Index

Index

www.ingramcontent.com/pod-product-compliance
Lightning Source LLC
LaVergne TN
LVHW011134300926
849160LV00008B/643